George Woodyard

Cultural Space and Theatrical Conventions

❖

IN THE WORKS OF

Oduvaldo Vianna Filho

The young dramatist. (Photo agency Globo, from the personal collection of Maria Lúcia Marins.)

Cultural Space and

Theatrical Conventions

IN THE WORKS OF

Oduvaldo Vianna Filho

LESLIE H. DAMASCENO

Wayne State University Press Detroit

Latin American Literature and Culture Series

A complete listing of the books in this series can be found at the back of this volume.

English language translation copyright © 1996 by Wayne State University Press, Detroit, Michigan 48201. All rights are reserved.

Original Portuguese edition *Espaço cultural e convenções teatrais na obra de Oduvaldo Vianna Filho,* copyright © 1994 by Leslie Hawkins Damasceno, published by Editora da UNICAMP, Brazil.

No part of this book may be reproduced without formal permission. Manufactured in the United States of America.

99 98 97 96   5 4 3 2 1

Library of Congress Cataloging-in-Publication Data

Damasceno, Leslie Hawkins.
Cultural space and theatrical conventions in the works of Oduvaldo Vianna Filho / Leslie H. Damasceno.
p.   cm. — (Latin American literature and culture series)
Includes bibliographical references (p.   ) and index.
ISBN 0-8143-2595-5 (alk. paper)
1. Vianna Filho, Oduvaldo, 1936–1974—Criticism and interpretation.   2. Vianna Filho, Oduvaldo, 1936–1974—Dramatic production.   3. Literature and society—Brazil.
4. Theater—Brazil—History—20th century.   I. Title.
II. Series: Latin American literature and culture.
PQ9698.32.I19Z66   1996
869.2—dc20   95-50722
CIP

IN MEMORIAM

Maude Elizabeth Lewis Hawkins and

Yan Michalski

Contents

Preface

Oduvaldo Vianna Filho was a key activist in the Brazilian national theater movement from his beginning work as a student in 1954 until his untimely death from cancer in 1974. Vianinha, as he is generally called, worked as an author and actor in theater, cinema, and television and was an astute theoretician whose assessments of Brazilian theater still speak directly to issues of debate in the 1990s.

This study of Vianinha focuses on theatrical conventions, juxtaposed with an analysis of the cultural space within which he lived and worked. Such an analysis entails an overview of the social, political, and economic factors that help to delineate the parameters of, and opportunity for, theatrical activity. Assessment of cultural space includes an analysis of cultural values and the social insertion of theater as these elements are incorporated into the "idea of theater" that Vianna Filho demonstrates in his practice.

By necessity, these considerations are treated in the continuum of contemporary Brazilian theater, and when applicable, to a broader world context. Within the primary discussion of Vianna Filho's use and understanding of theatrical and dramatic conventions, I examine conventions that may be said to be culture specific and those which are integral to the structures of dramatic literature and theatrical communication, thus entering into a discussion regarding methodological approaches to Brazilian and Latin American theater.

This twofold intention is facilitated by the accessible and easily documented relationship between Vianna Filho's theoretical intentions and preoccupations and his practice. Always at the center of the debate on national theater, he was a committed political activist who constantly appraised the efficacy of his theatrical activity, consistently questioning his own perceptions of the cultural and political possibilities for effecting social change in Brazil. At the same time, the close relationship between his theory and practice present the critical challenge of finding a structure and methodology that neither becomes subsumed in his critical discourse nor presents merely parallel analyses of the questions treated.

Thus, the structure of this study has been designed in part to provide a critical space and distance within the intertextuality inherent in a critical study of a playwright who was, himself, a theoretician. I have also attempted to allow for the complexities of issues of value systems and modalities of perception and reception, while attempting to avoid the sociological reductionism that a preponderantly thematic treatment of the plays would most likely give if joined directly to an analysis of cultural space. To this end, I have chosen to weave a back-and-forth structure between historical overview and cultural space, discussion of cultural values, theatrical theory (Vianna's, others', and my own observations), and textual and production analysis.

Chapter 1 describes the theoretical method I use within my definition of cultural space and theatrical conventions, setting up questions I wish to pursue in terms of cultural values and the social insertion of theater. This introduction is meant to organize some generalizations about theater in relationship to more complicated aesthetic concepts. Chapter 2 presents a systematization of Vianna Filho's theory and evolution of his principal theoretical concerns. Chapters 3, 4, and 5 accompany the development of his work from 1957 through 1974.

As indicated, my major focus is the interaction of the playwright with his specific historical moment, and with the audience of that moment. Therefore, with the exception of Vianna Filho's last and best play, *Rasga coração* (Rend Your Heart) (written 1972–74 and only staged in 1979), my analysis is limited to plays that were staged soon after they were written. Although this limitation excludes three of Vianinha's most interesting plays—*Papa Highirte, Moço em estado de sítio* (Young Man in a State of Siege), and *Mão na luva* (Pull Your Punches, or, Hand in Glove), which were first produced after the political opening in 1979—this emphasis is entirely appropriate to the panoramic aspect that my theory and methodology necessarily impose.

However, in a manner of being the exception to provide both

historical perspective and perspective to the methodology I have proposed, Chapter 6 is limited to an extensive discussion of *Rasga cora-ção*, which stands as a composite of the theatrical and dramatic conventions that Vianna Filho had come to value most. It is also a play whose "theatrical carpentry"—a term employed by its author—enters into intentional dialogue with the traditions of Brazilian theater.

Not all of the works discussed here have been published, and none has been published in English. When possible, I have used the published text, and have consistently followed the punctuation and accentuation of the original Portuguese text. There are a few caveats regarding translation. Limitations of length preclude commentary on the linguistic and philosophic intricacies provoked by the translations. Approximate translations of names of plays are given on first mention; thereafter I use the Portuguese title. Translations are not supplied for those words (titles, organizations, etc.) where Portuguese is similar to English. And verse is not translated with an ear to rhyme.

The important beginning research for this study was undertaken during 1980 and 1981, through the generous help of a Fulbright-Hayes grant. I would also like to thank Princeton University for various grants that have assisted in the research and writing of this book. Numerous people in Brazil, many of whom are noted in the interviews listed in the bibliography, made indispensable contributions to my research during this stage. I would particularly like to mention Maria Lúcia Marins, Sônia Farnstein of Editora Muro, and Fernando Peixoto for their always gracious help in finding sources and sharing material, much of which was still unpublished when I started my research, and also Deocélia Vianna, Yan Michalski, Carmelinda Guimarães, and Maria Sílvia Betti for their insights regarding this research, Maria Thereza Vargas and IDART (Department of Artistic Information and Documentation, now known as the Center of Research/Centro de Pesquisa of the Cultural Center of São Paulo) for the use of tapes of the production of *Rasga coração*, and the library of the SNT (CENACEN and now FUNARTE) for ample access of documentation. A modified version of Chapter 2 was originally published as "Oduvaldo Vianna Filho and Theatre Theory: Historicity as a Category of Representation" in *GESTOS* 7, no. 14 (November 1992). Part of Chapter 6 appeared as "Oduvaldo Vianna Filho: 'Pessedismo' and the Creation of the Anonymous Revolutionary Hero" in *Literature and Contemporary Revolutionary Culture: Jour-*

nal of the Society for the Study of Contemporary Hispanic and Luso-phone Revolutionary Literatures 1 (1984–85).

In the present reworking of this text, I would like to thank Sábato Magaldi, Mariângela Alves de Lima, and Maria Thereza Vargas for their close readings and critical comments. Photographs have been supplied by Maria Lúcia Marins, the Instituto Brasileiro de Arte e Cultura (IBAC, now FUNARTE) of Rio de Janeiro, and the Divisão de Pesquisa do Centro Cultural de São Paulo. Initial translation of Portuguese to English within the text was done by Stephen Berg.

The questions raised, or treated, in this study continue to provide renewed visions in Brazilian theater criticism. However, even though some retrospective critical commentary from additional bibliography has been incorporated beyond the period of the mid-to late 1980s, I have generally preferred to keep my arguments as they were formed within that temporal scope, since I feel that they conform to the tenor of the late 1980s: a moment when a utopian glimmer of democratic change surrounded campaigns for Brazil's first popularly elected president since 1961, and before the global changes that have altered so many cultural analysts' perspectives on the kinds of utopian projects that Vianinha espoused. In Brazil, among the unfortunate changes that have occurred in this interim are the lamented deaths of three persons whose contributions to Brazilian theater have also been essential to my study: Deocélia Vianna, Armando Costa, and Yan Michalski. This text hopes to honor them.

Theoretical Introduction:
Culture, Value Systems, and Theater

Theoreticians of theater and social philosophers since Aristotle have posited questions and definitions regarding the specificity of theater in relation to other arts and activities of social communication in terms of the cultural insertion and social utility of theater and drama, "cultural insertion" being understood here as how theater fits into the overall cultural activity of a society as well as what specific role of cultural mediation it plays. In times of relative social cohesion, when a society as a whole has a unified vision of itself and agrees with the written or unwritten laws, whether political or religious, as well as with the social mores and cultural values that sustain this unified vision, the communicative function of theater seems apparent to all, regardless of class or social divisions.

In such times theater celebrates and reaffirms the cultural values of a society; its specificity resides in its welcome as a necessary, live, and lively communal event. Theater is collective art that contributes to the intellectual and moral development of its public and its practitioners, as well as communal entertainment. There is a sense of socially sanctioned organicity between artist and audience, as both participate in the cultural mediation that theater can provide.

Organicity is compromised, however, when the economic, political, and cultural interests of different sectors of the society are antagonistic to one another. While dominant or elite cultural codes may continue to reign, there will be cultural and political ruptures. These ruptures, even incipient ruptures, become apparent in the dramatic text through the actions and attitudes of dramatic characters or through a challenge to prevailing theatrical aesthetics, perhaps to the extent that the work is censored or prohibited by those holding political power.

However, even more than being an occasion for outright censorship, elements of discontent will indicate that, in the broader social spectrum, there is no longer a unified belief in what a society purports to be and to do for its people. Cultural hegemony may continue to exist, but it cannot, without this consensus, fully explain or contain the social ruptures that will burst forth in times of political and social upheaval. Thus, if the sense of the social collective is precarious, the point of insertion becomes an issue for all the arts, including theater.

From a historical point of view, analytical models that speak to the cultural insertion and the social utility of theater stand in relation both to the functional concept of culture a society has developed and to a particular theoretician's definition of *culture*. For instance, inclusive definitions may apply the verb form ("to grow, to culture"), referring to the intellectual and spiritual growth of an entire society as well as to the artifacts and forms of social organization it generates. On the other hand, more exclusive definitions may select some particular cultural activity, designating as culture a set of artifacts (operas, oil paintings, tragedies, etc.) and establishing subsets of cultural activity as "high" or "low" according to narrow criteria of the artistic or cultural—which, in fact, inevitably reflect the values of a single sector or class of a society.

Definitions of culture are far too numerous to be discussed here.[1] However, given the complexity of the world we live in, the broadest possible definition seems desirable: culture is the "whole way of life, material, intellectual, and spiritual of a given society" (Williams, "Culture and Civilization" 273). This broad anthropological description allows for the various critical perceptions, not necessarily mutually exclusive, that guide our methodological approaches to cultural questions.

In this context, the question of how theater fits into the life of a society can be best approached by looking at the factors that organize theater's insertion into the culture at large. These factors range from the mechanics of theatrical production, to the cultural place ascribed to theater by the society, as well as to theater's role in promoting or contesting the value systems of the society itself. Within these general categories, a series of interrelated questions will clarify the parameters of theater as cultural insertion and will orient our future discussions. While these questions may be obvious, it is important to bring them to mind in an organized fashion as a point of departure.

We can begin with the theatrical worker. What is the role of the actor, the director, the author, and others involved in theatrical practice? Does the actor, for example, function as a kind of delegate of the audience, representing it while maintaining a specialized function as an artist?[2] What cultural mediation do actors perform, and how does society perceive this function? Are actors seen as shamans, artisans (religious or secular), court apologists, *artistes* in the sense of romantic alienation, or as celebrities, professional workers, or renegade experimentalists and political activists, as in more modern times? How are they integrated into the broader society? Are they fully accepted, partially or conditionally accepted, or seen as a caste apart (as in the times of Molière, when theater people were denied burial in consecrated ground)? Does a culture view those involved in making theater as part of a collective enterprise of interlocking functions, or are these functions hierarchically differentiated? Is a director considered more creative than his or her actors? Is a distinction between literature and theater assumed, in which the author is primarily a literary figure and only secondarily a theater worker?

These questions concerning the roles of theater practitioners are related to the questions of how theater is produced, and to what purpose. An investigation of the means and processes of production is fundamental to understanding what kinds of theater a society has and values (e.g., mainstream professional, alternative, collective, popular) and is also helpful in seeing the aesthetic options offered by a particular kind of theater.

Such an investigation will inform the analysis of cultural space and theatrical conventions made in the body of this study, but a few introductory points should be raised here, starting with a very basic question: how do theater people support themselves? How do they finance their activity? Can they work in theater full-time, or must they hold other jobs as well? If their energies are split by economic exigencies, how does this affect their work in the theater? In the larger context, how do the means of production of a specific theater relate to the economic and social organization of the general culture? Is theatrical activity subsidized or otherwise supported by the religious or cultural institutions of the state or society? If so, what ideological purpose does theater fulfill in exchange? If it is primarily an economic enterprise, how does theater juggle the economic exigencies of its production with its artistic, aesthetic, and social proposals? In other words, how does it obtain a significantly large enough audience to pay for its costs, and what kinds of shows will it produce to insure its economic viability?[3]

These considerations of production are inextricably linked to an analysis of who sees theater. What is the audience for theater, and how does this audience reflect the social organization of a society and its values? Is the audience constituted by a financial or social elite? The middle and upper classes or aristocracy? A cultural subgroup or minority? Or is the audience primarily a social or political fringe group that—regardless of class origin—contest the value systems or policies of the society? To what degree must a theater respond to the particular concerns of its audience? Are there artistic and moral values or ideological constructs held in common that when depicted by a work make it more generally acceptable, even though the work seems to speak out against its audience? (For example: "revolutionary" theater cast in an ethical mold.) And if a work treats a theme foreign to its audience, what values does it use to transmit it? (How is life in a black ghetto portrayed for, and received by, a middle-class white audience?)

In sum, what is the process of identification between play and audience? And to what extent does theater contribute to the development of self-image of an audience?

These questions pertain to the underlying values that are integral to social organization. But theater must also respond to modes, or modalities, of perception and reception, which also reflect value systems. What does a specific audience want and expect from theater? Entertainment? Intellectual, psychological, or spiritual instruction and stimulation? A sense of communal participation? Some combination of the above? How do theater groups and individuals assess and choose their audience in view of audience expectations? Is their assessment of these expectations in line with the goals and aesthetic form of the work they present?

When we look at what theater people aspire to do in their work, we must ask another question crucial to their reading of their audience: is this audience real or virtual? That is to say, does an audience already exist that understands and supports the aesthetic form and social content (in broad terms) of its theater? A virtual audience is one projected, or aspired to, by theater practitioners. Theater of aesthetic experimentation and/or political mobilization most often works in the problematic gray area between the real and the virtual. They begin with a core audience of like-minded persons, with the intention of building a larger audience. The discrepancy between real and virtual is one of the largest problems of politically oriented theater groups, especially those that which wish to do theater for and about a different class (for example, student groups that wish to do working-class theater among the working class.)

All of these questions regarding cultural insertion are applicable to some degree to any society's theater. They are especially pertinent to the theater under analysis here, for they come into play when we speak of the social utility of theater, both in general terms and in Brazilian theater in particular.

But, as formulated above, these questions would serve to delineate in broad strokes the sociological and economic structuring of theater, although the superstructural elements with which they interweave are indicated by placing them in abbreviated relationship to value systems. The dialectic between theatrical infrastructure and value systems is complex and will be treated gradually in this study, as it is best seen in reference to specific instances of theater.

The real or possible social utility of theater goes to the very heart of a culture's value systems and resides in the essential interchange theater establishes with its audience. This is a dynamic that calls, first, for a functional definition of theater in relation to text and performance. Working toward a definition, we can start with the broad question that indeed subsumes all of the ones previously asked: what is theater?

Eric Bentley proposes an answer in "What Is Theatre," arguing that theater offers opportunity for the "rediscovery of man" and investigation of meaning in an important way that only it can provide in the arts (*Theatre of Commitment* 47–98). He attributes this to the immediacy of communication that produces a social amalgam of "place," "actor," "I," and "we." He contends that theater must be seen in this necessarily vague and constantly changing social dynamic, and he muses, "There is something about ceasing to be merely an *I* and becoming, in this *place,* before that *actor,* a part of a *we*" (57).

Francis Fergusson relates this sense of community to shared

insights into a culture in his book *The Idea of a Theater.* He takes a historical approach examining how and why the compensatory "idea of theater" has replaced its original communal organicity. He signals place as of utmost importance to theater's role and cultural insertion, commenting on the organicity of the theater practices of Sophocles and Shakespeare, "both of which were developed in theaters which focused, at the center of the life of the community, the complementary insights of the whole culture" (2).

Fergusson goes on to say: "We do not have such a theater, nor do we see how to get it. But we need the 'Idea of a Theater,' both to understand the masterpieces of drama at its best, and to get our bearings in our own time" (2).

While this artistic organicity of communal sharing has become distanced in modern times, a residual idea only partially fulfilled, Fergusson believes that several elements have historically been basic to all successful theater. These elements involve the text-performance-audience triad that helps to define theater's specificity.

Fergusson bases his sense of theater on how dramatic action is structured to produce meaning and how this meaning is perceived by the audience. As with Aristotle, theater is the art of imitating action; by *action* Fergusson means not "the events of the story but the focus or aim of psychic life from which the events, in that situation, result" (36). He uses "action" as an analogical concept where the various components of action on the part of the dramatist—"plot making, characterization, and speech"—combine in the present of the performance with the "mimetic acts of the performers who reproduce, in the medium of their own beings, individual or characterized versions of the action the author had in mind" (230).[4]

The meaningfully constructed and produced play elicits a response from the audience that Fergusson calls "the histrionic sensibility," or the "mimetic perception of action." By this he means the immediate and discriminating perception of action that is quintessential to theater. He contrasts this with music: "dramatic art is based on this form of perception as music is based upon the ear. The trained ear perceives and discriminates sounds; the histrionic sensibility (which also may be trained) perceives and discriminates actions. Neither form of perception can be defined apart from experience but only indicated in various instances of its use" (236–37).

In fact, the immediacy of perception precedes and structures meaning. Fergusson paraphrases and then cites Aristotle in this respect: "it [apperceptive intelligence] is not naïve credulity but a recognition that we are aware of things and people 'before predication,' as he [Aristotle] put it." And Fergusson goes on to clarify that the "histrionic sensibility, the perception of action, is such a primitive and direct awareness" (230).

In closing his arguments, and his book, Fergusson defends the Aristotelian concept of mimesis as what distinguishes drama from the other arts and what gives theater its specific quality of social communication:

> the notion of drama as imitation of action is both possible for us and very valuable. We do actually in some sense perceive the shifting life of the psyche directly, before all predication: before we reach the concepts of ethics or psychology; even before imitating it in the medium of words or musical sounds. When we directly perceive the action which the artist intends, we can understand the objectivity of his vision, however he arrived at it; and thence the form of his art itself. And only on this basis can one grasp the analogies between acting and playwrighting, between various forms of drama, and between drama and other arts. (240)

I think that it is possible to restate Fergusson's argument in terms more appropriate to the tenor of this analysis and say that, according to his theory, production of meaning and production of feeling intersect and coalesce in the theatrical act as a result of an immediacy of perception that is unique to the theatrical experience.

In *Drama in Performance* Raymond Williams raises related issues regarding text and performance that merit brief examination here. Williams also takes a historical view to pose the question of how dramatic text and dramatic performance, which he calls the "written work in performance" (4), intersect. He places primacy on discussion of the "known general facts of performance and the existing texts" in his scholarly quest (6). These are the conditions of performance—the general social and political ambiance, scenic resources, and dramatic conventions of performance—as they are interpolated in the text. His basic underlying assertion is that "When a dramatist writes a play, he is not writing a story which others can adapt for performance; he is writing a literary work in such a manner that it can be directly performed" (170). In other words, the author includes a concept of performance in the text.

In his methodological approach, Williams employs several

terms that bear directly on the present topic of production of meaning and social utility. When talking about how meaning is produced in text and performance, he speaks in terms of structures, or patterns, of feeling. This term acts as a complementary term to Fergusson's idea of "histrionic sensibility" and goes far in explaining how apperception is affected by text and performance.[5]

The structure of feeling is the pattern that comes from the myriad and sometimes imperceptible emotional and psychological reactions of the audience. It can be also called a recognition, or the point where the elements of the pattern come together to structure a "feeling" of meaning. For Williams, this pattern comes mainly from the visual design woven between spatial and textual elements in theater, elements that encompass and organize scenic resources and dialogue.[6] He maintains that theater is a visual art that melds movement and speech. What allows the audience to perceive this design, and its meaning, are the conventions (forms and techniques of communication) a performance utilizes. In other words, meaning is intuitively and conventionally perceived and understood.

A brief example that will help to explicate this complicated idea of design can be found in Williams's analysis of the conventions and spatial design of the miracle plays. He comments that these plays are dramatically simple but that the dialogue often shows the "capacity of this drama to concentrate, at an attained point in the action, on a simple pattern of feeling, expressed through a rhythmic pattern of dramatic speech" (42). This pattern is spatially realized in a manner whose significance is established by tradition and religious conventions. Williams illustrates this by pointing out two "important elements of performance in this kind of resurrection play: the design of movement towards a known physical place, which is the essential dramatic structure of these plays, developed, though with critical changes, from the processional liturgy; and the design of *celebration,* when the place is attained" (36).

When using the phrase "structure, or patterns, of feelings," then, Williams uses feeling and the concretization of feeling as a linking force between text and performance, a force that is both understood within the dramatic conventions of a play and transmitted by these conventions. The social utility of theater—if this term may be applied by extrapolation here—is conventional: through conventions, theater establishes modalities of representation and perception that encapsulate a live form of communication that confirms or questions (explicitly or implicitly) the values of a society.

As used here, *conventions* is a rather loose generic term, referring as much to a dynamic of comprehension as to the specific dramatic and theatrical elements that create this dynamic. Williams also refers to conventions as methods, putting them at the center of theatrical communication:

> What has always to be emphasized is the profound relation between methods of writing and performance and particular views of reality. In each generation, the old methods are called conventional, but in an art like the drama the successful new method is in itself a convention. The writing and performance of drama depends on that kind of agreement—it need not altogether be prior agreement; it can be reached in the act itself—on the nature of the action being presented. What is called conventional, in the sense of an old routine, is a method or set of methods which presents a different kind of action, and through it a different kind of reality. (176)

The agreement of which Williams speaks is, of course, the one the audience reaches with the performance. Williams is careful to give the audience a living—not static—role in the evolution of dramatic traditions. He affirms: "An audience is always the most decisive inheritance, in any art. It is the way in which people have learned to see and respond that creates the first essential condition for drama" (176).

Within this kind of contract of comprehension, Williams is also careful to emphasize that, although he has used the term *method*, a convention "is not just a method: an arbitrary and voluntary technical choice. It embodies in itself those emphases, omissions, valuations, interests, indifferences, which compose a way of seeing life, and drama as part of life" (178). A convention, then, is not simply an aesthetic choice, but roots one in experience and works only when it corresponds to a way of seeing.[7]

Thus, when we speak of ways of seeing, we get back to the matter of values: the values a society gives to human enterprise, life, and feeling, as well as to those that are an integral part of the ontological, religious, or cosmological notions felt to govern or otherwise interface with human activity. It can be argued that the need to question the whys, wherefores, and wheretos of existence and experience is a universal human response that predicates artistic traditions. However, the phrasing of the questions and the modalities of response have changed radically throughout human history.

In theater, the questions and responses are transmitted by conventions. It is useful, when examining how this works, to make a distinction between dramatic conventions and theatrical conventions. Such a distinction helps us see how social structure and values inform, and are informed by, conventions. A basic, albeit mechanical distinction, comes from the obvious: dramatic conventions are those that pertain primarily to the text, to the act of authorship, and theatrical conventions are those used to stage the play.

However, this definition is not sufficient. As Williams, Fergusson, and many others note, the author is aware of the theatrical conventions of a projected stage and audience as he or she writes, and the author incorporates this awareness into the text. On the other hand, unless the director of a play decides to junk the text of a proposed production (which sometimes happens, often under the guise of recreating the feeling, or ambiance, in contemporary context), the production has to enter into some dialogue with the modes of understanding particular to the dramatic conventions of the text. In this sense, there is always an dialogue between the dramatic text and the performance text.[8]

A systematic exploration of how the value systems of contemporary Western culture are interpolated into dramatic and theatrical conventions is beyond the scope of this introduction. Even so, a few synthesizing statements regarding values should be made before proceeding further. I use *values* to connote the ideals and notions belonging to people and societies that organize and give meaning to individual and communal life.

The word reflects the dialectical process of interiorization and exteriorization of this organization in the dative proposition "to give value to." What one gives value to becomes imbued with value. Once valued, the object or concept has a place of its own, so to speak, and enters into a framework of personal or societal tradition, and the tradition may outlive the circumstances that gave rise to the tradition and the values integral to it, thus provoking a kind of functional disjuncture between objective reality and the perception of this reality.

A *value system,* as I use the term here, is the web of interrelated values that makes up the consensual view of life of a given society and sustains its coherence. As a rough example, medieval concepts of honor are integral to the authoritarian structure of the feudal system, where financial obeisance and allegiance to the highest earthly authority (the king, acting in the name of God) organized the social structure.

In his analysis of the key concepts of modern culture as they originate from the historical changes, including economic structuring, that predicate modernity, *Culture and Society,* Raymond Williams sustains the view that three major issues—industry, democracy, and art—delineate it.[9] Although he limits himself to England from 1780–1950, these issues are pertinent to our study. He defines industry as mass production and considers democracy to be the ideology of participation, art to be "imaginative truth" (xv). Williams notes how the contemporary meaning of such words as *class, mass, individual,* and *culture* intersect with these issues to provoke contradictions that reveal themselves in artistic conventions.

How these issues and concepts are valuatively manifested can be shown in a few examples that will also serve to show the intertextual dynamic of dramatic and theatrical conventions. The "fourth wall" is eminent among these.

Most critics concede that the concept of the fourth wall—that imaginary wall of the stage apron that encloses the stage set—began with the Italianate theater of the Renaissance period and expresses the burgeoning sense of individualism that characterized that era. In the theatrical realism, or illusionism, of the late nineteenth century—still significantly present in today's theater—the idea of a wall tends to persuade the spectators that they are witnessing a true representation of the life of the individuals on stage. They are demarcated from the audience by the presence of an imaginary wall; the separation of stage and audience is stressed.

Whether or not the play's theme may open up to explore the individual's broader relationship to social issues (as in Ibsen and Chekhov), the conventions are those of enclosure, reflecting, as Williams says, the "self-enclosed nature of action in (high) bourgeois drama, which gives primacy to reaction." He adds that "the emphasis is on the stasis of the individual, where resolutions of conflicts are interior" (*Drama in Performance* 182). The sense of enclosure permeates the text, and relationships are socially reductive rather than expansive: social questions are—with good reason, given the social structure of the audience—expressed and resumed in interpersonal family conflicts.

Physical enclosure, separation, and often isolation are textually indicated by the physical space called for in presentation: parlors, living rooms, and so on. In realistic stage sets, props and scenic design become emblematic of enclosure. The realism of the dialogue found in the dramatic text is accentuated by conventions of naturalistic acting. In effect, the dilemma of the individual protagonist is presented to the audience as an enclosed unit of experience, which the individual member of the audience accepts or rejects, generally as a result of identification or nonidentification with the character.

In the epic theater conceived by Bertolt Brecht, the fourth wall was one of the primary conventions of illusionistic theater to be challenged in his attempts to break with the evolutionary determinism and individualistic involvement of what he called "dramatic theatre."[10] It is possible to read Brechtian dialogue as a series of interchanges destined to be received as communication only by the actors on stage, although such a reading would be contrary to the textual indications of the conventions he wished to establish.

Brecht indicates the use of a series of scenic devices and acting techniques designed to break the reactive pattern fomented by the fourth wall and carry the discussion on stage into the audience, where response would be provoked by reasoning and argument, only secondarily by empathy. Placards are paraded interrupting dramatic sequences; songs, in stylized verse, are sung directly to audience; actors are trained not to identify with their characters, but rather to "recite" lines so as to emphasize their separation from the characters; and gestures are stylized to indicate a character's social status or class attitude, particularly a conflict between what is said and what is consciously or unconsciously thought.

The idea of the fourth wall as well as the desire to break it, or at least to use it as a metaphor for enclosure, is indeed central to modern theater. The illusionistic and Brechtian theaters invite further comment, but they serve here as broad examples of how dramatic and theatrical conventions can complement or be played against each other.

A more limited case, Hamlet's "To be or not to be" soliloquy, can clarify this further. The soliloquy was a convention common to Elizabethan theater, sometimes used to communicate the private thoughts of the character, but just as often used to impart information on action offstage or on action that the speaking character (or a confederate or enemy) had taken or was about to take. Seen through dramatic conventions, then, Hamlet's dilemma of oscillation is richer for playing off the soliloquy as an indicator of action.

However, there are many ways of interpreting Hamlet's speech. Whatever the director's and actor's reading of the motives for Hamlet's vacillation, the audience ultimately receives Hamlet's predicament through the conventions employed in the production: the overall environment produced, including the set, and most specifically, the actor's manner of delivering the lines. In effect, the actor's understanding of the speech is encoded in performance by such devices as phrasing, emphasis, gesture, intonation, movement, and stance, which must relate to the audience's conventional idea of how people speak and act in order for the actor's interpretation to be successfully decoded.

Regardless of the ideas and values presented in the dramatic text, in production the transmission of attitudes toward these ideas and/or values, as well as the efficacy of any intention to challenge or promote these concepts, is accomplished by the theatrical conventions used. Theatrical conventions also tend to be more culturally specific. For example, Oriental theater may be an exquisite aesthetic experience for the uninitiated Western spectator, but much more will be gained if the spectator has some comprehension of the cultural values, and the conflict of values, embodied in the stylized gestures.[11]

I have chosen to emphasize theatrical conventions in this study precisely because they are most revealing of a specific culture's values. I define theatrical conventions as the codes of communication used in the production of a play, a definition that includes the rhetorical devices in the text that indicate these codes. A playwright and/or theatrical production will utilize established conventions according to need but must develop new codes of communication adequate to new, or significantly different, ideas of what the playwright wants to say. The significance of these codes may be inductively perceived by the audience at the beginning, but if theatrically successful, may quickly assume conventional status.

Recognition of this dynamic is important to the analysis of any theater, but, I believe, essential to the investigation of Brazilian and Spanish American theater. Brazilian and Spanish American theater, at its best, is highly theatrical, rather than literary. There are several basic reasons for this. First of all, the strong and continuous tradition of national dramatic literature requires a certain sense of secure nationhood that, because of economic dependence and uncertainty and political instability, has been difficult to achieve in Latin America. Traditions do exist, but they are piecemeal. Continuity is the key word here. Within this framework, cultural coherence has precariously evolved in conjunction with debate and practice over questions of cultural dependency on European and, more recently, American traditions.

Secondly, the development of dramatic traditions requires

continuity of theatrical practice. Very little about theater can be taken for granted in Latin America. This is not simply a question of the individual author's financial stability, necessary to continue writing, nor of finding the money to have work produced. It is a question of the larger context for continuous theatrical activity: dependable performance spaces, backing, and resources, including a pool of trained talent to put on plays. In this last respect, it is rare to find, at least in Brazil, actors who have been able to train equally in the various areas of voice, movement, dance, and so on important to modern theater. Schools are few, and funding for students almost nonexistent.

If these preconditions of theatrical activity do exist at a given moment, there has been, historically, no assurance of their continuance. To the contrary. Particularly during the decades studied here, access to theatrical resources and to an audience were abruptly cut by political change or by censorship. Under these conditions, theater people who find themselves on the wrong side of the political fence run the risk of curtailment, exile, or even torture and death. It is a scene in which always present economic constraints (inflation, lack of resources) are exacerbated by actual or possible political circumscriptions.

Given the precariousness of its situation, Brazilian theater has of necessity become highly inventive, finding new forms of communication and developing or modifying conventions in accordance with the conditions of its performance. However, these are mainly considerations of a structural nature, as stated above. A sense of social and political intentionality prevails in contemporary Spanish American and Brazilian theater and reflects the historical and social problems of these countries.

Spanish American and Brazilian theater has been characterized by a commitment on the part of its practitioners for social change.[12] The emphasis on theatricality can be also seen in this light. Primacy is given to theater's capacity to render immediate social reality and to establish a dialogue with the audience designed to provoke thought and action directed toward social, political, and economic problems. Because of this focus, Brazilian theater, of the period discussed in this study, has tended to be situational, inventing theatrical responses to historical circumstances.

And it has evolved largely through groups and movements, as well as by the contribution of individual authors. This mode of growth may be attributed to a combination of factors: to the constant changes and limitations of its points of cultural insertion; to the necessity of collective action inherent in the political philosophy of its major practitioners; and to the difficulties of individual creation in regard to dramatic traditions.

For these reasons, it is a theater extremely conscious of its role of cultural mediation, and one can see in the highly documented and intense relationship between theory and practice in recent Brazilian and Latin American theater the genesis of much, or even most, of the artistic merit and aesthetic experimentation that characterizes it.

Therefore, an analysis that wishes to probe the evolution of the theatrical conventions of an author who shares these concerns, as well as to investigate how these conventions lay a basis for the evolution of his dramaturgy, must employ a methodology that can place his work within the factors that delimit his theatrical practice. This involves analysis of his ideas on the social function and utility of theater in conjunction with the ideas of theater held by his culture—ideas that necessarily entail discussion of the values of that culture.

Cultural Space and Theater

The methodological approach I have elaborated to organize these various factors is oriented by investigation of the cultural space that fixes the parameters of contemporary Brazilian theater. This concept is understood, in physical terms, as scenic space in relation to theatrical infrastructure. In its more inclusive definition, it considers the delimitations of communication within a society: how theatrical space is delineated by sociocultural circumstances (for example, censorship) as well as what aesthetic options are perceived and taken in the appropriation and utilization of this space.

This leads into a metaphorical level that is extremely important to my study. Cultural space also refers to the possibility of cultural debate available to theater and how theater people interpret that possibility. In other words, it is their reading of the degree of openness/ closure their society will permit for their work. This metaphorical sense also includes public response, or the flow of dialogue between public and theater. As the public responds, it helps form parameters of communication, largely determining how a cultural concept might exact a form in spatial terms. When this happens, the actual physical space occupied becomes a locus of cultural consensus, created by public demand and/or necessity (for example, the theatrical spaces that come to be associated with political protest).

The dimension of cultural space, even as it refers to a relatively fixed physical locale, is by no means immutable, but includes social fissures and the modes of access that one segment of a society has to another. It deals with the cultural interflow between different backgrounds and interests within a society (such as the spaces of communication created by groups of middle-class origin who wish to create links to the working class).

Analyzing theater in spatial terms provides a thread with which to interweave the theoretical interests and necessities detailed in this introduction. First of all, theater is defined by its utilization of space: what people do and how they move and interrelate on stage, the visualization of speech; how the author, director, and others represent the work in its scenic space; and the spatial relationship of the actors to the audience. Secondly, theatrical conventions arise mainly from spatial exigencies and from cultural values as these values are spatially demonstrated. Theatrical conventions, then, function as codes of communication that transmit values through spatial use.

Spatial concepts are physical, textual, performative, and authorial values that interrelate cultural values. They link a performance and play to the conditions of performance particular to the theater of the play's origin. In a world as complex as ours, where values and the conditioning elements of values shift so rapidly, a spatial study of theater allows a more definable way of investigating the cultural insertion of theater since it lends itself to the collaboration of an infrastructural analysis of theater with an analysis of the codes of communication of that theater. Finally, a study of spatial concepts in regard to cultural and social concerns is of particular importance to Brazilian theater given that its single greatest problem has been conquering the space for growth and continuity of its traditions.

Three interrelated spatial concepts will be discussed, all of which carry to some degree cultural connotations and all of which are influenced by cultural values. The first of these is physical space, the spaces that house, or otherwise demarcate, theatrical events. The second is scenic space, the specific use of the stage area made by a performance. The third treats the idea that the author, in the dramatic text, has of space. When speaking of physical space in the broadest sense, I consider a cultural space to be a place of communication and investigation of the traditions, artifacts and values of a given culture, in which the actual establishment of its physical parameters are emblematic of cultural concepts—confirming them or calling them into question. The use of space itself becomes a mediating term in the formation and perpetuation of modes of perception of a culture.

Theatrical locales may or may not be linked to officially recognized cultural institutions—such as state theaters—that subsidize the cultural work they house and that, therefore, to a large extent govern the cultural expression they support. However, whatever the specific physical parameters may be, the delineation and utilization of the space, at least in theater, represent a continual dialectic between superstructural concerns (cultural and ideological concepts) and economic infrastructure in the most basic manner: occupation of space represents choices and exigencies of the time, work, and money of its occupants and, depending on who has the power to authorize the use of it, indicates an often precarious relationship between who holds the means of production and who actually produces a work.

I don't think it possible to determine any precise formula to investigate how a certain space is empowered with cultural significance and what the relationships are between the elements of production of that significance. The points of intersection between an historical moment (sociocultural ambiance) and a specific artistic vision are too varied to make such a formula. However, as a means of analyzing the weight that use of space plays in this variation, I have come to perceive six categories of theatrical playing space in Brazil: professional theater houses; institutional spaces; university theaters; amateur spaces; cultural places that hold traditional significance (be it religious, historical, spaces traditional to popular presentations); and alternative spaces.[13]

These spaces are defined as much by the kind, or kinds, of theater done in them and by the way theatrical activity is funded as by their actual physical dimensions and locations. The borders between them and their cultural significance have been fluid in the history of Brazilian theater to the extent that the latter's traditions have evolved largely from the interpenetration of these spaces by theatrical forms not primarily associated with their adopted space (for example, the inclusion of popular theater forms in professional theater).

The growth of Brazilian theater has been characterized by a hybridization that reflects the cultural diversity found in Brazil. In this process, the transposition of theatrical elements particular to one cultural form to another theatrical space—as in the case of African rituals used in mainstream theater—often presents problems of artistic coherence, both on stage and in the dramatic text. But when successfully resolved, the scenic solutions of these productions lay a base for future theatrical conventions.[14]

The predominant idea of theater, and of theatrical space, is that of professional theater: large-scale commercial productions—be they comedies, social or psychological dramas, or musicals—that employ professional actors and hope to make a profit by extended runs in a fixed location. Professional, mainstream theater exists throughout Brazil but is concentrated in the major cities. In the years immediately following the political opening in Brazil in 1979, Maria Helena Kühner, in *A comunicação teatral,* counts fifty-eight major "casas de espetáculos" in the municipality of Rio de Janeiro in 1983. Seating capacity in these houses vary from 80 (Aliança Francesa de Botafogo) to 2,357 in the Teatro Municipal, but the average capacity is around 300–400. (The Canecão holds 2,400 but is used almost exclusively for concerts given by singers or groups.)

Of these theaters, at least forty-two were, and most continue to be, dedicated mainly to the production of plays or musical plays. As of the early 1980s, all but the eight federally or state-funded theaters were essentially run as impresarial ventures and therefore catered to the dictates of the market regarding the choice of plays produced. The major audience of these theaters is the middle class, and naturally producers select what they consider to be of interest to the audience. It is generally a cautious selection. This means a preponderance of shows of foreign origin, musicals such as *Piaf* being the most popular and profitable.

Limited subsidies are and have been given by municipal, state, or federal cultural entities to national plays, such as *Rasga coração,* put on in commercial theaters. However, in order to qualify for these subsidies, which are authorized against box office returns, these plays must be judged to be financially viable investments, which, in turn, means that they tend to fit within the aesthetic and thematic paradigms of professional theater.

The vernacular term that has served to designate this commercial theater is *teatrão,* an expressive word whose augmentative ending *(-ão)* ironically encapsulates a sense of largeness of production and grandeur that often exceeds the real capacity of human and material resources to fill that space adequately. It also connotes a certain mystification of theater as a spectacle of entertainment that is consecrated by the presence of popular TV soap opera actors who accompany *teatrão.*

It is rare to find small or experimental productions in these theaters. In Rio as in São Paulo and the other major cities, there are smaller ones linked with workers associations that, although they still work within the impresarial and commercial category, will from time to time house productions of aesthetic and thematic experimentation.

Since rents on these theaters are cheaper, the semiprofessional groups that tend to put on these plays can attract an audience.

Institutional theater spaces in Brazil have been created to strengthen professional theater and bridge the gap between professional theater and the more experimental amateur theater and university theater that has been the backbone of the growth of national theatrical traditions. The creation of the Serviço Nacional de Teatro (SNT) was decreed in 1937 by Getúlio Vargas, and it was made responsible to the Ministry of Education and Health. Reformed in 1981 as the Instituto Nacional das Artes Cênicas (INACEN), it maintained theaters throughout Brazil, organizing and administrating programs designed to strengthen national theater.

In Rio, in the early 1980s, five theaters were owned and run by INACEN. They have housed some professional productions but have tended to concentrate on national texts and give room to touring regional productions, many of which utilize folkloric forms particular to their regions. The actors and groups involved in these productions have been, in the main, semiprofessional or amateur. One theater, the Teatro Experimental Cacilda Becker, is dedicated to experimental and amateur productions. Another, the small 128-seat Aurimar Rocha, emphasizes puppet theater, which is a significant theatrical contribution considering the richness of the popular forms of puppet theater in Brazil, especially in the Northeast.

The then existing Fundação de Arte do Rio de Janeiro (FUNARJ), the cultural foundation of the municipality of Rio de Janeiro, owned and operated four theaters, the largest being the Teatro Municipal. It has housed opera, ballet, symphonic and jazz concerts, and concerts of internationally famous singers. The other downtown theater, the João Caetano, which has a seating capacity of 1,200, was, in the early 1980s, producing professional theater at subsidized ticket prices to encourage the working-class commuter population that congregates in its plaza to catch suburban buses. It also has promoted an outreach program of cultural events, mostly concerts, at popular prices. The other two theaters, which seat around 350 each, are located in the suburbs and continue to perform essentially the same function, although they also tend to house amateur groups putting on plays by contemporary suburban authors.[15]

The space used by university theater fluctuates widely and has not always been relegated to the auditoriums of the schools. University theater has been extremely important in Brazil, as will be discussed in chapter 3. Groups originating in the universities, some of them directly linked to theater schools, have grown to be subsidized by private or state funds and given spaces outside the university. Many professional actors come from this background, as well as from amateur theater, and a significant number of national authors started their dramatic careers within this framework.

Amateur theater has also made an important contribution to Brazilian theater. In the late 1920s and the 1930s, amateur groups formed predominantly by the cultured upper middle class organized sporadic performances, rehearsing in private homes and occasionally renting professional theaters for performances. (For instance, the Teatro de Brinquedo, organized by Álvaro Moreyra in Rio de Janeiro in 1927.) The quality of this theater varied greatly, but its existence as a place for apprenticeship and galvanization of interest in the monied classes regarding national theater—which had generally viewed acting and theatergoing in Brazil as lower-class entertainment—provided precedent and impetus for the growth of national theater that accompanied the period of industrialization in the 1940s. In recent times, particularly from the 1970s until today, amateur groups by and large occupy the same spaces as alternative theater.

The difficulty of obtaining professional training should be noted in regard to the relationship between professional and amateur theater. Although theater schools and courses have existed from the early years of the century,[16] their functioning is always at the mercy of economic forces. A major exception is probably at the University of São Paulo, the Escola de Arte Dramática (EAD). Therefore, in a country like Brazil where a consistent lack of resources has all but precluded definable stages of professionalization in the arts, the crossover and interpenetration of nonprofessional and professional theater has provided the breadth of artistic apprenticeship necessary to feed professional theater.

Traditional, or popular and folkloric theater, has fed the traditions of mainstream theater in a somewhat different manner. Popular theater forms traditionally dear to the urban working and lower middle class as well as to sectors of the middle class, like the *revista,* have always been performed by professional actors in commercial theaters, although these performances are given in the smaller and seedier theaters frequented by their audience. Rarely, if ever, are they performed in toto by the original actors on the professional middle-class stage, and within the dominant idea of theater in Brazil this theater has been considered marginal despite its large popular following. However, the theatrical conventions of cabaret and vaudeville as characterized in the *revista* filter into mainstream theater in productions that wish to broaden their appeal by inclusion of more popular forms or in the productions of directors and authors who demonstrate an intentional commitment to the use and exploration of autochthonous dramatic and theatrical traditions.[17]

A similar process of appropriation occurs with other popular forms. Brazil is indeed rich in popular theater forms, many of them, like the *bumba meu boi* and the puppet *mamulengo,* having precolonial origins in the Iberian Peninsula and Africa.[18] As popular theater, they are largely performed as part of festivals in public places, most often in rural communities. Carnival, religious dances, and processions—Catholic and African—also feed these traditions.

Popular festivals have their specific times and particularized utilization of public space, although these have become increasingly malleable in accord with the increasing commercialization of popular festivals. The performers in these festivals are not normally professional actors, although it often happens that a person will continue to portray the same character or allegorical animal throughout his or her life. Sometimes, roles are passed on within a family from generation to generation. At any rate, there is an artistic continuity that affords a "professional" quality that often surpasses nominally professional theater. The interior and rural regions of Brazil also abound with artisans and craftsmen who, master performers of popular theater, make a lifetime living touring small towns and communities.

Many Brazilian plays incorporate elements of popular theater, rituals, and beliefs, including them thematically, using them illustratively, elaborating dramatic and/or scenic structures based on popular forms and rituals, or appropriating the ludic tone and gesture found in Brazilian street theater. This is done with varying success and attention to authenticity, some productions also hoping to approximate the sense of community associated with these forms in their original settings.

The concept, or widespread use, of the term *alternative theater* is relatively recent in Brazil, born of the political repression of the 1960s and early 1970s in conjunction with the restrictions put upon professional space by the cultural and economic constraints of that era. Alternative spaces are delimited in opposition, or in contrast, to traditional and commercial ones and differ from the latter more in the conception those using them have of theater than in the actual kind of space used. Alternative theater tends to use small theater houses that run on minimal budgets, revamped commercial buildings, school or church auditoriums, union halls, parks and other public places, community centers, and also experimental spaces provided by state agencies.

Economic, ideological, and often aesthetic motives—or some permutation of these three—lead theater people to look for these other places in which to perform. When one thinks of alternative theater, one tends to think of low-budget theater of an aesthetically experimental and politically contestatory nature.

In the United States, cost of production is the most constant basic factor in the search for alternative spaces, although there are some groups motivated to use them for political and/or social reasons. Those dedicated to trying to make a professional living in theater rarely have access to the capital necessary to produce commercial successes, and often off- (or off-off) Broadway-style productions are the only way they can continue doing theater with remuneration. Small theaters rented several days a week, lofts, and storefronts are favorite spaces for such productions. Summer stock and dinner theaters provide a space for repertory and experimentation and, along with community theaters, may act as interstitial spaces for a flow of amateur and professional talent.

The economic delineation of space implies a desire for professional upward mobility into mainstream theater, which is often the case. Or, like off-Broadway, the availability of alternative spaces may give form to a loose community of theatrical talent that can create a parallel market to the large commercial-theater productions. This movement toward professionalization is also common in Brazil.

However, the functional attitude toward the economic structuring of mainstream theater of those dedicated to alternative theater (the theater that is of interest to this study and to the growth of theatrical traditions in Brazil and Spanish America) is inseparable from their understanding of the political and cultural context of their societies in determining where and what kind of theater is produced.

Politically contestatory and experimental theater spaces are chosen not just because they are financially viable, but because they are "independent," having minimal economic strings attached. Political and aesthetic options are greater outside the economic exigencies of professional theater. For example, persons wishing to do experimental or performance work that would never command a commercial audience may find that they can gather a community of like-minded people in the theater of an old school auditorium. As word spreads, the locale and work take on greater cultural significance as a gathering place for the interchange of ideas and theatrical practice. Cultural movements are born as a result of the appropriation of spaces that are peripheral to mainstream and institutional theaters (including those university spaces normally dedicated to theater), and often these movements are later integrated to some degree into what is conceded to be establishment theater.

For many groups wishing to do leftist political or social theater, alternative spaces represent a political statement. Structurally, they may signify a step in the transformation of modes of theatrical production from the capitalist toward the socialist. And they consider that the option for the noncommercial and for institutional independence is a move to construct an ideological independence that would permit both protest and an alignment with more progressive forces in society. This theater tends to see itself as a cultural arm of sociopolitical mobilization and works with unions, neighborhood and community entities, street people, sometimes churches and schools, and on occasion, within commercial spaces.

In times of overt political repression, the search for alternative locales is not an option, but a continual invention born of necessity. Within the context of this theater, the appropriation of space assumes even larger cultural significance, as it provides an opportunity for debate and testimony denied by authorities in sanctioned spaces.

Even in economic infrastructural terms, it is apparent that the borders between these six types of space are by no means clearly defined. Besides those economic factors that directly influence availability and that are to a large degree determined by the value systems and tastes of the audience, there are other institutional, or quasi-institutional, delimitations of communication within a society that serve to set parameters on the use of space. For example, institutions operate by a set of specified or unwritten guidelines in allocating room and money to groups. The web of relationships between these policies and the political-economic organization of a society as they bear on theatrical structure and space is, at best, complicated, and will be discussed with reference to specific theatrical productions in their particular contexts. In societies whose governments exercise direct control or censorship over the arts, theater productions suffer political, artistic, and economic restrictions. When political repression is severe, the possibility of torture and further loss of civil rights makes one very careful of what is said, how it said, and where it is performed.

In general, these spaces of theatrical activity and the process of interchange in their use have their parameters established by three factors: availability of space; appropriation of space; and the cultural significance that a space is imbued with. Availability is mostly determined by economic and political factors. Appropriation will depend on the economic and social resources of those wishing to do theater, as well as upon their aesthetic and political goals. The cultural significance of a space is usually interwoven out of the relationship between the first two factors.

The formation of primarily amateur or alternative theater festivals in Brazil and Spanish America is a particularly pertinent example of this relationship.[19] Theater groups may decide to organize festivals in some city of the interior because it is cheaper, there are accommodations and a natural stage space, the weather is good, or for myriad other reasons. Or in the case of Brazil in the early 1970s, because censorship laws did not apply to such "experimental" or "cultural festival" with the same rigor they did to productions designed for commercial or even alternative theater.[20] These festivals become regular events, and what was an improvisorially carved out space becomes either institutionalized or at least widely recognized as a site of cultural importance. In Brazil and Spanish America, festivals have become repositories of cultural interchange and integral to the concept of theater within those societies.

But when we speak of Brazilian theater, most specifically that of the 1930s forward, we can break these factors down into further points of analysis. Availability, appropriation, and significance of space are marked by poverty of resources; cultural restrictions imposed by political systems (especially important from 1964 to 1979); the functional understanding that theater people have of these political systems and their modes of discourse; positions taken regarding questions of national cultural identity and cultural dependency; and the intentional structuring of the participation of the public in the choosing and utilization of space.

Brazilian (and Spanish American) theater is truly a poor theater, where necessity is the mother, godmother, and midwife of invention. The necessity for theory has also been part of this birth process, and theoretical assessment of the above factors has been a determining element in the practice of politically oriented theater in Brazil, as these activists have worked to expand and give greater depth to the parameters of their practice. This is true not only of the search for and use of theatrical locales. Lack of funds and cultural restrictions not only hamper the availability and appropriation of stage, or production, possibilities in terms of theater space but also dictate, in large part, use of scenic space.

As will be discussed at greater length, in the context of specific movements and plays, theater activists have transformed their political theory on social organization and reality and possibility of change into aesthetic positions regarding scenic space and the choice of theatrical conventions used in that space.

As a preliminary definition of scenic space, we can say that it comprises the space of theatrical focus, that which the actors use in performance. In conceptual terms, the utilization of physical space reveals the idea of theatrical communication inherent in the production. The popular expression "set the stage for" conveys this sense of preparation and predisposition for a subsequent message or act.

Scenic space, as used here, is made up of the interrelationship between stage set, movement, and proxemics. The set is the arrangement of objects on stage: how a determined ambiance is conceived, designed, portrayed, and constructed on stage; what objects and props are used in this conception; how the style (realist, expressionist, for example) of the set enters into the conceptual transformation of scenic space; and how the mechanisms of production are disguised or highlighted in accord with the idea of theater held. (Does the set strive to be realistic, hiding scene changes? Are the bare bones of theatrical process intentionally exposed, actors changing the sets as part of the performance?)

Movement is, quite simply, how the actors utilize their space: how and where they move; what gestures they employ that indicate the parameters and significance of their effective space. Proxemics refers to the instance, or image, of spatial relationships between actors and actors, between actors and stage objects, and between actors and audience where the degree of distance or closeness serves to "freeze" a theatrical image for the spectator, transmitting a feeling of relationship (intimacy, participation, sociability, publicness, ostracism, etc.).[21] As Williams has pointed out, movement and proxemics in conjunction with stage design, or theatrical space, structure the feeling, if not the message, of a production.

When the basis of a performance is a dramatic text, scenic space mediates between the cultural concerns of the larger cultural space—which includes the factors that delimit availability of theatrical space—and the author's personal sense of space as we see it in the dramatic text. As a rule, an author has in mind a real or "ideal" playing space. He or she has an idea of the kind of theater space that will be used (commercial, alternative, etc.), of who the audience will be, and of how the audience should perceive the play. The kind of intimacy or distance the author wishes to promote between performance and audience is indicated by the theatrical and dramatic conventions written into the play.

The author may also envision the scenic space and mentally position characters as he or she writes in order to heighten the theatrical effect. The spatial disposition of the characters helps to establish the significance of the social and interpersonal relationships between them. Their individual placement on stage reveals something about them or about their dramatic purpose. For example: a monologue given in a dim spot in back of the stage may transmit profound social isolation, whereas one openly directed to the audience from the apron makes for more direct contact. Even a temporarily empty stage carries expectations about those who will inhabit it.

The author may write these relationships into the technical directions in the text. They will also be seen through the deictic functions of the dialogue. These are the references the characters make to themselves as speakers and to other characters (usually pronouns, such as *I, you, he, him, hers*) and the indicators of spatiotemporal coordinates of the characters (most often adverbs such as *here, there, now,* etc.).[22] Obviously, deictic words fulfill a practical function of providing information as to the whereabouts and relationships of the author's characters. Beyond this, however, they can also give the most poetically revealing instances of imagery. Depending on the intonation or emphasis given to the author's words, an *I* or a *here* can summon up a histrionic effect far beyond the verbal information imparted.[23]

In brief, the author's personal sense of space is the aesthetic of spatial concepts as seen in his or her work, in the elements of the text that invoke images that relate his or her personal vision to a cultural context. This happens on a variety of intertwining levels, including use or invention of conventions, understanding of theater, and the motives for the author's commitment to theater as mode of artistic expression.

It is a basic contention of this study that the most culturally significant theater—if not the best dramatic work—is born of the dramatic and theatrical tension produced in the process of finding coherence within the exigencies of these spatial categories of physical theatrical space, scenic space and the author's own sense of space.

The present study will investigate the tension and growth in the work of an author, Oduvaldo Vianna Filho, who struggled for artistic coherence, consciously grappling with concerns of cultural space, values and theater's cultural insertion and utility in a particularly turbulent epoch of Brazilian history.

Oduvaldo Vianna Filho:
Theory and Biography

Because he preferred to work collectively, Vianinha's[1] history as a playwright and activist is inextricably bound up with that of politically oriented theater groups. Starting his career in the Teatro Paulista do Estudante, he became an early core member of Teatro de Arena, a group founded by socially committed professionals and theater students, whose objective in the later 1950s included the ambition of providing a theater of national themes and texts in an alternative performing space that would eventually incorporate a working-class audience. In 1961, after leaving Arena in 1960, he and some other cultural activists created the Centro Popular de Cultura (CPC), an organization within the União Nacional de Estudantes. The nonprofessional groups of the CPC were committed to working-class and rural organizing, and their productions generally followed the spatial and thematic dictates of agitprop or situational theater. After the military coup of 1964 and the suppression of the CPC, most of the its members went back into professional or semiprofessional theater. Vianinha worked with the Grupo Opinião from

1964 until 1967 and then, like many other authors who continued to write plays that were produced when censorship and economic conditions permitted, he turned to TV as his only viable source of steady income.

Except for the CPC period, Vianinha's plays were written within the framework of professional theater and are explorations of the parameters of this theater both as a political forum and as entertainment. With regard to professional theater, his theory is remarkable in its relentless questioning—and self-questioning—of the communicative efficacy of committed theater in relationship to its real audience, and of the links and discrepancies between the real audience and the "virtual," or intended, audience of the play and performance.

It is precisely this coherence of theoretical vision and dramatic practice that places Vianinha at the center of the cultural issues that inform contemporary Brazilian theater. In brief, these issues involve exploration and experimentation of ways to create (or solidify) an autochthonous dramatic tradition that would speak to the social problems of Brazilian society.

Value Systems, Perceptual Modes, and History in the Theory of Oduvaldo Vianna Filho

From the beginning of his extant theoretical writings,[2] Vianinha approached the question of the specificity of theater in terms of its cultural insertion, speaking in more theoretically abstract language to the force art has to organize perception regarding value systems and concentrating on the possibilities of theater as a vehicle of political conscientization and transformation of the value systems operant in contemporary Brazilian society.

In a long discussion of the artist's and dramatist's role in society, "O artista diante da realidade" (The artist confronted with reality),[3] presumably written in 1960, Vianinha gives a general statement of what art—and by extension, theater—means to him:

> A arte para mim é a transmissão de vivências, relações, representações e valores, que se incluem no aparelho imediato de conhecimento com que enfrentamos a realidade—desenvolvendo nossa capacidade de reagir sobre ela, nossa capacidade de inteligi-la e representá-la. Arte não é útil—porque não ligada à produção de

bens materiais, não pode transmitir conceitos, nem pode definir e formar atitudes diante de fenômenos isolados—mas se inclui na cultura do homem, no seu aparato imediato com que representa os fenômenos sociais—determinando suas aspirações, sentimentos, e criando as formas de ação com que representa e apreende esta realidade. A arte coordena e desenvolve as necessidades objetivas de representação do mundo que determinadas épocas e classes têm da realidade.

[For me, art is the transmission of lived experiences, relationships, representations, and values that are included in the immediate apparatus of knowledge with which we confront reality—developing our ability to react to it, our ability to understand and represent it. Art is not "useful"—because, since it is not linked to the production of material goods, it cannot transmit concepts, nor can it define and form opinions when faced with isolated phenomena—but it is included in man's culture, in his immediate apparatus with which he represents social phenomena—determining his aspirations, feelings, and creating the forms of action with which he represents and seizes this reality. Art coordinates and develops the objective needs for representation of the world that certain periods and classes have of their reality.] (*Vianinha* 66)

Vianinha's concept of art is comprehensive, as his thought doubles back on itself and evolves this concept. The social utility of art is found in its power as a mode of knowledge.

A arte nasce na sociedade. No momento em que os sentidos juntam os dados imediatos da percepção—percebendo sua estrutura, relacionando-a a abstrações, a representações que já possui, a sentimentos que já possui—nasce a arte. É o conhecimento que cria sentimentos complexos—representações de alto nível de abstração—que—servindo e partindo da realidade concreta que o homem define para sua existência—volta sobre ela, modificando-a.

[Art is born in society. At the moment when the senses gather the immediate data from perception—perceiving its structure, relating it to abstractions, to representations that it already possesses—art is born. It is knowledge that creates complex sentiments—representations of a high level of abstraction—which—serving and starting from the concrete reality which man defines for his existence—turns upon it, modifying it.] (66)

The problem of determinism, or overdeterminism, of the relationship between art and society that plagues much of the theoretical writings of political activists constitutes a mainly subtextual dialogue in these early theoretical considerations and gains weight in his later writings. As seen here, he answers this problem by emphasizing art's role in organizing perception. Nowhere in his writing does he refer to art—or to theater—as a reflection of society. He contends that, although born in a dialectical relationship with society that constitutes artistic form, as a *mode* (not form) of knowledge *(conhecimento)*, art is not determined by the immediate circumstances of its cultural inscription and therefore promotes (or should promote) a critical distancing that gives it transformative power, as shown in this summarizing statement:

A arte é o mais importante instrumento do homem para a recriação de vivências e representações—desligadas de suas contingências imediatas—com as quais se define e atua sobre a natureza. Ela coordena, transforma em vivência objetiva, em sentimento, uma série de sensações esgarçadas que a natureza mesmo do movimento social instala na cabeça dos homens. A arte inventa vivências que vão coordenar ou anular sentimentos e representações que surgem a partir de necessidades históricas objetivas.

[Art is man's most important instrument for the recreation of lived experiences and representations—disconnected from their immediate contingencies—with which it defines itself and acts on nature. It coordinates and transforms into objective lived experience, into feeling, a series of faded sensations that the very nature of the social movement installs in the minds of men. Art invents lived experiences that will coordinate or annul feelings and representations that emerge from objective historical needs.] (67)

The universality of artistic endeavor resides in the dynamic movement of human consciousness as this movement constitutes knowledge.[4] According to Vianinha's theory, the aesthetic factor of art fits into the dynamic of consciousness as the appreciation the spectator feels in the participatory act of recognition of humanity in society. For Vianinha, what grounds this generalized movement in a specific historical time are the modes of perception that delineate and are promulgated by the aesthetic forms of an artistic tradition.

In this essay of 1960, Vianinha considers contemplation *(contemplação)* to be the dominant mode of perception in postindustrial, capitalist society. By this, he means the interior reflection, the solitary thought process, that is emphasized to an alienating degree by an ideology that stresses the individual. And he considers the aesthetic forms we have inherited to be those of contemplation. He believes that art forms such as painting, music, and literature that are most propitious to solitary contemplation have benefited greatly from this tradition. He attributes the effervescence of aesthetic experimentation that has characterized these forms in contemporary Western culture to the emphasis on individual creation and reception.

In sum, he feels that the space for creation and evolution of artistic conventions within these artistic forms has been enlarged, and despite the restrictions that the artist may suffer from competition in a market economy where cultural products are treated as commodities, the artist (and his or her art) have been particularly valued precisely because of the artist's individual isolation. In effect, the contradictions of the individual artist's social and cultural inscription have free reign to express themselves in art.

Vianinha says that this is not the case with theater, where vanguard experimentation is the exception, not the rule, and where the conventions continue to be those of early- and mid-twentieth-century realism. It is a pattern of artistic stagnation in which theater is caught in a double bind. As the most communal form of art, theater's primary material is the presentation of humanity *in* society. However, given that the sensitivity of the conventional mode of perception is geared to the individual's (usually the protagonist's) reactions to external events, the individual's relationship to society is generally portrayed as causal. The result is a theater of simplistic psychology, a theater whose legitimate time has passed, according to Vianinha.

This is not a double bind inscribed solely in the aesthetic realm of artistic intention and audience reception. It is manifested in, and promulgated by, the infrastructural nature of professional—and to some degree, alternative—theater. In contemporary societies, the survival of professional theater depends on the public's appreciation as shown at the box office, and, in order to insure an economically significant public response, productions must speak to the concerns of their public in an artistic form that the audience will both appreciate and pay to see.

Given the contradictions of what Vianinha calls a culture of contemplation, he feels that of all the arts, theater has most suffered in Brazil. On the other hand, because of its communal nature, theater has the greatest possibility of encapsulating and communicating the values of society:

> O teatro sofreu mais. Representação do homem como ser social—perde sua capacidade inventiva diante da solidão—não acompanha as monumentais transformações estéticas que sofreu a obra de arte. . . . O teatro era diferente—era empresa—bilheteria—não podia se separar do espectador—mas ao mesmo tempo—nas condições que surgem—talvez seja a forma artística que mais fortemente poderá se colocar na formação do mundo mental do homem—será talvez a arte que maior contribuição fornecerá para a modificação da atitude do homem diante da realidade. O artista de teatro—na sua manifestação—liga-se como ser econômico e político ao espectador—exprime os sentimentos que possui também diante das necessidades de transformação de sua própria condição de artista.

> [The theater suffered more. Being the representation of man as a social being, theater loses its inventive capacity when faced with solitude, it does not accompany the monumental aesthetic transformations which the work of art has undergone. . . . The theater was different, it was a business—box office—it could not separate itself from the spectator. But at the same time, under the conditions that arise, it perhaps is the artistic form that can most forcefully take its place in the formation of man's mental world. It is perhaps the art that will furnish the greatest contribution to the modification of man's attitude before reality. The theatrical artist—by his person and work—is connected as a economic and political being to the spectator—he expresses also his feelings about the need for transformation of his own condition as an artist.] (73)

Thus, Vianinha argues that the specificity of theater, at this historical moment, is to be found in the precarious dialectical relationship of the negative and positive aspects of its cultural insertion, at the point or points where the problematic of its commercial status intersects with its strengths as a form that shows human beings as social beings to a group representative of that society. This "modification of man's attitude before reality" is a tall order for any artistic endeavor to live up to, but it is an imperative that Vianinha followed throughout his life. His assessment of the "the conditions that arise" and their particular suitability to theater's taking a top role in influencing value systems will be discussed at length in following chapters.

However, it is useful to note at the outset how these concepts—albeit generalized and perhaps overly simplified as expressed in 1960—fit into the dialogue regarding culture and theater that obtained in this period. This was a moment of optimistic activity for politically committed cultural activists. The opportunity for discussion was great, and discussion often centered on the larger questions of political activism within the cultural realm: politics and theater, nationalism, class struggle and cultural dependency. How to implement a political vision in theatrical work was certainly debated and often vigorously answered in broad terms of "how to do political theater."[5] Subtle theoretical reflection on theatrical conventions was most frequently forgotten in the enthusiasm and real possibility of doing what one defined as political theater. It was an open field whose major problems were finding economically feasible ways to experiment with new techniques.

In the case of Vianinha, we find that his commitment to an efficacious political theater and his theoretical perspicacity as to conventions for that theater grow as the cultural space to practice political theater diminishes. In an article written in 1971, after some seven years of political and theatrical activity under an increasingly repressive dictatorship, we see that Vianinha has somewhat modified his theoretical reflections on theater in terms of perception and value systems.[6] Whereas before he spoke of perceptual modes within a culture of contemplation, he now speaks of a contradiction between unconscious and conscious perception as this contradiction relates to what he sees as historical necessity.

He begins by questioning what he calls "essa divisão estanque, cartesiana, compartimentada, do mundo mecânico" [This stagnant, Cartesian, compartmentalized definition of the mechanical world] (136). The division he refers to is one of perception according to categories of the unconscious and conscious mind, understanding, within the context of that suspect division, the unconscious mind to be that which governs feeling and spontaneous reaction, and the conscious to be rational thought. Furthermore, he alludes to the confusion produced by the variety of theories that pit the conscious against the unconscious, ascribing opposing qualities to them: reactionary versus revolutionary, conservative versus progressive, spontaneous versus repressive, and so on; according to one's point of view, the conscious and unconscious could be represented by either side of these qualitative pairings. Given these variables of interpretation of the unconscious and conscious, he accentuates the importance of these modes of perception within our Cartesian culture, declaring them to be at the very base of our cultural definitions. They serve as the "classificação e catalogação dos órgãos do sistema de representação" [classification and inventory of the organs of the system of representation] (136).

What does he mean by a "system of representation"? He does not define the term, but it is apparent that he considers a system of representation to be the way the organizing values of our lives are felt, perceived, and reproduced, as well as the manner in which we project these organizing principles of our worldview.[7] This is, then, a question of perception and [re]presentation.

By what he has said in earlier theory, it can be understood that he considers that ideology and cultural acts are both elements in the formation of a system of representation, in which sense they form a way of seeing, an identification of the values of a system (honor, e.g.), but also function as modes of seeing, of perceiving, where by cultural tradition we give primacy either to the "rational" or the "unconscious" as being the structuring devices of our perception.

For argument's sake, he admits that modes of organization of a system of artistic reproduction can be cataloged by emphasizing or weighing them in terms of having originated in the unconscious or conscious mode. Therefore, if we privilege either of these modes, then this is the view of life that is reproduced in our cultural representations. He applies this to two instances in theater.

On the one hand, he says that privileging the conscious mind will give rise to a kind of limited determinism where rationality perceives and articulates new values, pointing to a possible transformation of values, such as in the theater of Ibsen and Arthur Miller. And although he admires this theater, he also feels that it is limited by the rationality of its own discourse. On the other hand, privileging the unconscious will indicate an ahistoric, static, albeit turbulent, view of human activity in which the underlying assumption will be of life as a force of oceanic chaos. Vianinha contends that this view is held in the theater of Arrabal.

He goes on to state that Brazilian theater, since the decade of 1950 and until recently, has privileged the first approach, but is now (1971) involved in representing the world as an inherently chaotic force. He adds that to put aesthetic considerations in such terms as privileging the unconscious or the rational is a false contradiction, although a revealingly functional one:

> Estes setores predominantes no atual teatro brasileiro resolveram que a contradição existente é entre o rígido racionalismo e a força instintiva e inata do homem. O consciente que armazena prescrições e o inconsciente a acumular esperanças. Para um, o discurso lógico, correto, comportado, contido; para o outro, o discurso poético, desmedido, envolvente, inefável. A contradição não é essa. É da historicidade e da não-historicidade.

> [These predominant sectors in contemporary Brazilian theater decided that the existing contradiction is between man's rigid rationalism and his instinctive and innate strength. The conscious that stores up prescriptions and the subconscious that stores up hope. For one, the logical, correct, well-behaved, contained discourse; for the other, the poetic, unmeasured, involving, ineffable discourse. That is not the contradiction. It is between historicity and nonhistoricity.] (139)

When Vianinha asserts that the basic contradiction of representation is between historical and ahistorical vision, he does not reject the idea of unconscious and conscious modes of perception. He rejects the expressive roles assigned to them in artistic representation. He considers both the unconscious and conscious to be factors within a system of representation where history exists as a category of representation. He poses and answers the question of historical vision in the following manner:

> Se puséssemos a história como uma categoria que existe também no nosso sistema de representação? Ou seja—as formas de relacionamento humano modificam-se e estas modificações são registradas divididamente em todo o aparelho de representação do real que possui o homem—o consciente se divide entre representações promotoras e representações congeladoras do processo social. O inconsciente guarda também representações de promoção e de congelamento do devir. A divisão não é feita

entre nossos órgãos ou mecanismos. A divisão é feita entre nosso sistema global de representação e a realidade.

[If we were to define history as a category that exists also in our system of representation? Or rather—the forms of human relationship are modified and these modifications are duly registered in the entire apparatus of representations of the real that man possesses—consciousness is divided into representations that promote the social process and those that freeze it. The subconscious also retains representations that promote and freeze what is to come [becoming]. The division is not made between our organs or mechanisms. The division is made between our global system of representations and reality.] (136)

The problematic simplification implied here of history as reality as opposed to ideological constructs ("sistema global de representação") becomes more complexly answered as we consider Vianinha's definition of historical movement. He gives a definition of history:

A história é essa política de interesses e luta pela conquista de prerrogativas, a extensão delas para mais gente. Portanto é a caracterização dessas prerrogativas, a capacidade de distingui-las, reivindicá-las, negá-las—o poder de removê-las ou mantê-las. Este é o jogo mais intenso que mobiliza todo ser humano até o mais profundo de sua alma, todo o seu sistema de representação é feito deste e neste movimento, nesta oceanidade—nesta oceanidade o sistema de representação vagueia, soçobra, afunda ou encaminha, regula, dirige, humaniza, racionaliza, cria justiça.

[History is this politics of interests and struggle for the conquest of prerogatives, their extension toward more people. Therefore it is the characterization of these prerogatives, the ability to distinguish them, claim them, deny them—the power to remove or maintain them. This is the most intense game that mobilizes every human being to the depths of his soul, his entire system of representation is made up of and in this movement, this ocean—in this ocean the system of representation wanders, capsizes, sinks or guides, directs, humanizes, rationalizes, creates justice.] (137)

In essence, he asserts that history—both in reality and in our systems of representation—exists as a dynamic of its own projection, a dynamic that he sees as eminently dramatic in its projection, as evidenced in his description of it.

In another article, to which Peixoto gives the title of "A cultura proprietária e a cultura desapropriada" (Proprietary culture and disappropriated culture), Vianinha develops these arguments in the context of the economic structure of class conflict and underdevelopment.[8] Here, he uses terms that refer more to ideological movement, terms that relate more directly to a discussion of interpretations (implicit or explicit) of history as these interpretations form part of our system of representation.

To summarize the discussion as we are using it here: in our cultural products what is projected is a concept of history as either unalterable (where the "unconscious" determines social behavior), or as deterministically projected (where reason effects changes and new projections are then privileged). The latter view, in effect, is as inefficacious as the first in presenting any picture of social transformation. In its simplification of human emotions and motives, it does not yield any sense, or method, that would promote transitional values, nor would it facilitate the necessary incorporation of selected elements of old systems of representation that would be conventions essential to the successful transmission of new values.

Vianinha's thoughts transmit a decidedly evolutionary idea of theatrical traditions. He says:

> todo projeto novo deve conter em si as maneiras de incorporar a ele o máximo possível dos velhos comportamentos, atitudes, valores e representações que não são as legitamamente suas. Só assim ele é novo, porque transita na história e não somente na parte da história que é feita no nível de nossa pensamento, de nosso ideologia.

> [every new project must contain within itself ways of incorporating to itself the maximum possible number of old behaviors, attitudes, values, and representations that are not legitimately theirs. Only thus is it new, because it travels in history and not only in the part of history that is made at the level of our thought, of our ideology.] (138)

This idea of evolution is based on a concept of historical process that he defines in terms of our consciousness of, and participation in, historical movement.

He likens the movement of history to an automobile that both takes us to a destination and that we drive; it is exactly the fact that we can be immersed in a consciousness of being history, of not being able to be other than the history of now and here, that we can aspire to be another type of history. It is precisely the fact that, because we live a period of history in conflict, we can be aware of different positions (systems of representation) regarding our history. We can therefore be aware that different positions are not just conditioned but are options, albeit full of contradictions that must be consciously incorporated into our systems of representation:

> A história passa mais por cima de uns do que de outros. Esmaga, aniquila, não dá chances a um grupo e privilegia outros. Essas posições diferentes permitem enfoques diferentes. O sistema de representação dos agrupamentos mais desfavorecidos tende a procurar desesperadamente uma representação mais global, complexa e real do processo. Sabe que não tem o direito de se enganar, de fugir, de afrouxar sua precisão. Tem paixão para chegar ao osso da história, à moela, ao pâncreas. Não pode se submeter a essa aderência de fogo que a história exerce sobre nós—queima-lhe a pele.

> [History passes over some more than others. It crushes, it annihilates, it does not give chances to one group and favors others. These different positions allow different focuses. The system of representation of the more disfavored groups tends to desperately seek a more global, complex, and real representation of the process. It knows it has not the right to be mistaken, to escape, to loosen its precision. It has a passion to arrive at the bone of history, to its gizzard, to its pancreas. It cannot submit to this adherence of fire that history exerts over us—it burns its skin.] (137)

What is clear from a reading of his theory at this time, but somewhat murky in this segment, is that he is referring to a vanguard position toward historical movement and systems of representation.[9] He's not suggesting that the underdog, merely by the fact of having that perspective, will organize that perspective consciously. Indeed, one of the difficulties in ascribing any quantifiable role to ideology is the factor that dominant class ideology is also operant within the classes, or groups, whose interests, objectively, would not seem to coincide with the values proposed by dominant class ideology.

According to Vianinha, at the beginning of the 1970s there was an attempt to destroy the dominant system of representation characterized by explosive, and arbitrary advances. By this he refers to the theater of aggression that erupted in the political and cultural turbulence of the late 1960s.[10] While he gives this theater validity as part of a necessary process, he says that although this work calls into question the *projeto* of the dominant system of representation, it allows for no way to incorporate history; rather it calls for an escape from a historical perspective.

He calls for theater to take its place in a systematic exploration of representation, to go beyond reaction to link history to the experiential phenomena of historical context: "O teatro, elemento de formação do sistema de representação do homem, tem que ser o fiel intérprete da historicidade, da sua imersão no caos, na oceanidade— mas também tem que ser o intérprete de sua projeção" [The theater, formative element of man's system of representation, must be the faithful interpreter of historicity, of his immersion in chaos, in the oceanity—but it must also be the interpreter of its own projection] (138).

In other words, theater must take conscious control of the process of its projection; it must be analyzer and commentator of its own process.

What kind of theater could do this? Vianinha will reply: a theater of contemplation in which dramatic action is an aesthetic category—not a political or sociological category—would incorporate historical perspective. Although this emphasis on contemplation would seem surprising given his earlier views on a culture of contemplation, we can see it in the light of his continuing struggle to conceptualize a subtle dialectic between theater and social responsibility that would encompass theater's artistic specificity and guide his own praxis.

As a starting point in this formulation, Vianinha asserts that the necessity to evolve such a theater is indicated by the erroneous notion commonly held by political activists that, in the relationship between dramatic action and social action, the idealized purpose of dramatic action is to stimulate, directly, political action on the part of the spectator:

Nós encaramos o problema de maneira inversa—a ação dramática só se dá ao espectador na contemplação—um teatro será quanto mais revolucionário, quanto mais exigir do espectador a sua contemplação, a sua fruição, quanto menos exigir a sua ação física, imediata, liberatória. A ação dramática é uma categoria estética e não uma categoria política ou sociológica. É uma categoria estética que se dá ao sistema de representações do espectador. O objetivo é enriquecer e desenvolver o sistema de representação do espectador e não promover uma momentânea liberação dos arraigados valores do sistema de representação que possui o público.

Não se trata de uma ação psicológica, trata-se de uma ação estética.

[We face the problem in an inverse fashion—dramatic action is given to the spectator only in contemplation—a theater will be all the more revolutionary, the more it demands from the spectator its contemplation, its fruition; the less it demands his physical, immediate, libertarian action. Dramatic action is an aesthetic category and not a political or sociological category. It is an aesthetic category that gives itself to the spectator's system of representations. The objective is to enrich and develop the spectator's system of representation and not promote a momentary liberation of the deep-rooted values of the system of representation that the public possesses.

It is an aesthetic action, not a psychological one.] (140)

It is important to point out the continuum, and change, in the concept of contemplation in this theory. In 1960 Vianinha condemned the solitary nature of contemplation, stressing knowledge *(conhecimento)* as the primary element linking perception, theory, and practice. While the equation of contemplation with passive individualism and association of knowledge with collective action is often generic to youth, this theoretical opposition is particularly understandable within the context of Brazilian society in the beginning of the 1960s, when the political climate allowed optimistic activists premature leaps from theory to practice.

In his mature theory, Vianinha gives more recognition to the role of the individual spectator—in his individuality and as a member of a group. As will be shown in later analysis of his theatrical practice, Vianinha's changed emphasis on contemplation also reflects a more mature assessment of the theatrical conventions of Brazilian theater in relation to the cultural space available for politically oriented theater.

Vianinha uses *contemplação* as a conceptual construct of mediation that allows histrionic sensibility passage to thought. It is essentially a ruminative process in which aesthetic affect and cognition complement each other. In other words, when one perceives and then contemplates what one perceives (as opposed to immediate, or solely, visceral reaction), one is in the position to formulate and implement what one has perceived. Following this line of reasoning, theater will be more revolutionary to the degree to which it requires contemplation—as, in an extension of his earlier argument, it reaches and fuses both unconscious and conscious perception.

This fusion is not a matter of degrees or moments of intensity of audience reception, but rather one of quality, in Vianinha's view. In this sense, contemplation is synonymous with concentration:

Só com a total concentração do espectador para o ato estético esta energia [of enrichment] pode ser mais profundamente transmitida. Não se trata aqui do ato hipnótico de que falava Brecht ao comentar o teatro dramático—trata-se do ato estético, do ato de *espectare,* de presenciar um fenômeno humano que o envolve e ao mesmo tempo não lhe diz respeito—esta sistematização estética que é propria da ação dramática é o elemento de ligação cultural do teatro com o seu tempo.

[Only with the spectator's total concentration for the aesthetic act can this energy [of enrichment] be most deeply transmitted. We are not referring here to the hypnotic act that Brecht spoke of in commenting on dramatic theater—it is the aesthetic act, the act of *espectare,* of witnessing a human phenomenon that involves him and at the same time has nothing to do with him— this aesthetic systematization that pertains to dramatic action is the linking cultural element of the theater with its time.] (140)

Thus, he makes a categorical statement that places dramatic action as the main conduit of identification in this system of representation. As shown thus far, this is a neo-Aristotelian view in which dramatic action has aesthetic primacy in theater.

However, as we further observe how he delineates the role of dramatic action, we find that his concept is at least as much informed by Brechtian ideas. He defines dramatic action as the result of a shock between value systems: "o específico do teatro é a ação dramática, ou seja, a ação desencadeada diante do público pelo choque de dois diferentes sistemas de representação do mundo" [what is specific to theater is dramatic action, or rather, the action unfolding before the public by the shock of two different systems of representation of the world] (141).

He clarifies this by contrasting dramatic action in dramatic theater, (what is generally known as illusionistic, or at times Aristotelian, theater), and epic theater (in Brechtian terms). Obviously, dramatic action takes place in both dramatic theater and epic theater. However, in dramatic theater "os sistemas de representação entram em choque num ponto único" [the systems of representation clash on one sole point] (141), by which we can assume he means that there is a central dramatic conflict that organizes the conflict of worldviews. This is primarily produced by the interpersonal conflicts on stage. Regarding epic theater, "são as largas superfícies dos sistemas de representação que se chocam" [it is the large surface of the systems of representation that clash] (141). Here, we can assume that the social "gestus" of the characters indicate the deeper complexities of the contradictions and conflicts within a social system in a way that reveals its socioeconomic infrastructure (or of the shock between one established system and a proposed system).

A brief summary of the trajectory of Vianinha's theoretical practice would single out the (often difficult) attempt to juggle and progressively meld these two concepts of dramatic action as being the major characteristic of his artistic growth. (This is certainly the case in his last and best play, *Rasga coração*.) Furthermore, the fusion of these concepts form what could be considered an idea of mimesis:

> a maior força da comunicação estética no teatro—a sua característica de imitação da natureza—ou seja a ação dramática (categoria estética), tem uma forte semelhança com a ação humana, com o inter-relacionamento objetivo dos homens. Daí o seu fascínio, o seu encantamento—categoria estética e, ao mesmo tempo, forte aparência de realidade.

> [the greatest force of aesthetic communication in the theater— its characteristic imitation of nature—or rather the dramatic action (aesthetic category), has a strong resemblance to human action, with the objective interrelationship of men. Hence its

fascination, its enchantment—aesthetic category and, at the same time, strong appearance of reality.] (141)

In this idea of theater as an imitation of life, theater acts as a simulacrum, analogous to but separate from reality. It affords aesthetic pleasure from its properties of imitation and identification (a more Aristotelian idea), while it provides food for thought in its treatment of the objective interrelationships of human beings along the lines of Brechtian technique. Indeed, both these terms of pleasure and thought are transmitted by dramatic action, whether the staged treatment of this action tends toward Brechtian or neo-Aristotelian conventions. We see here the theoretical basis of Vianinha's attempts to use devices of epic theater to transmit the movement of conflict within and between systems of representation. This is a sort of meta-theatrical enterprise, since our system of representation is geared toward the Aristotelian. Brecht himself trod an uneasy path in his attempts to promote a system of representation that would provide commentary on the predominant ways of seeing.

The question of theoretical influences on Vianinha's thought deserves more attention than can be given within the present scope. The points his theory shares with those of Marxist theoreticians such as Brecht, Lukács, Althusser, Arnold Hauser, and of course Marx himself, as well as with those of sympathetic philosophers professedly in dialogue with Marxist concepts, such as Sartre, are striking.[11]

Although these points of communality are marked, it must be stressed that the evolution of Vianinha's theory should be mainly seen in a conjunctural light, rather than in terms of influence, as may well be the true of most pertinent Latin American theory. In Vianinha's case, the dialogue with Marxist concepts is not a matter of an "imported ideology." It arises from the necessity to understand the complex historical reality (or realities) of Brazil, and indeed, of Latin America, where Marxist theory is one tool to understanding the very real economic and spatial conscriptions of underdevelopment and repression, as well as the limitations these conscriptions place on cultural activity and growth.

Within such a framework, theory necessarily becomes to some extent metatheoretical, always questioning the applicability of its own theoretical formulations. For Vianinha, as with many other Latin American writers, theory also has the difficult task of assessing the interstitial points of connection between Brazilian dominant cultural thought as a secondary system of ideological constructs borrowed from more advanced nations, and this thought as it is integral to capitalist society in Brazil. We can summarize Vianinha's later theoretical positions in the light of these considerations.

Vianinha's insistence on analyzing the specificity of theatrical communication from a historical perspective allows him to see the conditioning factors that delimit Brazilian theater, its thematic concerns and its conventions. His insistence on including historicity as a category for our systems of representation allows him to relate a given dynamic of perception (how we see things) to an analysis of the value systems that inform dramatic action. Placing the latter as the primary factor in dramatic structure places humanity, effectively, in center stage. This is not to be read as simply humanity *in* society, but rather as an intention to show humanity within a specific historical context as individual and social beings constituting, as well as being constituted, by historical process. As a result, structuring dramatic action as a shock of systems of representation in the largest possible panorama of these systems is, for Vianinha, the most efficacious way of representing for serious contemplation the contradictions operant in contemporary Brazilian society. In effect, it is a question of analyzing and representing the historical imperatives particular to Brazilian society within the framework of cultural values. This theory allows him, in his own plays, to try to expand perceptual fields and propose social changes without ignoring the parameters of the already existent perceptual modes and artistic traditions.

This theoretical overview of Vianinha's thought is designed to organize and comment what I judge to be the major theoretical issues that inform, and are informed by, his theatrical practice. It is intended to focus on and systematize the importance he gives to the recognition of cultural value systems in his theater. Vianinha himself did not write a systematic theory of theater. Whether this lack of a theoretical volume was a question of time (he died at thirty-eight), or was the result of his need for constant immersion in practice, cannot be determined. He certainly was of an analytical bent, continually writing articles and giving interviews that analyzed world theater, Brazilian theatrical traditions, and also his own work within the context of its cultural space. Before discussing the evolution of his work in its context, however, it will be helpful to consider briefly several aspects of his early biography that have significant bearing on his practice and theory.

Biographical Considerations

The only child of Oduvaldo and Deocélia Vianna, Oduvaldo Vianna Filho was born, on June 4, 1936, into a tradition of theatrical and political activism.[12]

Oduvaldo Vianna (1892–1972) was one of the most popular and successful playwrights of his generation, as well as a movie and radio scriptwriter and journalist. He was active in promoting theater groups and was one of the founders of the SBAT, the Sociedade Brasileira de Autores Teatrais. His best comedies, *Amor* (Love) and *Manhãs de sol* (Sunny Mornings), are noted for their attention to theatricality. They center on the foibles and sentimental problems of the ascending middle class in an entertainingly satirical manner.

Critical evaluation of his work has not always been generous; he is often consigned to a place in a dubious tendency in Brazilian theater. This was the theatrical activity of the group of writers later known as the Trianon group, since most of their plays were staged in the Trianon theater in downtown Rio during the late 1920s and 1930s. Gustavo Doria sums up this tendency in the following terms: "O Trianon, . . . era o lugar onde se mantinha o fogo sagrado do nosso simplório teatro de dicção, [whose texts] cuidavam rotineiramente dos pequenos problemas sentimentais e domésticos das famílias modestas, moradoras dos subúrbios" [The Trianon . . . was the place where the sacred fire of our simplistic theater of diction was kept, (whose texts) routinely dealt with the small sentimental and domestic problems of modest, suburb-dwelling families] (20–21).

Another critic, Brasil Gerson, proffers the same opinion in 1928, citing Vianna as the sometimes exception to the rule:

Temos reparado que todas as comédias nacionais, exceto algumas de Oduvaldo Vianna, reproduzem cenas de subúrbios cariocas. As famílias que levam uma vida de terceira classe, na capital federal, é que vivem inspirando os sócios da Sociedade Brasileira de Autores Teatrais. O resultado disso não podia ser pior: o nosso teatrinho nacional é simplesmente ignóbil.

[We have noticed that all the national comedies, except some by Oduvaldo Vianna, reproduce scenes from the Carioca [Rio de Janeiro] suburbs. Families that lead a third-class life, in the federal capital, are those that are always inspiring the members of the Brazilian Society of Playwrights. The result of this could not be worse: our little national theater is simply ignoble.] (Qtd. in Doria 22)

This assessment may be merited if one contrasts this theater to the more technically and dramatically sophisticated urbane theater that came after, or to the desire for a more universal theater expressed by Gerson.

However, I think that the Trianon work deserves a more positive evaluation within the evolution of Brazilian theatrical traditions. As Doria himself points out, the audience for theater at the time was the lower middle class (21). The fact that these plays spoke to the concerns of this audience is not a negligible point, especially since one of the major intentions of many national dramatists of the early 1960s was to try to recapture a comparable audience. The position regarding dramatic language of the Trianon group should also be emphasized, for regardless of their dramatic merit, these plays incorporate a concerted effort to valorize Brazilian Portuguese as spoken by the audience for whom these plays were destined.

Throughout his life, Vianinha carried on a constant debate with the traditions expressed in his father's work. In the beginning of his career (1960), Vianinha condemns his father's dramaturgy as being facile, pandering to superficial conflicts within the petite bourgeoisie with little real analysis of the value systems of that class. He calls it a theater that

> fixa no ouro e na riqueza como espelho da desagregação humana. . . . Os valores que informam estas peças são de cerceamento do indomável poder criador que a necessidade exige do homem brasileiro. Não a investiga, aparta-se dela, satiriza, moraliza e pontifica sobre o que se perde. Os valores que possui não podem investigar a ação do homem, podem somente enunciá-la.

> [fixes on gold and riches as the mirror of human disintegration. . . . The values that inform these plays are of the sweep of the indomitable creative power that necessity demands of Brazilian men. It [theater] does not investigate it, it moves apart from it, satirizes, moralizes, and pontificates about what is lost. The val-

ues theater possesses cannot investigate man's action, they can only enunciate it.] (75)

He states that, in these plays, "Não há drama, propriamente, há bate-papos de espírito" ("strictly speaking, there is no drama, there are spiritual chats"), concluding this fierce judgment by asserting:

um teatro anti-metropolitano que não expressou a problemática dos valores que o homem possui para as circunstâncias, não poderia ser o ponto de partida para o teatro que se instala agora, muitos anos depois, numa metrópole, ainda desengonçada, mas industrializada, proletariazada e desenfreada.

[an antimetropolitan theater that did not express the problem of the values man possesses according to circumstances could not be the starting point for the theater that installs itself now, many years later, in a still disjointed, yet industrialized, proletarianized, and unrestrained metropolis.] (75)

His assessment of his father's legacy changes, both as his work matures and as he confronts his own problems with censorship. (His father worked under the constant possibility of censorship, largely because of his political activities.) Later in his life, Vianinha comes to see his father's work as innovative, valuing his father's commitment to popular speech and the high technical quality, which he calls the "carpintaria teatral" [theatrical carpentry] of his plays. We see that by the early 1970s, Vianinha comes to understand his father's theater in terms of the circumscriptions of its cultural space. In an interview in 1973 with Antonieta Santos, Vianinha speaks of his intention to adapt his father's play *O homem que nasceu duas vezes:* "Nem a censura, nem as pressões dos empresários impediram que Oduvaldo Viana se tornasse um inovador no rádio, no teatro e no cinema. Como ele, eu resolvi escrever para encenar hoje, agora" [Neither censorship nor the pressures of theatrical entrepreneurs prevented Oduvaldo Vianna from becoming an innovator in radio, theater, and film. Like him, I decided to write for staging today, now] (qtd. in Guimarães 20–21).

This reassessment of the cultural realities that prevailed during his father's time is not the only communality that he feels with his own work. He also reevaluates the conventions of theater, validating the popular comic elements and the *revista* elements of his father's plays. As we shall see, in his last play, *Rasga coração*, he intentionally constructs a theatrical carpentry that allows for inclusion of these conventions in a manner that would give them the depth of historical perspective he felt lacking in his father's plays.

His father's influence was not the only familial influence on his writing. His mother, Deocélia Vianna, was also a writer. As a youngster, Vianinha was accustomed to seeing his mother at the typewriter, composing scripts for radio shows. She would discuss them with him, asking his opinion (Vianna, interview by author; Guimarães 18). His mother and her work were a great influence on his own work in television, in his own tightly knit yet informal treatment of slices-of-life vignettes of Brazilian society.

Both parents were political activists and members of the Brazilian Communist Party (Partido Comunista Brasileiro [PCB]). In an interview Deocélia Vianna recalls that Vianinha was active in the party at an early age, helping in campaigns and demonstrations. He became a member of the PCB youth group at about twelve or fourteen years of age.[13] He remained a committed member of the Party until his death. And although he did not always agree with some of the PCB's positions, his theory remains in constant dialogue with the analyses and cultural positions taken by the Party.

Vianinha grew up in an ambience of political discussion and meetings, moving with his family to Buenos Aires for several years (1939–41) as a result of the political repression of the Estado Novo. His early life set a pattern of artistic and political participation and commitment. At three months of age, he was already acting, being cast in a film, *Bonequinha de seda* (Silk Doll). When he was two, he was in *Alegria* (Happiness), a film his father scripted. He wrote bits and pieces of stories as a child.

From these biographical factors one can see that Vianinha's positions regarding theater and politics are as much motivated by a lived sense of tradition as by personal options of worldview. His ties to his parents were tight, productive, and, from all accounts, positive and happy despite some theoretical disagreements. In a real sense, Vianinha's commitment was to the understanding and evolution of tradition. His mother accentuates this by characterizing the commitment of her son thus: "O compromisso de Oduvaldo Viana Filho era de usar a tradição. O partido é também da tradição" [Oduvaldo Vianna Filho's commitment was to use tradition. The Party is also a part of tradition] (interview by author). The intertwining of the values and traditions of the Brazilian Left, as expressed by PCB cultural figures, and the purposes of Brazilian theater will be a major subject of this study.

In 1953 Vianinha entered the School of Architecture of the Mackenzie University in São Paulo. He transferred to philosophy, in the third year (1957), but he didn't complete this course. He had already cast his lot in with the theater. In 1954 he became a member of the Teatro Paulista do Estudante, which joined with Arena in 1956.

Arena and the
Centro Popular de Cultura

Historical Overview

The Teatro de Arena was founded, in late 1953, by José Renato and other young theater people as a professional group dedicated to experimentation.[1] The *arena* (ring or theater-in-the- round) form was originally chosen both because of its aesthetic possibilities and because it provided an economically feasible space. This space is particularly propitious to farce and to experimentation with acting technique. The founders wished a circuslike atmosphere that allowed small casts to develop stage interactions. The arena was a more viable form, economically, for a young repertory group without a fixed home, since it dispensed with most of the staging and props required by the then traditional proscenium staging.

By 1955 the aesthetic proposals were well established, receiving critical acclaim. The theater had a following, particularly among students, and the company won the Governador do Estado award. It also was able to move into its own theater. As part of its cultural programming, the Arena began extending its activities into related cultural fields: plastic arts were exhibited in the theater lobby, and, most significantly, the traditional Monday night "dead space" was dedicated to theater production and music outside the nucleus group of actors.

Monday nights were mainly utilized by students of the Teatro Paulista do Estudante (TPE). The two most notable participants of the TPE, Gianfrancesco Guarnieri and Oduvaldo Vianna Filho (Vianinha), were young actors already politically active. In 1956, on his return from the United States, where he had worked with John Gassner at Columbia and with the Stanislavskian method, Augusto Boal joined Arena. These three were fundamental to the basic changes in the perception of the role of theater that followed.

About this time (1956) the emphasis shifted from artistic experimentation to investigation into what form a popular Brazilian theater might take, popular being defined at this stage as a looser actor-audience relationship that would eventually incorporate a larger and more diverse audience. In fact, the technical experimentation led to this new emphasis: the experience of intimacy in the theater-in-the-round with the audience in physical contiguity with the players had led to a type of democratization. That is, the spatial relationship introduced and exacted direct relationship with the audience; who were often literally sitting within the actors' space.[2] The actors utilized this proximity with the audience and began incorporating playful exchanges into dialogue or using already existent dialogue as direct communication, thereby enlarging the sense of identity with the audience. This demystification of the theatrical process could lead to a new interest and participation on the part of the audience. It was also felt that this identification was closer to the roots of Brazilian theatrical tradition, which has largely evolved around traveling troupes (known in Brazil as *mambembe*) and the circus.

At this point, although concern for popular theater had been growing, the process of elaboration of such a theater had remained mostly in the sphere of acting and staging. In 1956, the group reorganized administratively and structurally, giving new stress to theater research and teaching, and emphasizing collective participation in the decisions affecting the theater as well as in the distribution of tasks necessary to carry out the new program. There was a cultural department (headed by Augusto Boal), a children's theater department, and a department of publicity, as well as a general director (José Renato). A training course for actors, designed to last two years, was inaugurated, which would feed into Arena.

This enlargement of cultural activity, along with the consolidation of the group's purposes as both a theatrical and a learning space, led to the next step in its program: the preoccupation with the national dramatic text. Interchange with the audience evolved into gestural and linguistic patterns encoded within a Brazilian manner of communication: that is, a validation and exploration of a Brazilian way of acting. At the same time members of the group began looking for plays, more specifically Brazilian texts, that would lend themselves to the scenic and representational solutions that had created such energetic interchange with the audience. Very little was found.

The group sponsored a contest, an appeal to national authors to adapt for the stage four short stories by Brazilian writers. Two plays by members of the group had already been produced (*Escrever sobre mulheres* [To Write about Women] by José Renato and *Marido magro, mulher chata* [Skinny Husband, Dull Wife] by Augusto Boal). Although these activities found resonance in the comedy-of-manners style of Martins Pena,[3] they did not adequately reflect the theoretical investigations of the group, which increasingly questioned the social relationships of contemporary Brazilian life in terms of Brazilian economic structure.

Stimulated by the enormous success of Gianfrancesco Guarnieri's *Eles não usam black-tie* (They Don't Wear Black-Tie) and by discussion in group of the play, the creation of the Seminários de Dramaturgia (Dramatic Seminars) in 1958 was to deal directly with the problem of finding national texts. These seminars were organized both as theoretical sessions in which the problems facing a national dramatic literature were discussed in terms of the socioeconomic organization of Brazil and as drama workshops where members of the group (and also other interested people) presented their work for criticism. According to Fernando Peixoto, only four of the first twenty-one productions of Arena were by Brazilian authors. The twenty-second was *Black-tie,* which inaugurated a new phase of Arena (*Vianinha* 30).

Black-tie was a landmark for Arena and for Brazilian theater. It represented a social analysis of slum dwellers, members of the urban proletariat, in the context of a strike, establishing the dramatic conflict around the question of the necessity for the raising of political consciousness as well as for commitment to class struggle. Social themes had been presented before, but generally in the terms of farce or the even broader terms of satirical musical reviews, with also an occasional social melodrama.[4] However, the portrayal of the problems of the urban working class was new, as was the naturalistic staging and acting

Vianinha at six: foot on the ball, eye on the public. (From the personal collection of Maria Lúcia Marins.)

Vianinha as the romantic lead. (Photographic Archives:
FUNARTE/Documentation Center.)

The young dramatist. (Photo agency Globo, from the personal collection of Maria Lúcia Marins.)

Vianinha in an interview, shortly before his death. (Photo agency Globo/Ronald, Archives: FUNARTE.)

Vianinha reads the Corpo a corpo *monologue to his father. (From the personal collection of Maria Lúcia Marins.)*

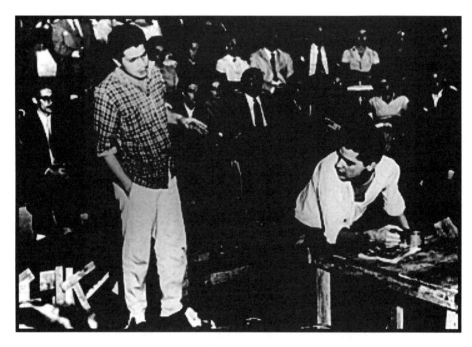

Vianinha (left) and Francisco de Assis in Gianfrancesco Guarnieri's Eles não usam black-tie. *This production of the Teatro de Arena, São Paulo, 1958, demonstrates a reduced distance between public and actor and the new relationship that the arena form allows. (Photo agency Hejo, Archives: FUNARTE.)*

Vianinha, Lélia Abramo, and Miriam Melher in Eles não usam black-tie, *1958. (Photo agency Hejo, Archives: FUNARTE.)*

The open space of the arena takes the closed form of a soccer club dressing room in Chapetuba Futebol Clube, Teatro de Arena, *1958. Included in the scene are Xandó Batista, Francisco de Assis, Vianinha, Arnaldo Weiss, and Milton Gonçalves. (Archives: FUNARTE.)*

Making the most of a lack of resources: Flávio Migliaccio and Francisco de Assis in Chapetuba Futebol Clube, *1958. (Photo agency Hejo, Archives: FUNARTE.)*

With musicians on an elevated level, the public surrounds the stage in
A mais-valia vai acabar, seu Edgar, *performed in the Teatro de Arena of the*
National Faculty of Architecture, Rio de Janeiro, 1960. (Archives: FUNARTE.)

As the players advance, the scenic space invades the public space, in Se correr o
bicho pega, se ficar o bicho come, *1966. (From the Archives of the Cultural*
Center Oduvaldo Vianna Filho, Divisão de Pesquisas-Arquivo Multimeios,
Centro Cultural São Paulo-SMC.)

Informal interactions and complicity between the actors and the public: Nara Leão, João do Vale, Ze Kitti, and Dori Caymi (with guitar) in Show Opinião, *1964. (From the collection of Derly Marques, Divisão de Pesquisas-Arquivo Multimeios, Centro Cultural São Paulo-SMC.)*

With the concentration of scenic space, emphasis falls on the actor's art. Maria Lúcia Dahl, Jayme Costa, and Vianinha in Se correr o bicho pega, *1966. (From the collection of Vladimir Sacchetta, Divisão de Pesquisas-Arquivo Multimeios, Centro Cultural São Paulo-SMC.)*

Agildo Ribeiro and Vianinha in Se correr o bicho pega, *1966.*
(From the Archives of CENACEN, Divisão de Pesquisas-Arquivo
Multimeios, Centro Cultural São Paulo-SMC.)

Rehearsal of Longa noite de Cristal, *1970, directed by Celso Nunes. The stage production leads the author to rethink the ambiguities of his theater. (From the collection of Celso Nunes, Divisão de Pesquisas-Arquivo Multimeios, Centro Cultural São Paulo-SMC.)*

The spatial intersections of the various moments of Manguari Pistolao (here played by Raul Cortez) in Rasga coração, *1980. (From the collection of Ruth Toledo, Divisão de Pesquisas-Arquivo Multimeios, Centro Cultural São Paulo-SMC.)*

The domestic scene frequently dominates: looking out from within. Raul Cortez and Sonia Guides in Rasga coração, *1980. (From the collection of Ruth Toledo, Divisão de Pesquisas-Arquivo Multimeios, Centro Cultural São Paulo-SMC.)*

The domestic present plays against the Bohemian past. Raul Cortez and João José Pompeu in Rasga coração, *1980. (From the collection of Ruth Toledo, Divisão de Pesquisas-Arquivo Multimeios, Centro Cultural São Paulo-SMC.)*

Papa Highirte: *a clash of opinion between official censorship and institutional recognition. (Divisão de Pesquisas-Arquivo Multimeios, Centro Cultural São Paulo-SMC.)*

that characterized the play. The visceral impact on the audience of this dramatization of Brazilian life was electric; it set up a current fed by and feeding into the particular sense of nationalism that characterized the Kubitschek years. (More will be said about this later.) In terms of critical response, most critics came to agree that theater could, indeed, have an express commitment to history without suffering aesthetically.

Black-tie ran in the Arena house from February 1958 to April 1959 and also toured throughout Brazil. During that time, Vianinha completed what was to be known as the other important text of the period, *Chapetuba Futebol Clube,* a drama that showed the social and economic relationships within a second-string (interior city) soccer club as it struggled to reinstate itself as regional champion. Treatment of such themes as small soccer teams opened up limitless possibilities in the perspective of creating Brazilian dramatic characters. These plays, naturalistic as possible in their treatment of the characters, authentically portrayed Brazilians as they lived, worked, and spoke, using language that reflected class and regional speech.

The seminars continued until 1960. While it was understood that research into the cultural reality of the Brazilian people was not in the least exhausted, it became clear that this phase of work had reached a plateau. Many members of the group wished to explore other channels of communication and began to see the naturalism of this period in terms of a "reproduction of national reality" that had served its purpose. A more critical theater was now demanded, much along the lines of Bertolt Brecht's theories of critical distancing and socially determined types. *Revolução na América do Sul* (Revolution in South America), by Augusto Boal, was staged in 1960, initiating this new emphasis on social types. As a farce, the life and trials of a migrant worker, it was made up of scenes that revealed the socioeconomic organization of the country as the latter affected the destiny of the dirt farmer who comes to the city hoping to improve his condition. Scenes of back-country politicians scrambling for position among city senators, intellectuals as ideological puppets of the system, and so forth, now began to people this new theater.

Inevitably, there was a break with a melodramatic tendency expressed in the plays put on up to this point, a break in favor of immediate and mobilizing communication. Exploitation was no longer shown through the development of individual characters but delineated as a process that forms characters who, in turn, change as social circumstances dictate. In point of fact, what had previously been criticism of the government and foreign intervention now became denunciation with a call to political action in favor of the Brazilian people seeking to control their own economic and political destiny.

Up to this point the audiences of Arena had essentially consisted of the liberal elite, students, and intellectuals of middle-class or lower-middle-class origins: people in the habit of going to the theater, with sufficient money to do so, and informed about artistic and political processes in Brazil.

In 1960 Arena made a larger commitment to reach and create a new audience: it was no longer enough merely to inform people about what theater is or could be as a popular art form (this had been done often before); it had now become necessary to demonstrate theater's possibilities in terms of political expression and mobilization for political action. Subgroups were formed that took skits and full-length plays to factories, suburbs, and union halls and that also traveled, primarily around the states of São Paulo and Rio. Three members of the group—Vianinha, Francisco de Assis, and Nelson Xavier—were particularly active in this enterprise, writing agitprop that put forth, for analysis by the audience in postplay discussion, such immediate concerns as agrarian reform, university reform, and the post-Kubitschek power struggle in national politics. Self-criticism of political and artistic positions became a constant part of the group analyses of the economic and political roots of the national crisis. Differing analyses, in conjunction with imperatives of a more personal nature, were to lead to a group split in 1961.

When assessing this golden age of Arena (1958–62), critics most generally compare its theories and practices with the Teatro Brasileiro de Comédia (TBC) (see *Teatro Brasileiro de Comédia* and Guzik). The TBC was, from 1948–64, São Paulo's most successful professional theater. Founded by Italian industrialist Franco Zampari, the TBC was this city's first stable repertory theater. Few plays by Brazilian authors were produced in the TBC's first years, and it was dominated by Italian directors, most of whom, such as Adolfo Celi, Luciano Salce, and Ruggero Jaccobi, immigrated after the war, having been called by Zampari to work in this theater. However, the TBC's contributions to Brazilian culture were considerable.

The TBC, with its continuing assessment of public reaction to its repertory, solidified a change in the structure of professional theater that we first see occurring, in any significant way, in Rio de Janeiro in the mid-1940s with the group Os Comediantes. This group composed of amateurs, many from university theater groups, began in 1938.[5] Its trajectory of professionalization in terms of presenting directions for national theater was marked by two presences. In 1940–41, Louis Jouvet, the French director noted for his sense of theatrical-ity and scenic innovation, lived in Brazil for two years and counseled Os Comediantes. When asked what path of theatrical growth they should follow, Jouvet promptly answered: stage plays by Brazilian au-thors (*Os Comediantes* 15–17)!

The other presence was that of a recent Polish emigré, Zbgniev Ziembinski, a director and actor schooled in expressionism who joined the group in 1941. Ziembinski's innovative and highly expressionistic staging of Nelson Rodrigues's text, *Vestido de noiva* (The Wedding Dress), in 1943 is considered by most critics to be the beginning of modern theater in Brazil, marking a renovation in concepts of staging, scenic design, and production. In late 1945, Os Comediantes became professional theater, with a regularly produced repertory and a number of very talented actors. In 1947 it became a theater cooperative, changing its name to Comediantes Associados; it closed permanently shortly thereafter.

Previous to Os Comediantes (late 1920s and 1930s), Brazil-ian professional theater had been dominated by groups that revolved around a particularly popular actor: most notably the groups of Pro-cópio Ferreira and Jaime Costa (both actors noted for their center-stage histrionics), and that of Dulcina and Odilon (who, in their theater, Teatro Dulcina, staged European and Brazilian boulevard comedies as well as serious Brazilian plays). In 1943, when Os Come-diantes—still an amateur group—presented *Vestido de noiva,* the atti-tude of professional theater toward amateur theater was one of open hostility (*Os Comediantes* 26), with the exception of Dulcina, who was more than helpful to the young group. Apparently, the professional groups considered the popular growth of amateur theater to be an incursion into its theatrical space and saw it as a threatening alternative to the star system that sustained its professional activity.

The prima donna system that had prevailed in previous pro-fessional groups was abandoned within the structure of the TBC: this break with the diva convention provided artistic growth for a genera-tion of new actors. Group production work behind the theatrical spec-tacle was valued, and the learning potential incorporated into the TBC was augmented by its open connection and communication with the Escola de Arte Dramática (EAD), also founded in 1948.

In effect, the TBC was the prototype of liberal contemporary professional theater in Brazil: means of theatrical production were controlled by the impresario-director hierarchy, but artistic and technical input from the crew of technicians and artists was valued, both monetarily and in terms of professional prestige; pay scales varied within the group (a modified "star system" prevailed), but economic security—relative to most actor's total lack of security—allowed for artistic growth. Outside artists and crew were often hired, and they, along with the EAD input, enriched group productions. Stable casts with a developed repertory allowed the TBC to be sufficiently sensitive to public reaction to replace plays that were not well received. The plays produced were geared to the demands of the existing market—essentially upper class for beginning TBC years—but there was also with an effort to create and expand this market. "Social" theater—slice-of-life theater of the existentialist or psychological bent—was presented, starting with contemporary European and American plays (Sartre, Tennessee Williams, Pirandello). These plays were enthusiastically received, and they helped to create a climate propitious to staging Brazilian plays of similar type.

The above evaluation of the TBC's contribution is the one generally held by critics today. However, it is necessary to consider also the virulent nature of the reaction to the TBC in the early 1960s by many dedicated to the growth of a Brazilian theater that spoke to national concerns. The TBC was attacked for being totally derivative and dependent on foreign theater. It was accused of having channeled national artistic resources into the service of upper-class or foreign capital. In short, it was condemned for having short-circuited the course of Brazilian theater. It was forgotten that the TBC had provided a theatrical structure and space to consider the country's problems and that its organizational experience and public following had provided the necessary conditions for Arena's growth.

It should not be forgotten that Arena was a professional theater and as such found its means of production determined in much the same way as did the TBC, although Arena did receive nominal official support and the TBC was supported mainly by the economic patronage of São Paulo's elite as well as by Zampari's backing. Even during the period of its political commitment to expand the parameters of popular theater, Arena maintained its home in São Paulo and was subject to the economic pressures associated with repertory theater. As members traveled more often in outreach programs, outside professionals were hired to fill in. Because of this impermanence many of the structural changes that had characterized the group's political commitment—those that had reinforced collective work and analysis—were abandoned, and Arena, in its São Paulo quarters, reverted to more impresarial lines.

But the virulent criticism of the TBC as well as Arena's activity must be put into a more specific, if abbreviated, perspective of the political and economic factors of developmental nationalism.[6]

The presidential election of 1955 was won by Juscelino Kubitschek, a strong nationalist with an acute eye to foreign investment, with João Goulart, heir to Vargas populist-nationalist policies, as vice president.[7] Resistance within the military and conservative elements of Congress to the Kubitschek-Goulart election was strong. A conservative coup was feared, and a group of "constitutionalist" military leaders, headed by Minister of War Teixeira Lott, intervened to assure the inauguration of the elected president.

Kubitschek drew his major support from the bourgeoisie, where a growing sense of nationalism accompanied the unprecedented economic growth of the early 1950s. In his speeches he repeatedly stated that the road to national independence was through economic development, creating the slogan "fifty years in five" to designate his ambitious plan of economic development. However, this nationalism was problematic, for large economic leaps relied heavily on foreign loans and foreign investment. Within this framework, however, domestic investments also reached an unprecedented level, reflecting, at least in part, the ebullient faith that attracted internal capital for his policies.

Industrial growth, particularly incentives to the naval and automobile industries, was one factor that encouraged a feeling of optimism in the country. Kubitschek also undertook a program of expansion and development in the interior that gave a decided sense of grandeur to the climate of fervent nationalism. The most important step in this policy was the creation of Brasília as the new capital of Brazil. This was an enormous project. Work was started on the new city in 1957 and continued day and night, seven days a week, for three years. In 1960 the capital was moved there. Located in Goiás over three hundred miles from the sea and created out of hitherto underdeveloped land, Brasília epitomized the government's commitment to expansion and development on a grand scale. Along with the creation of Brasília, Kubitschek also commenced work on the trans-Brazilian highway system. He also created Codeno (Comissão de Desenvolvimento Econômico do Nordeste)—later to be converted into Sudene—a commission dedicated to instituting new social and economic policies in the severely poor and underdeveloped Northeast of Brazil.

Obviously, these projects cost considerable money. Currency was printed in large quantities. Inflation spiraled. Although wages were repeatedly increased, real wages decreased. The International Monetary Fund complained. In 1959, Kubitschek broke off negotiations with the IMF, an act applauded by many nationalists as well as by the radical Left.

Despite the episode with the IMF, however, Kubitschek's overall foreign policy was one of conciliation, as can be seen in his encouragement of foreign investment. He was the creator and principal agent of the Operação Panamericana, an attempt to alert the United States to the real problems in Latin America. This plan was rejected by Eisenhower, but was the precursor of the Alliance for Progress under Kennedy.

Kubitschek's policies did not meet with unanimous support in Brazil, and conservative groups were more than wary of his developmental strategies. The radical Left also took an increasingly dim view of the growing economic hardships these strategies produced, particularly within the working class. Dissention within the Left and subsequent splits between liberals and the Left regarding both the ideology and practice of developmental nationalism is significantly expressed in the trajectory of the Instituto Superior de Estudos Brasileiros (Superior Institute of Brazilian Studies), the ISEB.

In 1955 the ISEB was founded. An autonomous research agency, a think tank that gathered together the most progressive of economists, sociologists, historians, and political theorists, the ISEB was federally funded and responsible to the Ministry of Education, a subministry of the Ministry of Education and Culture (MEC).[8] From 1955 to 1964 the ISEB formulated the ideological policy and economic programs followed, not always fully nor enthusiastically, by the government. In the beginning the ISEB functioned as a wide coalition of tendencies, incorporating political liberals as well as members of the Communist Party and other groups oriented to class analysis. A period of optimism and growth, stimulated by such projects of national development and internal investment as the construction of Brasília, the years 1955–59 were characterized by an exuberant and somewhat simplistic attitude toward self-determination and cultural affirmation. However, toward the end of the Kubitschek administration, some economists in the ISEB concluded that foreign investment had entrenched itself by placing capital at the disposal of national development plans and that there were only two options for continuing economic development: either to encourage further foreign investment, hoping to control it, or to reorganize the economy under socialist models. In the subsequent split over these methods, the ISEB became dominated by Marxist thinkers who supported the latter solution. This split occurred in 1959, on the eve of the election of Jânio Quadros, a political maverick running on the conservative ticket of the UDN (União Democrática Nacional), but actually under a coalition that hoped that Quadros could make the concessions necessary to continue development without further alienating foreign investment. Vice president elect was João Goulart, who ran on the ticket of the Vargas party.

In foreign policy, Quadros instituted a rhetoric of diplomatic independence that was quite different from Kubitschek's suave manner of conciliation. Quadros envisioned Brazil as the leader of a new South American power block. He alienated the Right by nationalization policies and by honoring Che Guevara. However, he refused to carry out "leftist" policies, claiming he required full congressional support. Quadros abruptly resigned on August 25, 1961, saying that his resignation was made to force Congress into giving him the power needed to preside effectively.

The result of this gesture in terms of public relations was chaos. He was not even supported by the Left, who considered his gesture self-indulgent and felt betrayed, as did the liberals, by his abdication. The resignation did polarize a political and civil situation that had been growing tenser. Quadros was not recalled by Congress, and it was only by reducing the powers of the presidency—instituting a parliamentary rule—that Goulart was allowed to take office. The liberal military again had to intervene in order to assure his taking office, and to forestall a rightist military coup.

Goulart inherited an administration whose effective power was crippled by a largely hostile Congress, as well as a situation of repeated military interference in national policies. The past two times interference had been in support of the constitution. In 1964 it was in abrogation of the constitution in favor of military rule. From 1962 to 1964, Goulart swung between radical programs of socialization and conciliation with those who based economic development upon further foreign investment. It became clear, at the end of 1963, that his only constituency, and only possible mandate, came from the Marxist Left, labor unions, and supporters of agrarian reform that called for land redistribution and other socialist programs. Goulart supported the leftist programs.

On March 31, 1964, the conservative elements in the army staged a coup, supported by rightist and even liberal civilians who feared more than anything the possibility of a Communist takeover.

Goulart left Rio on April 1 while the military proclaimed the success of what was to be called the revolution of 1964. The ISEB was disbanded, and many of its members subsequently were deprived of their political rights.

When one looks at the TBC-Arena trajectory in terms of the growth of developmental nationalism, one sees a progression of democratization toward radicalization both in terms of structural organization (means of production) and political consciousness of theater's social and cultural role. The TBC represents the relative democratization that accompanied the consolidation of the middle class and petite bourgeoisie as consumers of cultural products and arbiters of that product. Social concerns typical of the liberalism of that group began, at that time, to dominate TBC's repertory. This democratization process was taken up and expanded by Arena. There was no official link between Arena and ISEB. However, there is no doubt that Arena's political commitment parallels the radicalization process within the ISEB itself, as shown by the evolution of Arena from the epoch of the dramatic seminars until 1960.

In 1961 the members most involved with building a popular base (most notably Vianinha and Francisco de Assis) left the group. They argued that Arena was ideologically inbred, that is, it appealed only to leftists already in agreement with its politics and was incapable of acting as a politicizing force both because of its limited audience and because the means of production still followed the impresarial model controlled by petit bourgeois intellectuals. It is true that even in its heyday as a promulgator of popular theater Arena did not manage to incorporate the class it wished to organize within its ranks despite its pedagogical work in setting up theater workshops in union- and community-based groups. It did provide, however, the model for political theater for subsequent urban groups: theater done with few resources, with minimal staging and lighting, and presenting political analysis by a modified use of popular theatrical form, while most frequently underscoring the good/evil polarizations characteristic of this theater.

As previously stated, the touring groups of Arena during the early 1960s became increasingly involved in situational theater, geared to specific problems of its particular public, whether that public was rural or student. Although committed to working-class and rural organizing, these groups were student based and what funding they received generally came from the União Nacional de Estudantes (UNE), an open student union dominated in the 1960s by radical

Catholics and Marxists. The UNE was recognized and funded by MEC and had close political and research ties with ISEB.

In 1961, Vianinha finished a play on surplus profits, *A mais-valia vai acabar, seu Edgar* (Surplus Value Will Be no More, Mr. Shore), to be produced in the theater of the Architectural Students School in the Praia Vermelha branch of the Federal University of Rio. He contacted Carlos Estevam Martins of ISEB for help with the research for the play. The play, a musical farce along Brechtian lines, was a cultural landmark: students and the intellectual Left mobilized around the production, creating the Centro Popular de Cultura (CPC) from this mobilization. The CPC functioned as the cultural arm of the UNE and included people from all the arts. In its aspects as a research and information group, it concentrated on the assessment of popular cultural heritage as a basis for political organizing.

The importance of the CPC in the definition of national theater and as a model for alternative theater is only now being assessed. (The 1979 political opening allowed such discussion and research to begin.)[9] It gathered around it most of the radical leftists working in theater, particularly students, soon adopting a radical vanguard position as regards popular culture and theater. The major theorists for the CPC were Carlos Estevam Martins, Ferreira Gullar, Vianinha, and Francisco de Assis. Partly in reaction to the paternalism and co-optation of Vargas populism, where sections of dominating power promoted the participation of the dominated masses in order to maintain their (the masses) support of the regime, and in their optimism of effecting revolutionary change, these theorists took an extremely critical view about what was "popular." As we see in the "Anteprojeto do manifesto do CPC" (Pre-project for the manifesto of the CPC),[10] elaborated by Carlos Estevam Martins, the people (here mainly defined as campesinos or workers of rural origins) had in effect three artistic manifestations: *(a)* "arte do povo" [people's art], ludic ornaments without artistic/transformative value, representing the most common consumer level; *(b)* "arte popular," popular artifacts, representations of society with consciousness of artistic process but without transformative intent; and *(c)* "arte popular revolucionária," art that analyzed social conditions, with transformative intent. The question of aesthetic quality was subsumed into the necessity of social transformation.

In practice, the intent to change the public of theater from middle class to popular was not very successful, and the CPC ran into the same problems that Arena's radical theater program had faced.

Plays were staged for unions, but without audience; workers did not frequent union halls. The group met fierce police reaction, a reality of the discrepancy of rural and suburban police treatment from that of middle-class neighborhoods, as well as reflective of the governor's (Carlos Lacerda) antiradical policies. Staged plays (like *Black-tie*) were abandoned, and street theater and agitprop became the performing rule. However, increasingly the CPC theater moved back to its organizational base, student radical activity. On the eve of the coup (Vianinha's *Os Azeredos mais os Benevides* [The Azeredos and the Benevides] was scheduled to open in the UNE theater in several days), the CPC had in effect turned its energies primarily back to this constituency and back to writing full-length plays. At the time this was seen as a regrouping tactic, a time for more study of class struggle and popular organization.

Critics today consider the political analyses of the CPC naive, lacking a vision of the dynamic of popular culture, especially in its condemnation of the conservatism of the aesthetics of popular culture and in its simple position on art and culture as a means for organizing the masses. Members of the CPC, in interviews and statements, related this naïveté to a sense of political expediency and the urgency of pre-1964 Brazilian social reality. Despite these limitations, the legacy of the CPC remains very significant, particularly within the framework of post-*abertura* (after the political opening) critical activity. In the years immediately following the political opening of 1979, one could not read the weekly cultural section of any major newspaper without meeting the title of a book or article or a seminar investigating this legacy. The programs, experiences, and analyses of the victories and/or errors of the CPC have become the focal point for delineating possible lines for alternative theater dedicated to social change in Brazil. The CPC activity also solidified the link between the university and the movement for growth of a popular and national theater, stressing the emphasis on the necessity of theatrical practice as the basis for the growth of national dramaturgy.

This, then, is the general framework in which Vianinha began writing his plays. There are two other factors of international consequence that contributed to the radicalization of the Brazilian Left that should be briefly noted here. The first was the revelation of the Stalin atrocities in 1956 which, although creating havoc in the Brazilian Communist Party (PCB), had the renewing effect of provoking closer analysis of the means and ends of political activity on the home ground. The second, the Cuban revolution in 1959, encouraged a sense of optimism in Brazil in regard to the possibility of effecting revolutionary change there and on the continent.

As indicated, Vianinha's views on theater as well as of its cultural space become significantly radicalized. A look at his plays written and performed during this time will show the difficulties he encountered in elaborating theatrical conventions adequate to an increasingly complex, if not always accurate, analysis of Brazilian social reality.

Vianinha, Arena, and the Centro Popular de Cultura

During the time he was associated with Arena, Vianinha wrote two plays that, even as beginning works, well represent the two dramatic modes that characterize the modal oscillation of his later works: farce and realistic drama.

The first play, *Bilbao via Copacabana*, is an all-out farce. Written in 1957 and produced by Arena in 1959, *Bilbao* is a one-act play of moderate length with six characters that tells the story of the deception practiced on several inhabitants of a typical high-rise Copacabana apartment building by a traveling con man.

In the list of characters at the beginning of the play, the three middle-class (or aspiring to the middle class) characters are designated according to their farcical typification: the *marido* (the husband), the *patroa* (the wife), and the *vizinha* (the neighbor). In the dialogue, names are used that complement that typification. The husband, an architect with pretensions of being an artist, has the rather improbable name of Gronoldo Monfort. The wife is called Dulce, as befitting a sweet recent bride, and the neighbor, an Englishwoman who speaks broken Portuguese, is called alternately dona Matilde and Elizabeth (the name she gives to Dulce when they get to a first-name basis).

The other three characters are Pablo (the con man), Seu João (the janitor/doorman), and Rainha ("Queen," the maid). The con man is listed as Pablo, the name he uses while on stage. A large part of the farce revolves around his ability to affect different nationalities and accents, pretending to be separate people, while he sells the same nonexistent set of silverware to the inhabitants. He is successful in his impersonations despite large discrepancies in his stories, which, although they don't go unnoticed by his victims, he manages to cover up with ridiculous ease. Seu João is also taken in by Pablo, who proclaims himself to be a hardworking traveling salesman from Portugal, honest and desiring nothing more than to return to his homeland. It is interesting to note that, although Seu João is duped, his mistake is treated in a much less satirical manner. It is clear that the others who fall prey to the game—the wife, the neighbor, and the husband—are duped not only by their naïveté, but principally by their desire to buy, at a very cheap price, an item symbolizing aspirations of upward mobility.

The typification of these five characters remains constant throughout the play. As might be suspected from the political ideas of the author, the pivotal character of the play is Rainha, the maid. Her character is presented to invert, or probe, the stereotypical image of the maid and, indeed, has much in common with the comic tradition of the "gracioso/a." Her name, Rainha, is an irony perceived by the spectator that is underscored by her sad, but funny response to her boss: "Rainha não, patroa, Princesa só!" [Not Queen, ma'am, just Princess] (34). When we first see her, Rainha is presented as rather slow and stupid, unable (or unwilling) to follow quickly her boss's instructions. She speaks in uneducated, hillbilly Portuguese ("Pur que é que a senhora, quando subiu, já não levô ele?" (How comes you didn't take 'em up when you gone up?") [35]).

However, she is the first one to perceive Pablo's game. In the middle of the play, when her boss shows the "expensive perfume from Marrakech" that Pablo has given her, a freebie designed to demonstrate his good intentions of delivering the promised goods, Rainha states quite clearly that the perfume has the same unmistakable odor as a very cheap perfume popular in São Cristóvão, a poor suburb of Rio. When the others gather in amazement to try to sort out what has transpired, she is the first to understand and to laugh because they have all been duped.

The entire action takes place in the living room–bedroom of the small efficiency apartment of the young couple. It has modern furniture, with cubist paintings on the wall. The action opens with the wife, already visibly pregnant, trying to hang one of her husband's paintings as a surprise for their five-month wedding anniversary. The wife is frustrated by Rainha's seeming inability to understand her need for help. Seu João comes in, bringing with him Pablo. After Seu João leaves, the wife and Pablo commence a series of highly farcical and improbable interchanges that constitute the bulk of the play. They discuss her aspirations for her baby, his family, their lives. Pablo, in "espanhol macarrônico" [garbled Spanish] claims to be Spanish, of Italian descent, and born in Bilbao; hence the name of the play. It is clear to the audience that only a fool or someone who wished to be fooled would swallow his story of the family he left behind and the beautiful silver set and box from Arabia that he is selling to catch the next boat home.

The absurdity of these interchanges can be seen in the final protestation of friendship and honor Pablo makes to Dulce:

> *Pablo.* Se usted algun dia viajar para España, procureme!
> *Patroa.* Como?
> *Pablo.* Pablo de España. Todos me conocen. Procure Pablo. . . . me encontrará sin falta.

> [*Pablo.* If you go to Spain some day, look me up!
> *Patroa.* How?
> *Pablo.* Pablo. Pablo from Spain. Everybody knows me. Look for Pablo. . . . you'll find me easy!] (65)

It doesn't occur to Dulce to question this.

As proof of the existence of the silver, Pablo says that he sold the only set he had with him to the upstairs neighbor. He promises to ask the neighbor to come down and show it to Dulce. Of course, when Matilde enters, much confusion follows, since it seems that, pretending to be English, Pablo has also taken her money, saying that Dulce has the original. They finally realize they have been duped. At that point, Seu João enters, praising the wonderful Portuguese man who had sold him a silver set, followed by Gronoldo, who tells his wife about the fabulous present that he has just ordered for his wife from a Russian, an expatriate nephew of Lenin's.

Of course, by this time Pablo has disappeared. The play, however, ends happily with Dulce and Gronoldo thankful for the loving relationship they have.

As can be seen by the play's happy ending, the satirical elements of this farce are balanced by a genuine fondness for the characters. In all of his comedies that treat the middle and lower middle class, even when his underlying social analysis becomes more sophisticated and almost acerbic, Vianinha takes particular care to try to present them in a larger light, allowing them loving characteristics that mitigate their comic foibles. Although this is within the tradition of popular comedy, I believe this balancing of portrayal to be also a result of three other factors. First, Vianinha had a loving and humorous personality, reserving his worst criticism for himself. Secondly, his primary intention was not to lampoon this class, but to try to analyze, on stage, what were the social motivations of their aspirations. In this sense, although his characters share the values of conspicuous consumption satirized here, Vianinha wishes to tell us that these values do not originate with the characters but are unconsciously assumed as part of the baggage of a larger cultural value system. Admittedly, the analysis is slight in this farce.

The third factor is the most important in terms of his implicit reading of the cultural space of his theater. This was the ambience in which Vianinha was raised, even though, as pointed out, his parents' political consciousness was different from that generally held by the petite bourgeoisie. And this is also the class makeup of his real audience. The theatergoing public in Brazil at that time was the modest middle class, educated people with moderately paid, usually white-collar jobs who went to the theater for entertainment.[11]

In 1957, Copacabana was already a densely populated, teeming urban area. There were luxury apartments and hotels overlooking the Atlantic and extending a few streets in from the sea. The majority of the buildings were high-rise apartment buildings with modest and even minuscule units. Then, and even more so now, most of the first floors, and sometimes several up, were shops, small businesses, or professional offices, a large number of which catered to the tourist trade. Of course, there were numerous restaurants and some cinemas and theaters.

Most of the people (mainly the men of the family) worked in white-collar jobs, often as minor public functionaries, or were beginning professional careers and commuted to the center of the city for their jobs, a ten to fifteen minute bus ride, or longer depending on already crowded traffic.

In this farce the urban isolation inherent in this demographic setup becomes a mechanistic element of the plot. Pablo can safely work a whole building because the neighbors don't know each other. In fact, his game has a happy side in that it breaks this isolation, being the occasion for a new friendship between two isolated housewives who, although neighbors, were previously unacquainted. In the true sense of farce: all's well that ends well.

In other plays by Vianinha, the sense and reality of enclosure scenically indicated by a set consisting of one small room—usually a living room—emphasizes the concomitant alienation of this isolation. And despite his employment of various techniques to create fissures in the fourth wall, including the use of the arena stage (hard to imagine here with pictures on the walls), the fourth wall is very much present in most of his plays.

Although he doesn't speak in terms of the fourth wall in his theory, his later dramaturgy reveals an understanding of the conventions of identification associated with it. He wishes to use the illusion of realism created by this enclosure to establish identification between the individual spectator and the actors. At the same time, he will incorporate other dramatic and scenic elements that create holes in this wall that would provoke perceptual modifications in the spectator. In other words, the presentation of reality on stage is not questioned, but the audience is asked to analyze this reality in a way that would lead them to question the basis of their assumptions or perceptions of that reality. It is a matter of trying to turn a dramatic convention in on itself, to use it to investigate its own underlying cultural assumptions. This is indeed a hard task, and he accomplishes it with varying degrees of success, as will be discussed.

In an essay that figures as preface to *Bilbao*, Vianinha discusses the intentions and limitations of the play, justifying the implied contradictions between the play and his political vision. He says it is neither a farce nor a satire, but an exercise:

> Haveria, talvez, uma posição mais desenvolvida, mais marcada, caminhando então para a sátira, se Patroa, etc, representassem, com mais violência, a sociedade que detém os poderes intelectuais e sociais da época. . . . Não chega à sátira, não chega à farsa. Fica ainda regida por alguns princípios da detestável comédia realista.

> [There would, perhaps, be a more developed, more marked position, leaning toward satire, if Patroa, etc., represented with greater violence the society that holds the intellectual and social powers of the time. . . . It is not quite satire and not quite farce. It is still ruled by some principles of the detestable realist comedy.] (30)

Rejecting classification, Vianinha prefers to say that the play is "teatro e mais nada" [theater and nothing more]. He clarifies his idea of theatricality as applied to *Bilbao:* "Seu vigor está na teatralidade—nos efeitos—nas pausas—na quebra de ritmo constante . . . *Bilbao, via Copacabana* nada traz ao pensamento moderno, ao questionário filosófico e social que o homem se propõe. Ela brinca" [Its vigor lies in its theatricality—in the effects—in the pauses—in the constant break of rhythm . . . *Bilbao via Copacabana* brings nothing to modern thought, to the philosophical and social questioning that man proposes] (30–31). He also acknowledges a debt to the tradition of his father: "Antes de *Bilbao, via Copacabana,* Oduvaldo Pai e Martins Pena andaram dando lição, cada um no que mais dominava, de diálogos, de ritmo e de situação cômica" [Before *Bilbao via Copacabana,* Oduvaldo senior and Martins Pena taught lessons, each on the thing he was best at, in dialogues, in rhythm, and in comic situations] (31).

Severe self-criticism was a lifetime habit of Vianinha, as was an often ambivalent and defensive attitude toward the social role of comedy. As befits the tenor of the times, his justification of "a palavra cômica" [the comic word] in *Bilbao* is optimistic, as we see in the opening paragraph of his essay:

Eu admito a existência de comédias despreocupadas—comédias que, enquanto a condição humana é reduzida violentamente ao seu mais triste grau de expressão, envolvida por um sem-número de extorsões da sua dignidade, flauteiam, suaves, brejeiras, fazendo rir porque sim. Ainda temos tempo para rir. Só a perspectiva de futuro permite isso. Nunca analisei filosófica ou socialmente uma piada. Toda a piada é uma atitude inteligente. É comunhão. Corresponde sempre a uma visão nova de qualquer fato. O novo, a quebra de padrões estabelecidos e o riso caminham sempre juntos. Por isso o homem avança. Porque ri.

[I admit the existence of unconcerned comedies—comedies that, while the human condition is violently reduced to its saddest degree of expression, involved by countless extortions of its dignity, float, soft, mischievous, provoking laughter just because. We still have time to laugh. Only the perspective of the future permits this. I have never analyzed a joke philosophically or socially. Every joke is an intelligent attitude. It's communion. It always corresponds to a new vision of any fact. The new, the rupture of established patterns and laughter always walk hand in hand. This is why man advances. Because he laughs.] (29)

Almost as if in counterbalancing compensation for the high spirits and optimistic sense of community portrayed in *Bilbao,* Vianinha's next play with Arena is a serious, even pessimistic, realistic drama about an exploited community subgroup in full process of disintegration.

As stated earlier, *Chapetuba Futebol Clube,* a play about a regional soccer team facing a championship play-off, was written within the Seminários de Dramaturgia and staged in 1959. The major innovation of *Chapetuba* was thematic. It was acknowledged as the first time that soccer was given a major dramatic treatment on the Brazilian stage. Considering the popular passion for the game, this was a big step in the direction that Arena proposed of creating a national dramaturgy of quintessential Brazilian themes. In terms of dramatic structure, however, *Chapetuba* is a traditional drama in its basic form, containing three acts and a moderate-size cast of ten characters. Dramatic development follows chronologically within the conventions of traditional drama.

The first act introduces the characters: the players; the two promoters of the team; Fina, the girl who serves them in the boardinghouse; and Benigno, a reporter for the other team, Saboeiro. There is a verbal stimulus, or premonition of disaster to come followed by the entrance of Benigno, the character who provokes the betrayal that is at the center of the dramatic action.

The second act develops the conflicts between the characters, heightening the sense of climax that will occur in the third act, and ends with the offstage action that determines the events of the third act. Maranhão, the star player, feigns a sprained ankle, result of a pretended offstage fall, thus affirming complicity with Benigno, who has been sent to buy him off.

The first two acts take place in the dining room of the boardinghouse on the eve of the game. The third act transpires in the team's locker room during the last part of the game. Despite the generation of many subplots in the interpersonal conflicts of act 2 (a structural and thematic problem to be discussed later), the third act proposes nothing new in dramatic structure to resolve these conflicts, nor to leave them open in a dramatically provocative way. As can have been foreseen, Chapetuba loses the game during the last minutes of play.

Although *Chapetuba* was staged in the arena form, the use of scenic space presents no real innovations. Indeed, it reenforces and utilizes the inside-outside contrast common to much realistic social drama since Chekhov and Ibsen. The enclosure of the first two acts accentuates the doubts and personal conflicts taking place in the boardinghouse as contrasted to the euphoria of the mob of fans clearly heard outside. The sense of isolation in the locker room scene of the third act is augmented by the sound of the radio from which we as well as the players who square off in conflict in the locker room learn of the game's progress. The motif that links these scenes of enclosure to the outside is the impending birth of the child of a member of the team. Throughout acts 1 and 2, Zito calls to find out about his wife's labor. News of the birth of a boy is given at the end of act 3, a dramatic element clearly destined to give an optimistic twist and sense of opening to the dismal social microcosm depicted by the interactions of the players within their tightly circumscribed space.

Within these parameters of traditional drama there is, however, a substantial shift of emphasis in the dramatic treatment of characterization and action that serve to enlarge the theatrical conventions of Brazilian social drama. The interpolation of socioeconomic analysis through characterization and conflict at strategic points in the development of the dramatic structure of *Chapetuba* seeks to shift immediate audience interest from the subjective reactions of the characters (the conventionally established desired response) to an interest in, and analysis of, the objective social and cultural realities underlying and predicating dramatic action. We can see how this is meant to work in a brief act-by-act analysis of these aspects of the play.

The play opens traditionally enough. The players nervously joke about the game. Maranhão, the star player, declares that it's bad luck to call a game before it's played. Presentment of Maranhão's role in this bad luck is increased when we learn that he has a lame leg. With the entrance of Benigno, some ten pages later, we find that luck has nothing to do with it. In several pages of roundabout dialogue we learn from Benigno that Maranhão has serious financial problems and that Maranhão's character is suspect: it is insinuated that he once threw a game when he was playing for the rival team, Saboeiro. Maranhão resists, and it is made clear that the main motives for his betrayal will not be personal corruption, but rather a fatalistic capitulation to the dictates of political interests. As Benigno states, the Soccer Federation, backed by the coffee growers, prefer Saboeiro. It is clear by the dramatic emphasis given to Benigno's disclosure that this is the crux of the matter. Chapetuba's stadium is smaller than Saboeiro's (thus less profitable), and does not have the politically powerful backers that Saboeiro has.

The sense of futility inherent in being a pawn of a larger economic game is underscored by the other major character development of act 1. We learn the story of Durval, once a star player on one of Rio's major teams, Flamengo, and an international soccer hero, but now a has-been, reduced to technician and string player for Chapetuba. No longer an economically viable investment, Durval has been thrown aside. He is a drunkard who lives on past glory while anticipating the same fate from the owners of Chapetuba. Benigno uses Durval's example as his trump card in undermining Maranhão's resistance.

Act 2 elaborates on Durval's pathetic case, calling into question the economic underpinnings of the sport in contrast to its mass popularity. This takes place in an interchange between Durval and Zito, a rising young player who admires Durval. Durval is drunk, and alternately puts the blame for his fall on those who hold power over the sport and on the fans. Durval counsels Zito to save all his money and go into something else:

> *Durval.* Larga o futebol. Futebol é nada . . . futebol é vazio.
> *Zito.* É bonito, Durva.
> *Durval.* Não diz assim de novo! Quem manda é essa gente que fica sentada, torrando no sol. Essa gente que não sabe de nada! Eles querem berrá. . . . Gente que chora por causa de uma partida de futebol, nenê!
> *Zito:* Chora e ri. Isso é bonito, Durval. Futebol junta gente que nem se conhecem pra sê irmão . . . pra se querê. Tudo fica um!

> [*Durval.* Forget soccer. Soccer is nothing . . . soccer is useless.
> *Zito.* It's beautiful, Durva.
> *Durval.* Don't say that again! Who's in charge is those guys, the ones toasting in the sun. Those guys don't know nothing about nothing! They just want to yell. . . . People who bawl because of a soccer game, kid!
> *Zito.* Cries and laughs. That's what's beautiful, Durval. Soccer gets people together who don't even know each other. To be brothers . . . to like each other. All one!] (163)

Durval's emphasis on the bread-and-circuses aspect of the popular sport is understandable, given his history, just as Zito's optimism and faith in solidarity is part of his youth. The juxtaposition of these two attitudes, developed throughout the play, shows the social solidarity occasioned by soccer as perverted and limited by the economic structure within which the game takes place.

In act 3, Chapetuba plays a heroic game, even without their star player and despite the real injury of their next best player, Cafuné. They lose in the last minutes of the game by a bad call. The judge has also been bought, another item that Benigno had warned Maranhão of. In an extremely problematic sense, all circumstances converge to vindicate, or at least absolve, Maranhão's betrayal. His defection is explained as an understandable individual response to an overpowering system, much in the same terms of individualism versus solidarity that mark Zito and Durval's interchange in act 2.

This discussion in act 3 revolves around Cafuné and Maranhão. Although a seasoned player, Cafuné is still a determined innocent, as seen by his insistence on keeping his beard—a promise made to a saint—regardless of the club promoter's threats to throw him out if he doesn't clean up his appearance. Cafuné's first reaction to Maranhão's sellout is to decry his lack of solidarity: "Todo mundo é assim, seu? Todo mundo num é irmão? Ninguém liga nos outro sempre? Sempre de não acabá mais?" [Everybody's like that, man? Not all brothers? Nobody looks out for each other? Forever and ever like that?] (190). Maranhão finally responds: "A gente num tem nada pra fazê junto! É cada um no seu canto, sempre! Nunca se olhando direito . . . se desconfiando sempre! Não é assim? Não foi sempre assim?" [We got nothing to do together! Each guy in his own corner, always! Never lookin' the other in the eye . . . always suspicious! Ain't that how it is? How it's always been?] (192).

Cafuné calms down and considers Maranhão's response: "É sim. A gente que num sabe nada . . . que nunca vê as coisas direito. . . . Tudo aconteceu lá em cima" [Yeah, it is. We never know what's going on . . . never see right. . . . Everything happens up there] (193). The inference that what is not seen is the larger economic and political plan is made clear when Maranhão, directly after Cafuné's comment, tells Cafuné about the judge and the federation's preference for Saboeiro. Cafuné half-heartedly retorts that it still would have been better to try to win but soon resigns himself to accepting the validity of Maranhão's action within Maranhão's reasoning, even if he doesn't accept this response for himself.

It is Durval who encapsulates the contradictions of Maranhão's action. It turns out that he was also approached to throw the game and knew all about the judge and the federation but, for reasons of solidarity, refused. However, his condemnation of Maranhão ("Tu nunca percebe nada, nenê. Nunca?" [Don't you ever understand nothing, kid? Never?] [201]) is mitigated by his sense of reality: he advises Maranhão to retrieve the check (payment for his betrayal) that he has thrown crumpled on the floor. In essence, he forgives Maranhão's lack of character, blaming it on the economic realities of the game.

The ironic futility of Durval's personal honor, although sympathetically treated by the author, is underscored in the last scene.

Zito begs Durval to act as "padrinho" ("godfather") to his newborn son. Durval answers that he is really not fit for the responsibility, that he is no model to hold up to the next generation. His refusal puts into dramatic limbo any optimistic message that could be associated with birth and innocence at the end of the play.

There is another attempt to imbue the fatalistic tone of the play with a sense of opening. In the last scene, Bila (another player) asks Fina to leave Chapetuba and start life anew with him. Her response is neither affirmative nor negative, but left hanging in the pessimistic gloom. The play ends with Durval's absolving Maranhão, repeating through his tears, "Que cara é essa que tu põe, filho? . . . Tá certo, sim" [What kind of face is that, boy? . . . It's OK, yeah] (207). The curtain falls on Maranhão climbing the steps of the locker room. He has picked up the check but is limping. This final element is confusing, since Maranhão was supposedly not really hurt. It is to be assumed that this limp is symbolic of the injury he has done to his own humanity.

Considered in light of the analysis it proposes, *Chapetuba* is not just "an exposé of professional soccer in Brazil . . . [that] studies the social and political implications of the pastime as a business in an exploitive system." Nor is its principal theme "the corruptive influence of money on the characters of the play" (Schoenbach 368). It is meant to stand as a microcosm of Brazilian society, a realistic allegory of demystification.

However, its dramatic power is seriously flawed by subplots, most left unresolved at the end (for example, Bila and Fina's relationship, Paulinho's problem with his rich father, Cafuné's feelings). This looseness of structure could be attributed to inexperience; in Vianinha's first major play, he included more conflicts that he could handle. As Sábato Magaldi remarks in a review of the play's opening, "O pecado em *Chapetuba* é de excesso. . . . Nota-se que o autor se escravizou à noção de conflito, segundo a qual devem sempre estar contracenando opositores permanentes ou ocasionais" [The sin in *Chapetuba* is one of excess. . . . The author has noticeably become a slave to the idea of conflict, according to which permanent or occasional opposites ought always to be on stage] ("Problemas de 'Chapetuba F.C.' ").

This criticism is undoubtedly true. However faulty the resolution of conflicts, on the other hand, the intention behind Vianinha's inclusiveness is important to understanding the trajectory of his work. Throughout his career, Vianinha stretches characterization to include as many points of view as possible, incorporating a variety of cultural attitudes. He gives dimension to systems of values, contrasting the positive and negative aspects of a system so as to implicate the social and economic conditions that inform it.

In *Chapetuba* this results in a weird scenic democracy. The play is overloaded by the necessity to give each character a chance to state his or her case. On the one hand, characterization is opened up, allowing an ample vision of personal contradictions and values. On the other hand, this burden of conflict creates structural problems and leaves a confused message regarding social change. Magaldi puts it succinctly: "Como está, o texto converte em pessimismo duradouro o pessimismo de um momento" [As it stands, the text converts into lasting pessimism the pessimism of a moment] ("Problemas" n.p.).

In sum, despite its intentions of staging an analysis of the microcosm it presents, the play remains more contestatory than critical and analytical. In the same review, Magaldi relates Vianinha's difficulty to his being part of a generation still searching for a path of action: "Mas o substrato profundo de nossa geração ainda são os descaminhos, as inquietudes sem resposta, o mundo insatisfatório. *Chapetuba* reflete com seriedade essa herança intelectual e daí o resultado da peça ser menos o de um processo em marcha que o de uma triste verificação" [But the deep substratum of our generation is still made up of misdirections, the uneasiness of no answers, the unsatisfactory world. *Chapetuba* reflects with seriousness this intellectual heritage; hence the play's result as less an ongoing process than a sad confirmation].

The critical reception of *Chapetuba* was mixed, the most pertinent evaluations pointing to questions of the contemporary cultural space and conventions of Brazilian theater. It is emblematic of the growth of national theater that both the pros and cons in critical reactions were to a large extent accurate. The discrepancies in response reflect the problems of a theater looking for its own conventions and cultural space.

The most enthusiastic responses signaled the production as a giant step in the consolidation of Arena's work in capturing a significant place within the framework of professional theater for treatment of political, and politicized, national themes, as the critic Luiza Barreto Leite recorded in her articles of that moment (Leite).

Approbation of this conquest was not unanimous, however. Patrícia Galvão, writer, activist, and theater critic and director, saw the tendency toward national themes as limiting the aesthetic growth and options of Brazilian theater: "A criação artística e só ela salvará o teatro brasileiro do melodrama e da grosseria, de Gimba [another play by Guarnieri that portrays the *favela* (slum)] e Chapetuba" [Artistic creation alone will save Brazilian theater from melodrama and crudeness, from *Gimba* and *Chapetuba*] (qtd. in A. Campos 227). By her analysis, professional theater was too constricted, by its economic exigencies and the expectations of its real audience, to provide significant opportunity for experimentation. The professional stage almost inevitably led to a reductionist treatment of innovative themes. It was her opinion that only the independent, or amateur, groups had the artistic and economic freedom to experiment with national texts (she cited Ariano Suassuna's *Auto da Compadecida*) and balance that search with a vanguard selection of more universal texts.

Paulo Francis discusses characterization in *Chapetuba*, astutely pointing out that its greatest strength is also its primary weakness:

> há uma autenticidade de tipificação que quase distrai o espectador da peça. Ele, o espectador, fica tão surpreendido de encontrar em cena gente que viu, talvez, faz poucos instantes, na rua, que corre o risco de não se interessar pelo resto, isto é, pela peça. Seria um erro de sua parte. . . . Assim, o texto é conceitualmente exato dentro do ponto de vista político e social do autor. Ninguém, a que eu saiba, escreveu sobre futebol com tanta percepção até hoje entre nós. É uma percepção que se estende ao linguajar apanhado na rua, organizado sobre uma base popular tão complexa de maneiras e costumes, que abrangem uma pensão e um vestuário de campo no interior do país. O espectador não precisa de mapa para saber que está no Brasil.

> [there is an authenticity of types that nearly distracts the play's spectator. He, the spectator, is so surprised at finding people onstage whom perhaps he saw a few moments previously on the street, that he runs the risk of not being interested in the rest, that is, in the play. This would be a mistake on his part. . . . Thus, the text is conceptually exact within the author's political and social point of view. As far as I know, until today no one among us has written about soccer so perceptively. It is a perception that extends itself to street talk, organized on such a complex popular base of manners and customs, that include a boardinghouse and a rural locker room in the interior of the

country. The spectator does not need a map to know he is in Brazil.] (Qtd. in *Vianinha* 43)

These qualities of characterization and popular language are what makes José Renato, then director of Arena, observe in retrospect: that *Chapetuba* was the best text produced by Arena, the one that "mais conseguiu um gesto brasileiro" [that best captured Brazilian gesture] (interview by author, 1981).

However, the impact of *Chapetuba* within Arena can best be seen in an interview with the author and Augusto Boal, the director of the play, conducted right after its opening. It is interesting to note that in this interview Boal defends the play against Vianinha's harsh criticism, whereas Vianinha feels that he has failed to produce the social analysis he wished. In answer to the interviewer's question, "Você acha, então, que na fase atual de sua dramaturgia, você se volta mais para a reportagem teatral dramaticamente bem realizada" [So you think, then, that in the current phase of your work you are tending more toward theatrical reporting dramatically well realized], Vianinha categorically states:

> É. Quer dizer, não foi essa a minha intenção. Eu, quando escrevi, estava certo que era isso que eu tinha que fazer. Inclusive o Brasil, de dia pra dia a gente muda, tem tantas coisas novas. E a gente passa por um processo tão violento de amadurecimento, que foi a partir de quando eu terminei a peça, que eu fui analisar por que eu tinha escrito sobre futebol. . . . Então, foi a partir daí que eu pude chegar mais ou menos a essas conclusões. Realmente, a peça é um pouco cronística, um pouco reportagem como você diz. E realmente sem uma pesquisa de valores, não digo humanos, mas de valores culturais. Afinal de contas ela não é baseada em nenhuma idéia, ela não se fundamenta em nenhuma pesquisa de cultura.

> [Yes. I mean, that wasn't my intention. When I wrote, I was certain that was what I had to do. Even in Brazil, from day to day people change, there are so many new things. And we go through such a violent process of maturation that it wasn't until I finished the play that I got to analyzing why I had written about soccer. . . . So, it was from there that I was more or less able to arrive at these conclusions. Truthfully, the play is a little anecdotal, a little journalistic, as you say. And really devoid of

research on, I wouldn't say human, but on cultural values. After all, it isn't based on any ideas, it isn't founded on any cultural research.] (*Vianinha* 37–38)

In essence, Vianinha finds that his play registers cultural values but does not investigate them. In an article written shortly after that evaluates Arena's contribution to Brazilian theatrical history, Vianinha also faults *Chapetuba* for proposing an incorrect identification between the leading character, Maranhão, and the audience. In reflective reference to Paulo Francis's observation that Arena's plays always seem to put a traitor in center stage (*Vianinha* 43), Vianinha offers the following autocriticism:

> *Chapetuba Futebol Clube* tem os mesmos defeitos de *Eles não Usam Black-Tie*. O homem que pensa, que procura racionalizar—trai. Há um susto de teoria no Teatro de Arena, ele que põe uma teoria, ainda que simplista, do teatro brasileiro. A objetividade, o real, é confundido com sua descrição, não com sua síntese. (*Vianinha* 51)

> *Chapetuba Futebol Clube* has the same faults as *Black-Tie*. The thinking man, the one who attempts to reason—betrays. There is a fear of theory in the Teatro de Arena, which theorizes, albeit simplistically, Brazilian theater. Objectivity, the real, is confused with its description, not with its synthesis.

Boal answers Vianinha's objections to *Chapetuba* by speaking to problems of characterization and identification, asserting that the playwright's assessment of the play is overly harsh. Mentioning self-criticism as part of Vianinha's personality, Boal also says that severe criticism was endemic to Arena's group process at the time (interview by author). He echoes Vianinha's statement that they were passing through a "processo violento de amadurecimento" [violent process of maturation], attributing the play's faults to the vicissitudes of apprenticeship.

Boal does not think the play is mere "reportagem"; rather, he sees a disorientation between the social (the play's ideas) and the emotive levels, which the play fails to associate well enough. The play presents a unified social critique, but the relationship between the microcosm of soccer and the macrocosm of the social problematic is not sufficiently in evidence. Boal argues that this problem and that of overidentification between problematic characters and audience is inherent in the form of dramatic theater, "que não permite uma análise mais profunda do desenvolvimento de um processo que o Vianna quis fazer na sua peça" [which does not allow a deeper analysis of the development of a process that Vianna hoped to perform in his play] (Vianinha 42). Boal takes this opportunity to reiterate the need to study Hegel, Aristotle, Brecht, and Piscator.[12]

At this time, Vianinha was unhappy with his own work and with that of Arena. He felt himself constricted by the parameters of professional theater as designated by an "individualistic culture of contemplation." In its zeal to make a political theater, Arena had fallen into the trap of economistic reductionism and thereby, paradoxically, reinforced patterns of perception rather than challenging them. Despite or because of its superimposed political analysis, Arena's essentially maintained a fatalistic portraiture of humanity against society.

Such a vision does not provoke an audience to question its own assumptions about individualism and the social order, nor does it provide perceptual models leading to any transformation of values within its principal audience, the middle class. Vianinha would have Arena put the middle-class spectator in perspective within the larger, mass, society:

> Afinal, não há uma visão que fundamente a necessidade de uma transformação cultural, dê um giro nos valores éticos predominantes para a área da produção, para a área do homem social.
>
> O Teatro de Arena continua a manter o homem como ele é; sem procurar discutir como ele não é. A perplexidade do homem diante da sociedade é espantosa. Ele pensa, age, sente, em termos de indivíduo. O Teatro de Arena não procurou golpear e demolir o indivíduo, e jogá-lo dentro da massa e dos seus problemas e sentimentos como massa. A idéia de que o indivíduo desaparece pode assustar a pequena burguesia.

> [There is, after all, no vision to substantiate a need for cultural transformation, to give a twist to the predominant ethical values in the field of production, the field of social man.
>
> The Teatro de Arena continues to maintain man as he is; without seeking to discuss him as he is not. Man's perplexity before society is astounding. He thinks, acts, and feels in individual terms. The Teatro de Arena did not attempt to strike and demolish the individual (individualism) and throw him into the

masses and into his problems and feelings as the masses. The idea that the individual disappears can frighten the petite bourgeoisie.] (*Vianinha* 49)

In an article on national theater written in 1960, shortly after these statements, Vianinha elaborates on the shortcomings of Arena's work. It is not enough to "fotografar a realidade aparente"—a limited and even illusory act of political contestation—for what appears to be reality on stage is distorted by the predominant cultural ethic. To restate the argument in slightly different terms, one's interpretation of a realistic photograph has more to do with the values one applies than with the subject matter. A static treatment of reality gives the subliminal message that change is impossible, and although viewers may lament the protagonist's social fate, they come out of the theater reinforced in their feelings of the primacy of the individual. The spectator is not really asked to consider the individual as part of a group, in relationship to the economic structure that oppresses him or her, nor is the viewer challenged to see how the predominant ethic filters down through the class system. In short, the viewer is let off the hook, and the political analysis proffered by these plays is diffused within the extant system of values.

To counteract this static vision, Vianinha proposes a theater that would capture reality in movement. It is important to point out that Vianinha does not refer to political movement, but to cultural movement in the broadest sense of the word. He does not think of theater as a political, but as a cultural, act. Theater's point of social insertion is in the cultural realm. It is an act of cultural mediation. He ends his arguments with a kind of manifesto for Brazilian theater for the early 1960s:

Um teatro brasileiro que faça viver o homem, o sentido de sua responsabilidade na criação dos valores a que se encontra submetido, não é um teatro político—é um teatro que vai ter que se incluir na mediação que o homem tem da realidade concreta, para poder aguçá-la, e permitir uma intervenção precisa. O problema brasileiro é de cultura—política e teatro ganham fenomenal importância. As condições estão dadas para a modificação. É preciso que isto ganhe a consciência. Esta é a nossa tarefa.

[A Brazilian theater that can bring man to life, his sense of responsibility in creating the values to which he finds himself submitted, is not a political theater—it is a theater that will have to be included in the mediation that man has of concrete reality, so as to sharpen it and allow a precise intervention. The Brazilian problem is cultural—politics and theater gain phenomenal importance. Conditions for modification are given [are here]. It is necessary that this become conscious. This is our task.] (79)

When he asserts that "o problema brasileiro é de cultura," Vianinha is speaking of the cultural face of underdevelopment. In his assessment, the Brazilian Left has been caught in a reactive bind against the European and American cultural paradigms that inform elite Brazilian culture and consequently does not question effectively the contradictions this cultural process poses for Brazilian society. When he affirms that the conditions are ripe for modification, we must remember that in 1960 profound structural change in Brazilian society seemed possible. Thus, when he establishes a correspondence between the importance of political activity and theater, he isn't necessarily aggrandizing theater's role. In 1960 and up through 1968 theater did in fact play a leading role as a mediatory voice militating for social change.

What was lacking for the "intervenção precisa" in organizing cultural values that Vianinha saw as the "tarefa" of theater was a clear analysis of social and cultural conditions. Better said, there was no lack of analysis: analyses proliferated, helter-skelter, but were implemented without full theoretical consideration of how the infrastructural problems of Brazilian theater intersected with dominant cultural values.

Vianinha felt that Arena, caught up in administrative problems, could not see the larger picture. The solution to both organizational problems and shortsighted analysis would be to form links with entities that had established forums of political intervention, expertise in infrastructural analysis, and organizational skills:

A solução para mim é a imediata ligação de Teatro de Arena a entidades que facilitem e ampliem a capacidade administrativa do Arena. Não imediata—de hoje para amanhã—mas feita de estudo, de relações, de ligações lentas e necessárias. ISEB, FAU, sindicatos, partidos políticos que expressem ou procurem expressar sua intervenção política na realidade—da mesma maneira que nós queremos intervir culturalmente.

[For me, the solution is the immediate linking of the Teatro de Arena to groups that will facilitate and amplify the administrative capacity of the Arena. Not immediate—as in today to tomorrow—but made from study, relations, from slow and necessary connections. ISEB, FAU [Faculdade de Arquitetura e Urbanismo da Universidade de São Paulo/School of Architecture and Urbanism of the University of São Paulo], unions, political parties that express or seek to express their political intervention in reality—in the same manner in which we wish to intervene culturally.] (78)

Although his call to seek help from like-minded political parties is encompassing, he is of course alluding primarily to the PCB. He becomes more specific: "Não digo que o Teatro de Arena deva ser subsidiário do Partido Comunista. A ligação porém seria fecunda— mantidas as independências. Os contatos seriam abertos por ele. Ele auxiliaria a administração do Arena" [I am not saying that the Teatro de Arena should be a subsidiary of the Communist Party. The connection would be fertile, though—were independence maintained. Contacts would be initiated by it [the Party]. It would assist in the Arena's administration] (76). At the time Vianinha's political stance was actually to the left of Party policy, a factor that gives curious credence to his earnest call for solidarity.

Vianinha strove to be realistic in his strategies to implement his always optimistic (and often idealistic) vision of the future. He knew that these parties had an organizational basis in the working class, as well as political power higher up, that could not only broaden Arena's sphere of activity, but also facilitate needed structural changes in theater. Vianinha wished to go to the infrastructural heart of the matter and reform the structural base of Brazilian theater by utilizing these proposed contacts:

> É preciso um grande plano de reformas radicais na estrutura do teatro brasilerio. É lento, mas precisa ser feito em cima de conhecimentos seguros e possibilidades efetivas. Trabalho de coligação da classe teatral—que fosse permitindo o pagamento e o aparecimento de funcionários comuns, interessados no desenvolvimento do teatro brasileiro. As companhias teatrais brasileiras estão sumindo. É preciso enfrentar o problema de frente.

> [A great plan of radical reform in the structure of Brazilian theater is necessary. It is slow, but it needs to be based on secure knowledge and effective possibilities. Theatrical class coalition

work—which would allow for the payment and appearance of ordinary employees, interested in the development of Brazilian theater. Brazilian theatrical companies are disappearing. We must face the problem head on.] (78–79)

Indeed, throughout the evolution of his theoretical analysis of the cultural space of theater, Vianinha's most important contribution is his questioning, at each step of the way, how theater's infrastructure responds to and delimits its aesthetic and political projection. The precedence he gives, in 1960, to thorough overhaul of theatrical organization, beginning with a solid base of full-time functionaries, reflects the widely held view that such reorganization was possible in the larger Brazilian social and economic reality.

However, Arena, as a practicing whole, was not in agreement with Vianinha's proposals. Already involved in Arena's cultural outreach programs, Vianinha took advantage of a move to Rio to strike out on another direction of theatrical activity that would come closer to forging the organizational links he wished to create.

In the interview on *Chapetuba* from 1960, Vianinha mentions that he had just completed a one-act play, "uma tentativa, uma experiência muito rápida, tentando escrever sobre um determinado problema econômico da nossa sociedade" [an attempt, a very quick experience, trying to write about a given economic problem of our society] (40), called *A mais-valia vai acabar, seu Edgar* (Surplus Value Will Be no More, Mr. Shore). At this point he was still an active member of Arena. According to Chico de Assis, the director of *A mais-valia*, Vianinha formally disconnected himself from Arena only when he decided to join the cast of the play (Oduvaldo Vianna Filho/ 1 Teatro 215).

Whatever the precise chronology of his departure from Arena, it was agreed among those involved in the play that Arena was not a viable forum for their concerns. Chico de Assis, in his preface to *A mais-valia*, remembers the step that the play represented: "Todos nós sabíamos que era preciso dar um passo à frente do Arena. Tínhamos chegado a um ponto onde a diversificação era desejável. *A mais-valia vai acabar, Seu Edgar* foi o início de um dos vários movimentos que tentaram estabelecer uma proposta de teatro popular naquela época" [We all knew we needed to take a step beyond the Arena. We had reached a point where diversification was desirable. *A mais-valia* was the beginning of one of the many movements that attempted to establish a proposal for popular theater at that time]

(214). A look at the play's aesthetic and political proposals in combination with an analysis of the cultural space it generated and occupied will show the limitations of the "proposta de teatro popular" of that epoch.

A mais-valia was a political musical whose structural base, as Chico de Assis points out, was that of the *revista* of the Praça Tiradentes, including Brechtian techniques with added "formas estratificadas pelo cinema americano" [forms stratified by the American cinema] (215). As in the *revista* form, the play presents a series of ludic sketches. In them, everyday scenes alternate with didactic (Brechtian) scenes that teach the theory of surplus value. In the production (although not specified in the text), a series of slides amplified the underlying realities the play wished to show by contrast to the ludic. Characters are presented unidimensionally, stressing identification with Brazilian types, a unidimensionality that probably had as much to do with the work on characterization done in the Dramatic Seminars of Arena as with the approximation to the popular type-characterization of *revista* techniques.[13]

The tone, structure, and use of scenic space for the critique of surplus value that the play presents are established in the first several scenes. The play opens with the actors directing themselves to the public, declaring, in verse, what the play will and will not be:

> Atenção! Vai começar a função!
> Não será o melhor espetáculo da Terra,
> Pobre de terra como ainda será.
> Mas:
> Não faremos chorar porque o croquete sobrou,
> Rir não faremos porque o croquete faltou.
> Queremos cantar o que sabemos,
> Apesar de pouco sabermos;
> Queremos fazer vocês rirem
> Da graça que ninguém tem.

> [Attention! The play will begin!
> It won't be the best spectacle on Earth,
> Poor Earth that will always so be.
> But:
> We won't make you cry because the croquettes were left over,
> Nor make you laugh because the croquettes are gone.
> We want to sing what we know,

Even though we know little;
We want to make you laugh
About the charm (or wit) no one has.] (224)

The actors then take their places as the first chorus begins:
the three capitalists in front of a painted panel depicting a luxurious
swimming pool; four workers *(desgraçados)* in front of a machine from
which issues a series of "objects"—a woman, chewing gum, a pillow,
cigars, lighter, all symbolizing what the worker doesn't have time for.
The chorus of *desgraçados* sings its fate:

Não mandamos, não fugimos, não cheiramos,
Não matamos, não fingimos, não coçamos,
Não corremos, não deitamos, não sentamos:
Trabalhamos.
. . . . . .
HA MIL ANOS SEM PARAR!

[We don't give orders, we don't flee, we don't smell
We don't kill, we don't pretend, we don't scratch,
We don't run, we don't lie down, we don't sit:
We work.
. . . . .
A THOUSAND YEARS WITHOUT STOPPING!] (226)

In the action that immediately follows the song, the workers,
who have been given a two-minute break, find that when they try to
sit down they no longer know how. The accompanying comments
and mime elaborate a slapstick technique utilized throughout to underscore the curtailments of basic physical pleasures the play portrays
as integral to the economic system it criticizes. The workers then protest, calling for two more minutes of break.

Enter the capitalists. As with the *desgraçados* who are referred
to onstage and in the text as "*Desgraçado* 1, 2, 3, and 4," the capitalists are 1, 2 and 3. However, there is dissention in the ranks of both
the capitalists and the workers. In this scene, capitalist 2 declares that
all are created equal. Capitalist 1 is frightened by his statement, saying
that it is dangerous to tell such lies, because the workers might believe
him and revolt. Capitalist 2 answers to the effect that these lies are
necessary, besides which, he has already taken precautions that the
"house won't fall on his head" (a Swiss bank account?). He tries to

enlist sympathy by inventing a parable on his life: born in a cabbage patch, forced to read at three days of age, he worked every moment, selling his own blood in order to get where he is; he learned to buy cheap and sell high. Of course, the message he wishes to impart is that happiness depends on being totally subjugated to work. The capitalists then stage a contest to see who is the happiest man in the land, offering a trip to the United States as the prize.

The workers refuse to settle for these explanations or "compensations" and set off to find out what happens to the money. D3 leaves, declaring, "Eu quero saber por que é que existe lucro!" [I want to know why profit exists!] (245), but his investigation is short, and he accepts the bosses' absurd story that profit is generated by centrifugal force as the world turns.

The play focuses in on its theme as D4, unsatisfied by D3's explanation, goes off to find the *lucro*. He also suspects C2's explanation of profit, reasoning that if C2 bought cheap to sell high, so did others, and therefore profits can not be solely obtained by the pricing of commodities. First he enters a car dealership. Playing the fool, he tries to buy a super model car with a letter from his grandmother, a rhetorical gesture designed to show that what might be worth much in emotional terms (the letter) rarely has any exchange value.

A didactic interruption follows: an actor enters saying that the truth should be found in an economic congress. This playful didactic scene shows a group of decrepit academicians confronted by a tongue-tied youth. The young economist, stammering, proposes that profit is determined by the work time put into an object. The others guffaw. Losing his stammer, the youth then quotes Marx (called here "Karlão" [Big Karl]) to make his point.

The point is not lost on D4, who goes back to his companions with what he has learned, devising his own scheme to teach them the lesson. He asks D1 to follow him in his imagination to a market where everything is bought for the price of the labor used in the production of the object. They enter the imaginary scene, which is, of course, represented as real on stage. A doorman gives them tickets according to the hours they have worked. D1 is excited and wants to buy everything possible, but D4 reminds him that, according to their previous arrangement, D1 can only buy what he normally would buy during a day: beans, a little milk, and so on. D1 begrudgingly conforms to this, although he sees that he still has tickets (work hours represented) to spend. They do their shopping and start to leave.

At the door, the doorman requests their remaining tickets.

D1 rebels, protesting that the tickets are his. D4 says no, that is the profit and therefore it must remain in the market, to which D1 replies: "A gente vende a gente, não é?" [We sell ourselves, right?] (272). D4 gives the name to game: "Sabe como é que o Gaguinho [the young economist] disse que chamava isso de ficar com as horas que a gente trabalha? . . . Mais-valia" [You know what Gaguinho said this keeping-the-hours-we-work bit is called? . . . Surplus value] (273).

The workers then confront the capitalists in a verbal battle about the injustice of working for surplus profits. Then turning to the audience and speaking "personally" to them (using common names such as Toninho, Ricardo, etc.), the workers tell the audience that by the logic of surplus profits, everything is theirs since their labor paid for it all. For example, D1 calls out: "Joaquim—o sapato é teu, o pão é teu . . . tambor é teu, navio é teu, avião é teu" [Joaquim—the shoe's yours, the bread's yours—drum's yours, ship's yours, plane's yours] (277). This rapid-fire dialogue is interspersed with the capitalists' chorus, which first proclaims "É mentira—é meu" ("It's a lie—it's mine"), then modifies its position (confronted by the workers' insistence) to "É nosso" [It's ours] (277). The curtain falls quickly on the whole chorus crying out "A vida é tua!" [Life is yours!] (277). From behind the curtain, an actor pokes his head out, gives three jumps and the war cry: "A mais-valia vai acabar—seu Edgar!"

In his critique of the play, Paulo Francis applauds Vianinha's experiment, as a young author who risked a lot "num teatro onde quase todo mundo quer jogar certo" [in a theater where almost everybody wants to play straight (get it right)] (qtd. in *Vianinha* 43). But then he adds: "Mas fica pouco de teatro do seu texto. A molecagem—uma das mais intensas tendências da dramaturgia brasileira—é uma das exceções" [But there's not much theater in your text. The con man attitude—one of the most intense tendencies of Brazilian playwriting—is one of the exceptions].

The theatrical good spirits of the production are evidenced in the text of the play, and this spirit of *molecagem,* or artful chicanery, will be used even more successfully by Vianinha later. However, as an explanation of surplus profits it leaves a lot to be desired: the text lacks depth even within its own intentions. It captures "reality in movement" only in the broadest possible sense. *A mais-valia* gives a beginner's lesson on the economic structure of underdevelopment, but it does not challenge cultural values by questioning perceptual patterns as Vianinha wished to do, according to his theoretical statements in 1960. In fact, the play has much the same limited appeal that Vianinha criticized in Arena: it essentially appealed to a like-minded audience, confirming rather than questioning assumptions.

The overt political thematic and theatrical treatment of *A mais-valia* might seem to contradict Vianinha's earlier statement that he did not want a "political theater," rather one of cultural mediation. When one looks at the more recent (1979–present) judgments on the simplistic definitions given to popular theater of the play's era, these contradictions seem more glaring. But this is hindsight.[14] If we look more closely at the cultural space *A mais-valia* created and occupied, as well as at the movement it was instrumental in generating, we will see how Vianinha's idea of cultural mediation fitted the reality of the times despite its problematic assertions.

One of the most significant intellectual and student movements in Brazil's recent cultural history was created in the process of the production of *A mais-valia*. Intellectuals such as Carlos Estevam Martins of ISEB applied their theory to theatrical practice. In a sense, the play provided an ambience for interdisciplinary interchange, where intellectuals found specific ways to interface with the artistic realm. Links with other arts were strengthened as Carlos Lira came in to do the music and Leon Hirschman brought his cinematic talent to the play.

The method of elaboration of the show, in combination with the use of scenic space, was of prime importance in the convocation of the people who were to form the CPC's core group and supporters. The play was staged in the theater of the architectural school of the Urca home of the Universidade Federal do Rio de Janeiro. It was an open-air theater with a capacity of about two thousand and had housed the first bossa nova shows. Thus, it was a locale already imbued with a tradition of the convocation of large-scale cultural participation.

The scenery designed for the play by the director and crew was enormous. Fifteen meters high, it utilized the large stage space, dividing it into several levels to accommodate the scenes and the band of the political musical. With little money to carry out the project, work on this huge set was labor intensive. It was truly a community project. Chico de Assis notes that besides the twenty actors involved in the play, a core group of seventy worked on the production (215). There were three months of rehearsals, all open to the public and marked by constant discussion with spectators. The play opened with a full house and with little publicity ran about eight months, with a median house of four hundred spectators, as Chico de Assis relates.

This was indeed a large public, contending with that of the most successful professional productions of the time.

According to Carlos Estevam Martins, the idea to form the CPC came from the communal work and discussion associated with the play's production (qtd. in Berlinck 11). In March 1962 the CPC was legally constituted as the cultural organ of the União Nacional de Estudantes, maintaining administrative and financial autonomy. Its work was initially financed by individual donations and later augmented by occasional subsidies by MEC or municipal funds.[15]

The theatrical arm of the CPC sought to reach a broad audience with its political messages, utilizing theatrical forms most appropriate to the spaces available to them. In Rio, they performed in the auditorium of the UNE building at 132 Praia do Flamengo, reaching mainly a student and intellectual audience with full-length plays such as *Eles não usam black-tie* and long satirical sketches. Besides playing other small theaters, they took these plays to union halls, community cultural halls, and theaters and schools in the suburbs, reaching a lower-middle-class and working-class audience.

The larger part of the theatrically innovative work they did took place in the streets. In 1963, after some mechanical problems, they managed to construct a moving stage on a large wagon pulled by a jeep. This stage gave them the mobility to take some of the plays that required more sophisticated equipment (such as light reflectors, slides, recorded sound) to the *favelas* (slums) and open public spaces such as parks and squares. They performed skits at political rallies, both in support of candidates (these were requested and paid for by the candidate or his party) and, in some cases, against the policies of a candidate. Under the orientation of João das Neves they embarked on a program of "teatro de agitação" (agitational, or agitprop, theater), also called "comício dramático" ("dramatic rally"). These were short plays or skits immediately elaborated on current political items in the news, giving comment or offering interpretation of the items and taken directly to the streets of the city, its suburbs and *favelas*.

This activity was not restricted to Rio and its environs. By this time the CPC had spawned affiliates in all of the major cities of the country, and most of them engaged in some kind of theatrical practice. There were also two national tours, called UNE-Volantes, that took the artists to all the capitals and larger cities of Brazil. The first tour, in early 1963, included the participation of politically active theater groups from the CPC. The second tour, some months later, demonstrated the split already occurring in the UNE: the CPC, in widening disagreement with the more conservative directorate of UNE, refused to take their productions on tour, and the UNE had to hire professional talent to complete the tour.

Political differences had reached a crisis point in Brazil. Even so, the CPC had a large following, with sympathy, if not significant financial support, from both the private and public sectors. Most of the plays were financed against profits, meaning that they received private or governmental subsidies or loans that were to be repaid, fully or in part, by box office profits. Their truck was financed by private donations. Individual theatrical impresarios lent a hand. Union leaders, politicians, and candidates contracted for shows. Shows put on in theaters owned by federal or state entities were either bought or subsidized. The Serviço Nacional de Teatro provided the financial backing for the construction of the CPC theater in the Praia do Flamengo building. The Companhia Aérea gave them the resources necessary to carry out the two UNE-Volantes.

The depth and breadth of this support reveals that the interest (or at the very least, tolerance) in the programs of social reform that the CPC espoused was shared beyond the CPC's projected and real audience in the student, radical-left, and working-class populations. Although the CPC and its theater groups did not set out to antagonize anyone, it was always clear in positing its Marxist, anti-imperialist orientation.

But by the eve of the coup, exhausted by financial burdens (subsidies went to pay for production, while most work was volunteer), hampered by internal dissent within the UNE, and somewhat discouraged by their only partial success in working-class organizing, the theater arm had begun to turn its primary interest back to its original point of cultural insertion: student radical activity. The problems of its outreach programs were numerous: rural and suburban police reaction; trouble with Rio's then governor and staunch conservative, Carlos Lacerda; and difficulties in reaching rank-and-file audiences even though relations with politicized union leaders were excellent and productive.

It is important to stress that this evaluation of the partial successes of the theater activity of the CPC lies within the context of the CPC's own hopes, intentions, and proposals for social reform and popular mobilization. The importance given to their work by the organized Right at the time cannot be underestimated. The Right took the CPC's work seriously indeed, considering it a significant threat to their conservative policies. This attitude was concretely demonstrated in one of the very first acts of right-wing violence after the coup. On April 1, 1964—the day the coup's success became known—the CPC-UNE building at the Praia do Flamengo was burned to the ground.

Besides *A mais-valia,* Vianinha wrote three other plays that formed an integral part of the CPC's repertory. In February 1962 he wrote *Brasil—versão brasileira* (Brazil—Brazilian Version), a long satirical sketch using *revista* techniques that told the history of industrialization and imperialism in Brazil from the point of view of the communist worker. In an article entitled "Teatro de rua" (Street theater), Vianinha explains the importance of the option for the *revista* form found in this play and in many of the other short sketches that the CPC produced:

> O CPC da UNE resolveu-se inicialmente pela revista, procurando reavivar e manter uma tradição de sátira impiedosa, de crítica de costumes—espetáculos com quadros isolados, com uma ligação dinâmica que permita a permanente chamada de atenção do público, com música, poesia e as formas mais variadas que permitam sempre uma mudança no tom do espetáculo. Esta adaptação às condições objetivas nos parece fundamental em todo o tipo de realização de trabalho de cultura popular.
>
> [UNE's CPC initially decided in favor of the *revista,* attempting to revive and maintain a tradition of pitiless satire, criticism of social customs—shows with isolated sketches, dynamically connected in a way that would permanently hold the public's attention, with music, poetry, and the most varied forms that might always allow for a change in the show's tone. This adaptation to the objective conditions seems to us to be fundamental in carrying out every sort of work with popular culture.] (*Vianinha* 98)

His other two major plays written during this time, *Quatro quadras de terra* (translated literally, *69.696 Square Meters of Land*) and *Os Azeredos mais os Benevides* (*The Azeredos and the Benevides*)[16] do not conform to the idea of conventions to be used for popular theater described above. Rather, they point to his continuing struggle to be comprehensive in his approach to theater as a tool of cultural mediation. They are full-length plays more significant as departures from his other work than for their dramatic merits or experimentation with theatrical conventions. Both depict social, political, and economic conditions in the *latifundário,* or absentee landlord, system of the Brazilian Northeast. Analysis of the dramatic structure and theatrical conventions of these two plays would add very little to the purposes of this study, since both are essentially realistic dramas within the mold of social theater of Arena, with a strong tendency toward melodrama, although *Os Azeredos* uses a chorus and has dialogues sung in verse interspersed in the text. Characterization in the plays presents no innovation from *Chapetuba*.

On the other hand, the theme of these plays points to two aspects of Vianinha's idea of cultural mediation that were of substantial importance given the prevailing political reality. First of all, considerable hope for revolutionary change was centered on the drought-ridden and poverty-stricken Northeast. This hope, fed by the Cuban example of revolutionary mobilization in the countryside, was not without solid basis in Brazil.[17]

Secondly, this thematic treatment enlarged the scope of the cultural and political message of the CPC theater work. Put on in the industrialized cities of the South, these plays aimed at raising the consciousness of urban and suburban audiences regarding the social and economic situation in the Northeast. Depicting these conditions and the possibility of reform or revolution also aimed at instilling a greater sense of national cohesion in the struggle for social change. In addition, these plays and thematically similar ones by other CPC playwrights were not performed solely in the industrialized cities where the CPC was most active, such as Rio and São Paulo. They were also performed by theater groups of cultural entities in the Northeast, an area that already had a rich theatrical tradition of its own that used popular conventions to treat social realities (see *Dionysos* 17).

As shown thus far in this chapter, the political and cultural agitation immediately preceding 1964 was indeed significant and affected the whole country, and the contradictions between the political and aesthetic proposals of this theater must be seen within this context of agitation and upheaval. A summary of how Vianinha saw his work and that of the Centro Popular de Cultura at the time, in contrast to his reflections on the movement shortly before his death, provides an important perspective on the cultural space of politically motivated Brazilian theater.

In an article published under the title "Do Arena ao CPC" in 1962 in the UNE journal *Movimento*, Vianinha discusses the necessity for a new kind of theater. Again he paves the way for his point of view with a critique of Arena. He says that, within its circumscription of middle-class professional theater, Arena was reduced to commercializing its content in much the same way that other companies commercialized their form. Because it did not expand to include the audience that its thematics implied, Arena "não chegou a armar um teatro de ação, armou um teatro inconformado" [didn't quite set up an action theater, but rather a nonconformist theater (of limited protest)] (qtd. in *Vianinha* 93). In essence, in its nonconformity, Arena still subscribed to models of theater dictated by the dominant culture.

Vianinha envisioned a popular theater where the definition and functional efficacy of art would not be determined by categories consecrated by the dominant culture, but gained by practice among the people:

> O importante é que um movimento de cultura popular se enriquece com a obra dos grandes artistas, mas não vive deles. . . . A questão não é pesquisar o que é arte e o que não é; a questão é pesquisar quais as que servem ao homem e quais as que o alienam. . . . Não se deixa o título de artista quando nos dirigimos à praça pública. Lá se consegue ou não o título de artista.

> [The important thing is that a popular cultural movement is enriched by the work of great artists but does not live from it alone. . . . The question is not to research what is or is not art; the question is to research [those things] that serve man and those that alienate him. . . . You don't abandon the title of artist when you walk into a public square. That's where you do or don't obtain that title.] (94)

While this makes perfect sense in theory, it raises serious questions of a theatrical form and content consonant with its theoretical purpose. As Vianinha saw at the time, these problems were at best only very partially resolved by imposing conventions of popular theater on a social thematic, regardless of the audience one managed to reach. Shortly thereafter in the same article and in response to a criticism made by Guarnieri of Vianinha, that "quer fazer equação e não teatro" [he wants to make equations, not theater], Vianinha criticizes his own search for form and content. This autocriticism bears substantial quoting, for it reflects the artistic and political turbulence of the times and contains real but embryonic elements of analytical clarity:

Parti para buscar uma nova forma. E fui alienado à procura da forma. Se a um novo conteúdo devia corresponder uma nova forma, comecei a procurar a nova forma e não o novo conteúdo. Para mim era e é evidente a passividade humana das minhas peças e das peças de realismo. . . . Guarnieri tinha razão. Todos os dados para que o espectador seja sensibilizado por uma peça devem estar dentro da própria peça. Não pode haver cenas, acontecimentos, personagens, situações que necessitem de uma visão de mundo que esteja acima e fora do mundo teatral criado. As peças ideologicamente perfeitas podem ser mudas para o povo se não lhe dão meios para a compreensão. É preciso um teatro ajustado à capacidade intelectual do povo brasileiro. Um teatro com formas já consagradas pela percepção popular. A forma nova será nova historicamente, será nova em relação à situação cultural da sociedade—não será necessariamente nova na história da arte.

[I set off to find a new form. And I was [became] alienated when [as] I went off to look for it. If a new form should correspond to a new content, I began to seek the new form and not the new content. The human passivity of my own plays and the plays of realism was and is evident to me. . . . Guarnieri was right. All the information the spectator needs in order to be moved by the play must be in the play itself. There can be no scenes, events, characters, situations that necessitate a world vision above and outside the created theatrical world. Ideologically perfect plays may be mute to the people if they are not given means to understand them. A theater adjusted to the intellectual capacity of the Brazilian people is necessary. A theater with forms already acclaimed by popular perception. The new form will be historically new, it will be new with regard to society's cultural situation—it will not necessarily be new in the history of art.] (94)

In the last months of his life, Vianinha reflected repeatedly on his early attempts to make accessible the ideology that informed his work, whether through use of popular theatrical conventions or the expansion of the thematic conventions of essentially realistic theater. As he points out in February 1974 in an interview with Ivo Cardoso, the space for cultural debate and practice in the years immediately before 1964 "era institucional, era orgânico, fazia parte da realidade, não era uma coisa que você tinha que impor à realidade e lutar: fazia parte da realidade, debates constantes, conferências, assembléias, cursos, trocas de impressão, seminários de dramaturgia, laboratórios de interpretação" [was institutional, organic, part of reality, not something you had to impose on reality and fight: it was a part of reality, constant debates, conferences, assemblies, courses, exchanges of impressions, playwriting seminars, acting laboratories] (qtd. in *Vianinha* 185).

Vianinha describes how the "organic" quality of those cultural debates extended beyond the middle-class intellectuals, crossing class lines and encompassing other sectors of the society. He attributes this interchange to the cultural conditions specific to the period before 1964 that permitted "a possibilidade do contato entre as classes, que nunca foi tão fervente, nunca foi tão 'trânsito' " [the possibility of contact between the classes, which had never been so fervent, so "in transition"] (175). He goes on to say:

> ao mesmo tempo que nós bebíamos das classes trabalhadoras todas as infomações sobre a sua situação, sobre as suas condições de lutas, sobre as suas aspirações (e essa era uma coisa não literária, mas vivida, uma coisa real), nós tínhamos possibilidade de tentar levar a eles os instrumentos culturais que são privilégio de setores minoritários na sociedade.

> [at the same time that we drank from the working classes all of the information about their situation, about the conditions of their struggle, about their aspirations (and this was a nonliterary thing, a lived thing, a real thing), we had the possibility of trying to bring to them the cultural instruments that are the privilege of minority sectors of society.] (175)

He then sums up the CPC's trajectory and importance:

> Sem dúvida o CPC ajudou um pouco a horizontalização da cultura. Mas eu acho que a massa trabalhadora é que ajudou esses intelectuais a dimensionar melhor os problemas. Realmente havia muito de aspiração, muita ingenuidade no CPC da UNE. Depois esses intelectuais se organizaram em torno da UNE e se ligaram ao movimento estudantil, que estava diretamente ligado e empenhado na batalha cultural.

[Without a doubt the CPC helped to horizontalize culture somewhat. But I think that it was the working masses who helped those intellectuals to have a better dimension of the problems. There really was a lot of aspiration, a lot of ingenuity (with possible meaning of "naïveté") in the UNE CPC. Afterward, those intellectuals organized around UNE and linked themselves to the student movement, which was directly connected to and committed to the cultural battle.] (174)

Vianinha's critical assessment is, on the whole, accurate and well founded, although the "horizontalization" of culture probably affected intellectuals much more than it did their working-class audiences. As indicated, the artists came to realize the utopian and even paternalistic component of their efforts. He states, "Atingir o povo realmente era uma visão utópica em relação ao processo real da sociedade brasileira" [To affect the people was really a utopic vision insofar as the real process of Brazilian society was concerned] (175). By this, he is indicating the naïveté and romanticism of putting on ten-minute skits that proposed to show the workers problems that they already knew too well, along with the imposition of solutions to the problems.

There is another factor integral to this lack of cultural and political vision. The very amplitude of this opportunity for cultural interchange made it difficult to institute a continuity of work necessary to reach a clear perspective on its gains and limitations as popular theater. For one thing, the frenzy of debate consumed a lot of the time that could have been put into broader community work. This was largely unavoidable, since theoretical discussion and agreement were necessary preliminaries to work. After all, the CPC theater was trying to create strategy that only had schematic precedents in Brazil in such quasi-contestatory forms as the *revista,* certain experiments of alternative or university theater, and in some of the sporadic work done in working-class theater (mainly the anarchist theater of the earlier part of the century in São Paulo).

Perhaps even more importantly, the work process of the CPC theater groups did not allow them to establish continuity with a specific audience that would have given them a deeper understanding of how that community perceived itself or what the cultural problems or elements specific to that community were beyond those shared with the larger spectrum of Brazilian society. Vianinha reminisces: "Eu acho que realizei espetáculos teatrais em praticamente todas as favelas do Rio de Janeiro. Mas eu devo ter realizado um ou dois em cada uma. Isso significa uma total descontinuidade" [I think I put on theatrical events in practically every slum in Rio de Janeiro. I must have put on one or two in each one. That means a total lack of continuity] (175).

In another interview in 1974 (with Luís Werneck Vianna), Vianinha indicates how, by late 1963, the failures of the CPC had led them to reevaluate the aesthetics of political expediency that characterized their work:

> O CPC . . . no seu esvaziamento, já nos deu as indicações de que o artista tinha que participar lutando no campo das transformações estéticas, na atualização cultural do teatro em relação ao seu tempo, em relação aos seus problemas mais complexos, as suas ambições as mais altas. Quer dizer: em nome do povo o artista tem que ambicionar a mais alta complexidade e não o contrário.

> [The CPC . . . in its emptying [draining], had already given us the indications that the artist had to participate in the field of aesthetic transformations, in the cultural modernization of the theater with regard to its time, with regard to its most complex problems, its highest ambitions. That is to say: in the name of the people the artist must strive for the highest complexity and not the opposite.] (*Vianinha* 163)

There is no way to assess nor even imagine how this would have been put into practice with time. The continuity of the CPC theater work was curtailed by the events of 1964. But certain essential theatrical conventions and ideas were developed within the wide, if somewhat frenetic, space available to the CPC that would be transformed into more solid work after the coup circumscribed activity. On the practical level the theatrical conventions of massive cultural convocation and mobilization begun with *A mais-valia* would be immediately put to use after the coup.

On the ideational level the debates regarding popular theater, theater's cultural insertion, and the need for new theatrical conventions that had predominated theatrical thought during these years assumed even larger importance as the military dictatorship delimited cultural space. Lately, in the process of review and analysis of cultural history that has captured the attention of post-*abertura* critical thought—a debate that has revolved around the multiple question of "what happened and why, when it all seemed possible"—theatrical theorists continually return to an analysis of the mistakes and successes of Arena and the CPC in order to pose their questions and look for realistic solutions to the problems that confront Brazilian theater today.

Given the political and cultural importance of the era, it is no wonder that Vianinha also continually returned, sometimes obsessively, to the Arena-CPC period in his own theoretical work. The limitations of Vianinha's plays at this time and the discrepancies between them and his theory should, therefore, be seen in the dual context of theatrical apprenticeship and the cultural and political conditions of 1956–64.

Contesting the Coup: 1964–1968

Historical Overview: The Military Coup
and Theatrical Space

When considering the often apparently contradictory nature of space left open or appropriated for cultural activity after the military coup of 1964—especially the enormous creative surge of a culture of contestation in the 1964–68 period—it is most important to look at the complex process by which the military regime legitimized and consolidated its political power. A simplified look at the goals of the Brazilian Revolution, the term the military used to designate the regime set up after the coup, will show that the military justified its intervention in the political process by two related factors: the need to stave off a leftist takeover of the government, or, in other words, the need to curtail the incursion of communism; and the necessity to provide political stability for economic expansion within the capitalistic mold.

Although the military overtly controlled political power from 1964 until 1985, the establishment of authoritarian rule in Brazil did not take place as an immediate result of the coup. For one thing, at the beginning there was no consensus within the armed forces regarding the kind or degree of intervention needed to effect its goals. There were hard-liners who advocated full martial rule and moderates who considered the coup a kind of interim government that would relinquish power to civilian rule once the country was stabilized. Within the continuity of the military government, there were a number of alliances with civilian political power that answered to the economic concerns of the private sector, pro forma conciliations with pre-1964 legislative processes, including several rewritings of the constitution, as well as to a series of decreed acts that ultimately formalized military control of the political process, abrogating civilian rights.

In their analysis of the trajectory of authoritarian rule as it contended with civilian political structure Sebastião C. Velasco e Cruz and Carlos Estevam Martins make the important point that authoritarianism in Brazil should be seen more as a variable than as a constant. Comparing it to other military dictatorships in Latin America, they observe:

é forçoso reconhecer que o regime, apesar de ter-se tornado agudamente autoritário em diversos momentos, não só nunca chegou a atingir os graus extremos de intensidade registrados em outros países capitalistas periféricos (Chile, Argentina) como até mesmo assumiu, em certas oportunidades, características próximas às da normalidade republicana, tal como essa expressão é contemporaneamente entendida. As idas e vindas do regime foram, ademais, facilitadas pelo fato de que nunca se chegou a implantar um conjunto plenamente estruturado de instituições autoritárias, respaldado por uma ideologia inambígua, frontalmente avessa a compromissos com o credo liberal-democrático.

[one must recognize the fact that the regime, despite becoming acutely authoritarian at several moments, not only never achieved the extreme degrees of intensity registered in other peripheral capitalist countries (Chile, Argentina), but even assumed, when certain opportunities arose, characteristics similar to those of republican normalcy, as this expression is currently understood. The regime's comings and goings were, furthermore, facilitated by the fact that a completely structured set of authoritarian institutions was never implanted, backed up by an unambiguous ideology, frontally opposed to compromises with the liberal-democratic credo.] (14)

Velasco e Cruz and Martins by no means negate, here, the extreme and violent measures taken at particular moments during the military regime, measures clearly outside of "institutional limits" and justified by "a chamada 'excusa da necessidade'" [the so-called excuse of necessity] (14). On the other hand, they wish to emphasize that the very absence of "uma congruente cobertura normativa e valorativa" [a congruent normative and evaluative coverage] contributed to an "exorbitant" exacerbation of repressive practices in these critical moments. They conclude this argument by concurring with Juan Linz that "o caso brasileiro constitui uma *situação* autoritária mais do que um *regime* autoritário" [the case of Brazil constitutes an authoritarian *situation* more than an authoritarian *regime*] (cited in Cruz and Estevam Martins 14).[1]

Given the miasmic quality of the Brazilian situation, they rightfully consider it more useful to emphasize the discontinuities, or breaks and reformulations, of power in order to understand the flux of authoritarianism in Brazil. Looking at the "sucessivos arranjos institucionais, cada qual combinando, em dosagens diferentes, elementos avulsos de autoritarismo, militarismo, corporativismo, liberalismo e democracia" [successive institutional arrangements, each combining, in different doses, sundry elements of authoritarianism, corporatism, liberalism, and democracy] (14) that Brazil has passed through since 1964, they advance three preliminary hypotheses to capture the dynamic of these institutional arrangements that go far to explain the political confusion that allowed such a large opportunity for contestatory cultural activity in the 1964–68 period.

All three of these ideas contest the often-made assertion that the changes in civilian society came about as a direct result of the military takeover of 1964. In the first instance, the authors argue that the moments of intensification of authoritarianism did not occur in "linha direta do golpe de 64" [a direct line from the 1964 coup] (15). (They cite the enactment of Institutional Act 2, in 1965, and of Institutional Act 5 in 1968, which will be discussed later.) They see these moments as interstitial points of the meeting of distinct factors, of "processos parciais que redundaram em recrudescimentos do autoritarismo" [partial processes that resulted from outbreaks of authoritarianism] (15). In other words, these moments were not easily predictable but rather arose from contradictions whose elements were not necessarily available for analysis, thereby catching many otherwise astute observers of the political scene unprepared.

As their second hypothesis, Velasco e Cruz and Martins discredit what they consider the Manichaean concept that attributes all positive or democratizing steps to the political opposition, thus relieving the opposition of responsibility in the growth of authoritarianism. On the contrary, the authors stress the part played by the continuous reformulations of alliances according to party, or group, interests of the opposition—including the Left and the Brazilian Communist Party (PCB)—in the political dynamic that allowed, or impelled, the military to take extraordinary measures. The subtlety of this view is important: many cultural activists adhered to specific party lines, or based their analyses to some degree or another in disagreement or agreement with the line of action proffered by a particular political group. In effect, the instability, vulnerability, and shortsighted analyses that characterized the coalitions formed by the political opposition were pervasive in the artistic community as well, regardless of the real cohesion of that community behind its statements of protest.

As their third point, the authors contend that blaming the coup for all the events that followed it obscures "o avanço de processos mais profundos de natureza estrutural" [the advance of the deepest processes of a structural nature] (15). They prefer to see the structural changes that occur in Brazil in the more global light that refers as much to the exigencies of contemporary capitalism, where economic growth required a larger participation on the part of the state "na produção de mais-valia e na reprodução da força de trabalho" [in the production of surplus value and the reproduction of the labor force] (15), as to the coup itself. The question of the reformulation of private sectors in line with governmental bureaucracy and of the ideological and institutional shifts that accompany these reformulations is not, then, unique to Brazil, although the Brazilian case will naturally take characteristics specific to its internal dynamic and to its position of "desenvolvimento na periferia do sistema mundial" [development in the periphery of the world system] (15). They also cite the rise of communications technology and the growth of governmental information systems as being a factor that has called into question civil rights throughout the world, causing crises in concepts of law, in party, and parliamentary organization.

The sophistication of this retrospective view stands in contrast to the comparatively crude developmental models of economic structure and policy that predicated the operant concepts of national culture informing a great deal of cultural activity before the coup. In an important sense, leftist cultural analysis lagged behind events from 1964 to 1968, not solely as a result of finding themselves, abruptly, in a situation that called first and foremost for them to mobilize protest against the coup. Operating on simplified models of development, cultural activists applied them to analyze the coup, seeing the crisis as one of direct confrontation of forces, and on the whole overlooked how the complex internal political dynamic both allowed the room for their protest and foreshadowed its subsequent closure in 1968.

Velasco e Cruz and Martins assert that the major point to be underlined when looking at the political opposition was their "quase total incompreensão com respeito à natureza da ruptura verificada com o movimento de 64" [almost total incomprehension with respect to the nature of the break verified with the movement of 1964] (23). Despite evidence to the contrary, the opposition acted as if the military intervention would be of short duration. Proceeding with the traditional political model of effectuating change, the opposition did not see that the military's observance of certain legislative formulas was strategic rather than a real compliance with the pre-1964 political process.

A brief look at this "strategy" from 1964 to 1968 reveals the military learned well from its failure to stop João Goulart's presidency in 1961. As indicated before, the 1964 coup was successful because the broad nature of the goals expounded by proponents of the "revolution," goals that, emphasizing ideals of "ordem e progresso" ("order and progress" being the inscription on the Brazilian flag), facilitated cohesion within the various tendencies of the military and attracted both sympathetic reaction from the Right and centrist public as well as the adherence of rightist and some centrist politicians. Because of this broad base of support, the coup was easily effectuated. Obviously, after initial victory, the finer points of disagreement within these forces would call for attention. What might appear as concessions of the military to the complaints of the opposition regarding legislative and political procedure, then, was in reality a juggling of position and power within the forces that had initially supported the coup.

Humberto de Alencar Castello Branco, who assumed the presidency in 1964, was considered a moderate within the military, or as Velasco e Cruz and Martins point out, a "legalista histórico" who supported the Sorbonne school concept of economic expansion through a tight liberal-democratic regime legally constituted with political powers of decision to protect itself against internal subversion.[2] He was elected president by vote of the National Congress and worked an uneasy balance between observance of constitutional procedure and promulgation of hard-line juridical acts designed to strengthen the military's hold on power. At the beginning of his presidency, acting in accord with the limits of interventional powers stipulated in the constitution of 1946, he signed "cassações de mandatos," the suspension of political rights of civilians, but insisted in observing the legally stated cutoff date of June 1964 for the exercise of these "exceptional" measures, also refusing to institute a state of siege.

Nevertheless, despite the suspensions of political rights of important opposition leaders (including Kubitschek) immediately after the coup and despite strategic federal interventions in state affairs, the opposition managed to win five of the eleven states—including the key states of Minas Gerais and Guanabara. This propelled the hardliners to insist on the passage of the second institutional act (October 1965). Institutional Act 2 decreed the extinction of political parties, set up procedures for the indirect election of the president, and established the Serviço Nacional de Informações.

From then on, whatever liberalizing proposals that Castello Branco may have wished to institute—there is considerable difference of opinion regarding his motives and true wishes—were reduced to defensive measures. In this respect, it is important to note that the expiration date of Institutional Act 2 was March 1967, when a new president would assume power.

However, there was no real return to democratic process inaugurated with Arthur da Costa e Silva in 1967, even though his inauguration coincided with a new constitution that nominally reestablished the rights of representative government. Real reform was countermanded by limiting legislation, and the passage of a new Lei de Segurança, or security law, in 1967 took over where Institutional Act 2 left off.

Given the complexity of these political and juridical machinations, it is quite understandable that cultural activists erroneously assessed the nature of the space available to them. But they took full advantage of those they could appropriate. 1966–68 saw a continual rise in manifestations against the military regime, whose increasingly repressive methods were marked by the death of the student Edson Luís in a confrontation with military police on March 28, 1968. The situation reached crisis levels, which culminated in the promulgation of Institutional Act 5, in December 1968. This act abrogated all civil rights, including that of habeas corpus, and effectively instituted a state of siege in Brazil.

In respect to theater, we see that the varying implementation of censorship is one of the factors that most clearly traces the relationship between the political and cultural realms throughout the dictatorship.

The censorship laws invoked against the theater after 1964 originated with the decree 20.493, of January 1946—formulated during the Estado Novo, but put into law somewhat later. In brief, this decree sets up the Serviço de Censura, responsible to the Ministry of Justice, with powers to censure, in part or whole, works offensive to public decorum or religion, works that advocate criminal activity or subversion of the Brazilian government, or works that would be harmful to relations with other peoples. These laws were rarely invoked until 1964. It is estimated that from 1964 until about 1976 about four to five hundred plays were censored, although it is impossible to verify any such statistic since archives remain closed (Michalski, *O palco amordaçado* 43).

For theater, there were two types, or stages, of censorship: of text and of performance. In order to be staged, a play had to have its text cleared. From 1964 to 1968, texts were read by state boards, which at least facilitated direct contact with censors (most theater people not having the time or money to carry on battles with Brasília). After that the censorship service centralized in Brasília. Criteria in censorship were almost totally arbitrary, although it was almost uniformly right-wing, and the ignorance of censors was notorious (Brecht and Sophocles were both asked to appear before the board). Texts were often held without response, *engavetados* (put into drawers), neither officially prohibited nor released. It was difficult to get a liberation date for a text. In the meantime, in order to fulfill economic obligations and temporal commitments, plays had to go into rehearsal pending their liberation. Even when liberated for presentation, plays were subjected to censorship at any time in rehearsal and by most any authority figure (DOPS [Departamento de Ordem Política e Social/ Department for Political and Social Order], federal police, or the actual censor) who happened to object. Dress rehearsals were obligatory for final clearance, and many plays were closed or cut the night before they were to open. Besides this official censorship, productions were prey to harassment by rightist vigilante groups, their actions were tacitly or openly supported by the police.

This situation obtained from 1964 to 1979, although stages of aggravation and loosening paralleled changes in the political climate and in economic programs. A brief look at these years will show that censorship was arbitrary and became increasingly heavy, but that until 1968 it was still possible to make political statements in theater and possible for theater people to have public discussions about theater's role as contestation against the coup. From 1964 to 1966 the coup still had the support of the majority of Brazilians who wielded any political influence (elite to middle class). In late 1966, with the inauguration of Costa e Silva, political control loosened and a new constitution restored some electoral rights. However, as the failure of anti-inflationary economic policy became more apparent, forces of protest gained support from the middle class. And there was a sharp rise in urban guerilla activity as well as in rural organization.

Institutional Act 5 severely curtailed artistic expression. During the Médici administration, paroxysms of arbitrary censorship and extremes of repression often entailed imprisonment and torture of those in the theater considered dangerous to the regime. From 1974 to 1979 there were still some notable examples of severe censorship, but with *distensão* (the relaxation of special measures), protest was again possible. In any case, during this period economic conditions and self-censorship had exhausted most of the will to produce controversial works.

Some details of protest activity will provide a background to tendencies of national theater and theory at this stage.

1965–68 was marked by nationwide protest, beginning with students, radical unionists, and liberal or radical intellectuals but extending to the middle class, which had previously adhered to the coup. 1965 saw many manifestations of opposition to censorship, and a letter signed by members of the artistic community was sent to the United Nations Educational, Scientific, and Cultural Organization (UNESCO). In January 1968 an organized Week of Protest against Censorship (Semana de Protesto contra a Censura) took place in Rio, sponsored by the Associação Brasileira da Imprensa, culminating in a manifesto signed by one thousand intellectuals. In February of that year, the theaters of Rio and São Paulo went on a three-day strike. In reaction to these protests by the artistic community, and in view of growing unrest in the general public, a committee was formed, within the Ministry of Justice in Rio, to review censorship laws and to draw up modifications that would allow theater to function economically. Several representatives of the theater community were included in this committee. In September 1968, Justice Minister Gama e Silva sent the recommendation of this committee to Costa e Silva. However, the recommendation was in effect negated by an addendum that maintained interdictory censorship and reversed the recommendation of censorship by classification (by age, etc.).

The functions of the official cultural institution that dealt with theater, the Serviço Nacional de Teatro, was also affected by censorship. Founded in 1937 by decree of Vargas, the SNT's activities included subsidizing theatrical productions. In 1963 the national playwriting contest was instituted, which turned out to be the most consistent, if sometimes problematic, program of support for national dramaturgy. Although its value in terms of economic support of national theater was limited by slight funding, the contest came to have much symbolic value during the years of repression as a result of the consistent censorship of plays awarded prizes.

The SNT-sponsored contest continued under the dictatorship. In 1968 *Papa Highirte* (by Oduvaldo Vianna Filho), a parable portraying the declining years of an exiled South American dictator and his struggle to regain power, won the prize but was immediately prohibited. With the promulgation of Institutional Act 5, the contest was suspended until 1974. Up until this point, SNT policy had been to award prize money in the form of subsidy of production costs. The juries for these contests were made up of newspaper critics and several representatives of the SNT.

When we speak of the activity of the "theatrical class" in Brazil—especially in these crucial years of 1964–79—it is important to note that the antagonism between critics, impresarios, artists, and institutional functionaries that so often prevails in cultures with more clearly defined divisions of interests and work had been relatively little evidenced in Brazil. Lack of resources and problems of technical training have made it necessary for most artists to work a variety of theater jobs. Actors are impresarios, directors, scenographers, producers, and vice versa. Most theater critics have had training with theater groups or teach in dramatic-arts schools. A large number of people holding institutional jobs, whether these be with the SNT or with state or municipal entities, have been in some way directly related to theatrical production, and a significant number of authors have paid their bills as functionaries of the SNT while they continued to write. Thus, despite differences of opinion that may be weighted by specific theatrical functions, as well as by aesthetic or political visions, a sense of solidarity and common purpose prevailed to the extent that participants refer to themselves as a "classe teatral."

After 1964, this solidarity manifested itself in the acts of protest mentioned. Even so, divergences of opinion regarding the significance of the coup to the social and political life of Brazil and to the development of national theater soon became manifested in the definition of distinct theatrical tendencies that arose as political and aesthetic responses to the curtailment of civilian rights. It bears repeating here that the diversity of response reflects the room for maneuvers left open by the political indecisions, or manipulations, of the 1964–68 period.

The theatrical scene of 1964–68 saw several important innovations that, as a direct consequence of censorship, have since become an integral part of professional traditions. One of the most important was the introduction of the dramatic musical show. Right after the coup, many members of the CPC (most active being Vianinha, Ferreira Gullar, Teresa Aragão, Armando Costa, and João das Neves) reformed as the Grupo Opinião in order to continue political theater work. As an immediate response to the coup the group put on a show, consisting of the personal statements of three popular singers—Zé Keti, João do Vale, Nara Leão—who represented three class orientations in popular Brazilian music: the samba of the suburban margins, forms such as the *desafio* and *incelença* popular among those who migrated from the Northeast to the economic center, and the bossa nova, associated with the urban middle class. Songs, all of a protest nature, were interspersed with commentaries by the singers that showed the link between personal experience and political conscientization. The *Show Opinião* always played to overflow houses, and critical acclaim was unanimous. Many critics took advantage of the opportunity to discuss the nature of popular culture as protest and to register their stance against censorship.

Many shows along these lines followed, most notably another production of Opinião, *Liberdade, liberdade,* a musical review whose book—a collage of famous statements made about liberty—was written by Flávio Rangel and Millôr Fernandes. These shows were often produced in professional theatrical spaces, but they were conceived within the alternative modes of the late Arena and CPC work. They also received the approbation of the theater class, and mainstream people and actors, such as Paulo Autran, contributed their time and talents free or for nominal salaries. *Liberdade* made an extensive tour under often precarious conditions, reflecting the actors' commitment to the value of protest in such plays, since many of these actors could easily have found stable and better-paid work in São Paulo or Rio.

In theater destined for long-run productions in major or semiprofessional houses, a tendency toward metaphor gained ground as a way to outwit censors. These plays often relied on music or verse as well as heavy farce to camouflage political commentary (example:

Se correr o bicho pega, se ficar o bicho come [Caught If You Run, Eaten If You Stay], by Vianna Filho and Ferreira Gullar). Arena, under the theoretical direction of Boal, developed a system that he called *coringa* (joker), in which tales of historical heroes were told in music and verse (example: *Arena conta Tiradentes* [Arena Tells Tiradentes], by Boal and Guarnieri). The hero in these plays was the only participant to remain in consistent character. The other actors played various parts, changing roles in a pattern that emphasized the economic and social interests that determined the dramatic action.[3]

Episodes of Brazilian history that suggested parallels with the period after 1964 were also dramatized in more traditional (illusionist) form, for example Dias Gomes's *O Santo Inquerito* (The Holy Inquisition) (first produced September 1966). Popular themes were used as metatheatrical devices to draw political parallels, as seen in Dias Gomes and Ferreira Gullar's *Dr. Getúlio, sua vida e sua glória* (Dr. Getúlio, His Life and Glory), (produced August 1968), where a play within a play shows a samba club in the midst of an internal power struggle. The play culminates in the suicide/murder of the populist president of the club, representing a *samba-enredo* (musical plot) of Vargas's life.

The new theater of aggression—which spoke for the agitated 1960s in all the Western world, following a theoretical line between Brecht and Artaud—had a manifestation in Brazil. In 1967 the São Paulo group Oficina, under the directorship of José Celso Martinez Correa, put on *O rei da vela* (The Candle King) (a play written in 1933 by Oswald de Andrade and published in 1937), which clearly posits the relation of imperialism with internal, Brazilian monied interests. The farcical elements of the play were heavily emphasized; gestures and props both politically and sexually provocative to the audience were employed to elicit response, if not thought. This political aesthetic of aggression differed from the American (example: Living Theater) and European (example: Peter Brook) in its underscoring of Brazilian stereotypical images. Zé Celso's agitational proposal is an analytical and critical one, and his theatrical style was noted for the grotesque caricaturing of the "exotic-erotic" common to foreign or even elite Brazilian conceptions of Brazilian reality, especially as these conceptions had become internalized and assimilated into Brazilian popular culture.

The work of Zé Celso and his group Oficina was extremely important to the Brazilian stage at this time, as well as to subsequent conventions of Brazilian theater. This tendency to exuberant exaggeration of Brazilian stereotypes later becomes what is termed *tropicália*, a looser revitalization of Brazilian music, art, and theater that parallels the hippie movement. In Zé Celso's work, emphasis on spectacle and on direct interaction with the audience questioned the efficacy of predominant conventions that, despite incursions of Brechtian technique and use of folkloric forms, relied mainly on the spoken word *(a palavra)* to transmit theatrical responses to the political situation.[4]

However, the richness of the theoretical discussion in the 1964 to 1968 period can best be resumed by a look at special issue of the *Revista Civilização Brasileira* entitled *Teatro e realidade brasileira.* Published in July 1968, almost half a year before Institutional Act 5, this journal is an indispensable document, since it compiles the polemics that agitated the theatrical class. Indeed, the fact that this polemical and radical issue was published and widely circulated attests to the strength of protest on the eve of Institutional Act 5, as well as indicating that protest was still possible. It will be noted that these articles are all of leftist political persuasion.

An article by Dias Gomes, "O engajamento: Uma prática de liberdade" (Political activism: A Practice of Freedom), presents the case for theater's being a social engagement a priori by virtue of its nature of means of communication. "Um teatro em tempo de síntese" (A Theater in a Time of Synthesis), by Maria Helena Kühner, enlarges this argument and gives a summary of recent trends in Brazilian theater. The respected "old guard" is represented by Joracy Camargo, who contrasts past and present trends in Brazilian social theater. Class analysis by the Communist Party, at a time of great optimism concerning the outcome of class struggle in Brazil, was represented by Nelson Werneck Sodré, who wrote on theater's role in mass organization. The article most representative of the thought of the new radical Left (those sympathetic to guerilla warfare), "Quem é quem no teatro brasileiro" (Who's Who in Brazilian Theater), by Luiz Carlos Maciel, lambasts what he considers the capitulation of Brazilian theater to authoritarian principles, relying on a neo-Freudian analysis of theatrical tendencies as reactions to authority.

In the essay "Elogio fúnebre do teatro brasileiro visto da perspectiva do Arena," (Funeral Elegy for the Brazilian Theater Seen from the Perspective of the Arena), Boal presents his theories of the *coringa*, proclaiming the death knell of Brazilian theater as then constituted. He justifies Arena's recent emphasis on, and identification with, the national hero (Zumbi, Tiradentes) in terms of the historical moment, ending his critique by paraphrasing Brecht: "Brecht cantou: 'Feliz o povo que não tem heróis.' Concordo. Porém nós não somos um povo feliz. Por isso precisamos de heróis" [Brecht sang: "Happy the people who have no heroes." I agree. However, we are not a happy people. Therefore we need heroes] (251). In a cogent response, Anatol Rosenfeld criticizes these theories as a new mystification of the hero in "O herói humilde" (The Humble Hero).

In an interview with Tite de Lemos, José Celso Martinez defends his theories of a theater of aggression, and in another article Tite de Lemos expands on this defense, painting a picture of current Brazilian theater as doomed to political inefficacy because of its leftist paternalism and because of its aesthetic attitudes conciliatory to the middle class.

Articles on regional/popular and minority theater as forces for social change are included, Hermilo Borba Filho and Luiz Mendonça contributing articles on northeastern popular theater and Abdias do Nascimento contributing an article on his theatrical experience that served as a manifesto for black theater: "Teatro negro do Brasil: Uma experiência sócio-racial" (Black Theater in Brazil: A Socioracial Experience).

Analysis of the class background of the theatergoing public in terms of theatrical infrastructure is made by Fernando Peixoto. Paulo Autran, basing his statements on his touring experience with *Liberdade, liberdade,* reports public enthusiasm about Brazilian themes ("O público reclama a realidade brasileira no palco" [The Public Demands Brazilian Reality Onstage]). An opinion poll of five people involved with different aspects of theater production (actor to impresario) reveals a variance of opinion about these topics. The volume also includes, as documentation, a synoptic history of the fight against censorship as well as the delineation of the principles supposedly guiding censorship, giving recommendations for legal revision that could be demanded even within the political restrictions of 1967.

However, the article that provoked the fiercest debate among theater people was "Um pouco de pessedismo não faz mal a ninguém" (A Little "Pessedism" Won't Hurt Anyone), written by Vianinha. It calls for a united front of the theater class, minimizing the differences in social class and in interests among theater people. The only effective policy would be the umbrella unionization of theater workers, since at that time (1968), Vianinha felt that the very economic survival of theater was in danger. Sectarian and divisive fights such as the one between proponents of more professionalization and proponents of alternative collective theater were economically disastrous and only weakened theater's influence by confusing and dividing a public that clearly wished to support a national theater, as well as support this theater in its protest. The communality of basic interests of all members of the theater class is an idea still being hotly debated, some critics considering it naive and others realistic. At the time, Vianinha was almost ostracized by the student and radical Left for his position, but this article (and his subsequent theory) laid the theoretical base for structural changes within theatrical unions and set the model for official collaboration between the various entities of the theater class.

How Vianinha arrived at this analysis through his theatrical practice will be the subject of the second part of this chapter. As can be seen by the vast variety of responses to the limitations of cultural space outlined in this overview, a number of questions would preoccupy him in this search for his own aesthetics of protest during this period.

Grupo Opinião and "Pessedismo"

Although Vianinha between 1964 and 1968 wrote two full-length plays *(Moço em estado de sítio* [Young Man in a State of Siege] and *Papa Highirte)* that were produced only after the political opening of 1979,[5] the work that immediately integrated his ideas on the Brazilian stage after the coup was done in collaboration with other authors in the Grupo Opinião. In 1964 he, along with Armando Costa and Paulo Pontes, wrote the text for the *Show Opinião.*[6] In 1965 he coauthored *Se correr o bicho pega, se ficar o bicho come* with the poet Ferreira Gullar.

Opinião, which opened on December 11, 1964, at Arena's Rio theater in the Super Shopping Center on Siquiera Campos, was the first major theatrical response to the military takeover.[7] However, the significance of the show was not limited to the strong element of protest it presented. The history of the conception and elaboration of *Opinião* represents a broader reorganization of the cultural proposals that engendered the show.

The idea of forming a new theater group that would carry on, as much as possible, the work under way in the CPC was conceived by the latter's directorate right after the coup. Since the União Nacional de Estudantes had been declared illegal, the CPC no longer had access to the theatrical spaces it had carved out from 1962 to

1964, nor could it count on the audience support that it had mobilized within the relatively mass organization of the UNE. Thus, the founding members of what was to become the Grupo Opinião—Gullar, Vianinha, Teresa Aragão, Armando Costa, Denoi de Oliveira, and Paulo Pontes—realized that they would have to restructure along the lines of professional theater. As Gullar remembers: "Para continuar aquele trabalho precisávamos de um teatro, de um grupo, de espetáculos pagos, mantendo o tanto quanto possível o espírito da atividade interrompida, dentro das novas condições" [In order to continue that work we needed a theater, a group, paid performances, maintaining as much as possible the spirit of the interrupted activity, under the new conditions] ("O alvo da repressão") (The Target of Repression).

The idea for the show came from discussions at Zi Cartola, a samba club and favorite meeting place in Rio for intellectuals interested in popular culture. A dramatic show structured through popular music offered several important interrelated advantages. First of all, the immense interest in popular music and musical shows—an interest that crossed (and still crosses) class barriers—would assure the fledgling group box office success. Secondly, the show wished to demonstrate a sense of cultural unity throughout the various sectors of Brazilian society through an emphasis on popular music. Rhythms marked by a mixed racial heritage and lyrics that emphasize and mesh the private and public concerns of the Brazilian people make popular music a distinctly national cultural expression. Foreign musical influences may prevail in mass culture, but like the combination of jazz and samba of the bossa nova, they are often absorbed into indigenous forms. The third advantage spoke to the political purposes of the group. Characterized by strong elements of social protest, popular music offered both direct and metaphorical messages of opposition to the military regime.

Opinião was written in conjunction with taped interviews of the three original singers: Nara Leão, Zé Keti, and João do Vale. Their stories were testimonies of how they became interested in popular music, giving references to their class origins and regional backgrounds. The authors then went to other composers and singers (examples: Cartola, Sérgio Cabral) and researched regional music that would complement the sambas chosen. They also included music of Pete Seeger and verses of José Martí to add an international element to the "statements" they wove into the production. The text and musical sequence were modified by the singers, the musicians, and the director, Augusto Boal. The show was structured to include allusions to moments in Brazilian history. The idea was to present a collage of elements, to give depth and a sense of historical continuity to the protest.

As indicated, the basic "opinion" proffered fuses the artistic with social commentary: according to *Opinião*, popular music is most expressive when it gives an opinion, when it helps people see the need and possibility of social change. However, the communication of protest against the military regime is the underlying statement of the show, an identification between singers and public facilitated by historical reference.

A look at how opinion is structured in the two parts of the show demonstrates the theatricality of the production and the dramatic possibilities of the collage technique. *Opinião* does not pretend to be a dramatic work.

The show opens on a dark, empty stage to the sound of a *berimbau*. The *berimbau* is a twangy instrument of African origin used in capoeira, the fluid martial art–dance developed by slaves in the Northeast, mainly in Bahia. This sound evokes a dual connotation, of popular culture and of rebellion against slavery. This heritage is intended to encompass the larger Brazilian society. The first words sung by Nara Leão—representative of the urban middle class—are "Menino, quem foi seu mestre?" [Who was your teacher, boy?] (15). The intention to go to the roots of Brazilian culture is thus stated and generalized.

The lights go up on João do Vale, representative of northeastern migration to urban centers, singing an entertaining ditty popular in the Northeast, "Peba na pimenta." João explains to his urban audience that the peba is an armadillo hunted by poor people of his region. The song tells of a highly peppered peba dinner prepared for forty people, and of one guest's complaint that, although it's great, it burns like the devil. This witty song carries the serious messages later elaborated on: poverty, resourcefulness, community and solidarity (the large gathering), and the vicissitudes of survival (pepper). Zé Keti—"a voz do morro," or opinion of the urban marginal—enters, and all three singers, now onstage, do a medley of verses composed by Zé and João.

The singers then identify themselves and their musical affiliations, placing their socioeconomic background and professional status. This set of testimonial speeches, all made directly to the audience, is the first in a series of similar *depoimentos*, or statements, that intersperse the text. João comments that his best-known music is that which only entertains, but he counterbalances this by observing: "Minha terra tem muita coisa engraçada, mas o que tem mais é muita dificuldade pra viver" [There are a lot of funny things in my country [region], but mostly there is much difficulty in staying alive] (19). Zé Keti recounts the economic problems of his profession as *sambista*.

Nara Leão alludes to her confusion about what should be done in Brazilian music. She feels that being a middle-class resident of Copacabana should not limit her to interpreting only one musical style (a reference to bossa nova). She answers her own preoccupation with a statement that serves to unify the three singers in their opinion: "eu quero cantar tôdas as músicas que ajudem a gente a ser mais brasileiro, que façam todo mundo querer ser mais livre, que ensinem a aceitar tudo, menos o que pode ser mudado" [I want to sing all the songs that help us to be more Brazilian, that make everyone want to be freer, that accept everything except what can be changed] (20).

This initial set of *depoimentos* brings up, in an experiential way, the problematic relationship between popular and mass, or commercial, culture, a theme that will receive a more specific socioeconomic treatment in the second part of the show.

A long intercut medley focusing on poverty and drought follows, after which the performers make a second set of statements, again emphasizing their personal relationship to music in the context of their social environments. Historical reference comes into play with Zé's explanation of how "Zé Quieto" became "Keti": "Aí, eu comecei a escrever com K, que estava dando sorte—Kubitschek, Kruchev, Kennedy. Mas agora, meus camaradinhas, acho que a sorte michou. Michou" [Then I started to write it with a *K*, which was lucky—Kubitschek, Khrushchev, Kennedy. But now, my little friends, I think we're out of luck. We ran out of luck] (30).

Thus far, the testimony and interchange of song establishes the opinion that all three—and by extension, all Brazilians—have a right to a national culture and are not bound by specific backgrounds. At this point, the only other "character" of the show makes its presence known: an offstage recording gives a brief history of the *desafio* (a battle of verse improvisation), from colonial times to its most renowned modern practitioner, O Cego Aderaldo, a blind singer. This sets up Nara and João's rendition of a *desafio* between Cego Aderaldo and another singer, Zé Pretinho, Little Black Joe. In the *desafio*, the theme of the social conditions of poverty and formal illiteracy are contrasted with the richness and inventiveness of the verse. The use of the authoritative recorded voice "legitimizes" popular music. The juxta-position of the *desafio* with its historical legitimization gives a contem-porary association to the word: the use of the term for northeastern musical competition comes from bellicose origins ("to defy or chal-lenge") and reverts back to them in response to the dictatorship.

The metaphor of discrepancy between official (allowable) in-terpretations and personal understanding of historical events is under-scored by the samba that immediately follows. In "Noticiário do jornal," Zé sings: "Eu digo o que leio, não digo o que vejo / Porque o que vejo não posso dizer" [I say what I read, not what I see / 'Cause what I see, I can not say] (37). The newspaper talks about economic and educational opportunity. What Zé sees are unreported facts such as "99 por cento do povo / Não passa nem na porta da faculdade" [99 per cent of the people / Don't even pass through a college door] (37).

The *depoimentos* that come next further delineate the per-sonal ethic of each singer. Remembering his painful, but necessary, decision to leave the poverty of the Northeast, João reads his parting letter to his father, which begs his father's forgiveness and asks his blessing. This is intercut by Nara's interpretation of "Carcará," a song about a bird of prey indigenous to the region that "pega, mata e come" [preys, kills, and eats] (40). Initially used as a symbol of the poverty of the Northeast, the *carcará* is converted into a metaphor of repression, coming to symbolize the military government by the end of the show.

Zé Keti declares himself, in "Samba do morro," a marginal *brasileiro.*[8] His personal ethic, however, shows a careful attention to society's rules, knowing that as a marginal, he has no protection against infraction of these rules. A funny scene in which Nara plays a marginal zonked out on marijuana illustrates this. Since his subculture equates *ser valente* (being valiant) with use of drugs, Zé pretends to be stoned. Nara looks at him, doubting his act since his eyes are not even red. Zé then brings down the house with his politically loaded response: "O, meu camaradinha, não fica falando em vermelho, não, que vermelho tá fora de moda. Fora de moda" [Hey, little buddy (comrade), don't keep talking about red 'cause red is out of fashion. Out of style] (43).

The tone of the show abruptly changes to references of death, with the inclusion of an *incelença,* a song sung in wakes based on verses beginning with letters of the alphabet. As João comments, "Morte é coisa de todo dia" [Death is an everyday thing] (46). Be-

sides stressing the presence of death, the *incelença*, using as it does
the alphabet, alludes to the inventiveness of the *povo* [people] when it
does get access to formal education. The link between popular culture
and dominant culture is asserted by the insertion of verses by João
Cabral de Melo Neto, one of Brazil's most sophisticated poets, who
also used popular themes and verse forms.

In the reprise that ends the first part of the show, all three
singers join together to affirm their opinion of the cultural sovereignty
of the *povo:*

> Eu sou o samba
> A voz do morro sou eu mesmo, sim senhor
> Quero mostrar ao mundo que tenho valor
> Eu sou o rei dos terreiros.

> [I am the samba
> The voice of the hill is me, yessir
> I want to show the world how I'm strong
> I'm the king of the *terreiros* (courtyards where Afro-Brazilian
> religions are practiced).] (49)

Thematically, the first part establishes the shared opinion of
the singers: the traditions of the *povo* are the *mestres*, or masters, of
both art and life. Thus, the cultural roots of protest are signified. In
the second part, the call to protest becomes internationalized; economic and ideological factors that structure Brazilian culture are ex-
amined, and moments in Brazilian history are juxtaposed to this more
global view.

Nara starts by singing Pete Seeger's "If I Had a Hammer."
She sings it in English but interprets the meaning she finds in it. She
says the hammer "É o martelo da justiça" [the hammer of justice];
the bell "o sino da liberdade" [the bell of liberty]; and the song "uma
canção que fala do amor entre todos os homens da terra" [a song that
speaks of love between all men on earth] (53). She puts the song in
the North American context of the struggles for racial equality during
the 1950s and early 1960s. Then example of Cuba is then invoked by
the singing of "Guantanamera."

The internalization of the search for social justice is immediately contrasted by a view of cultural imperialism where, for economic
reasons, the models promoted for cultural imitation are representative
of the blandest possible common denominator of American music.

The lights dim, and the dark stage emphasizes the solemnity of the recorded voice ("Play Back") which intones:

A partir de 1940, com o incremento do rádio e do disco, chegam ao Brasil em grande quantidade as músicas estrangeiras. É mais barato para as companhias gravadoras vender um só tipo de música no mundo todo. Para isso as músicas precisam ser despersonalizadas. Até hoje, o que há de pior na excelente música americana é que disputa o nosso mercado. Naquela época virou mau gôsto ouvir samba.

[Beginning in 1940, with the increase of radio and records, great amounts of foreign music arrived in Brazil. Recording companies found it cheaper to sell one kind of music worldwide. For this to happen the songs must be depersonalized. Until today, it is the very worst of otherwise excellent American music that has vied for a piece of our market. In those days it became bad taste to listen to samba.] (55–56)

The aesthetic impoverishment of Brazilian popular music caused by the domination of the foreign market is pointed out in a burlesque medley of Brazilian verse set to American rhythms. Imitating the Platters as a doo-wop group, Nara and João sing "o melhor do meu sertão" [the best of my sertão (backlands)]. The ridiculousness of this thematic and stylistic pairing is heightened by João's final, acerbic, encapsulating allusion to the voracity of the foreign market, "Comeram o boi" [They ate the ox] (59).

The imperializing role of foreign cultural models is linked to political dominance. In a stylistic echoing of "Play Back's" speech ("A partir de 1940 . . ."), Zé introduces an anecdote about his non-participation in the World War II effort with, "Em 1943, o Brasil entrou na guerra" [In 1943, Brazil entered the war] (59). He recounts how his friends of that time all ended up on the *Baependi,* the Brazilian warship sunk by the Germans off the coast of Brazil. Corresponding directly to João's statement "Comeram o boi," Zé's story implies that the energies and resources of Brazil have been siphoned off to serve foreign political and economic interests.

The division of energies is then put into a national context that pits the poor northeastern farmer against the *latifundário.* Nara and João sing the farmer's lament:

Eu sou um pobre caboclo
Ganho a vida na enxada
O que eu colho é dividido
Com quem não plantou nada.

[I'm a poor *caboclo* (mix of white and Indian)
I earn my living with my hoe
What I reap is divided
With those who planted nothing.] (61)

In the refrain of this song ("Sina de caboclo" [Fate of the *caboclo*])
the farmer affirms his resolve: "Mas pra dividir / Não faço mais isso,
não" [But to divide . . . / I won't do that anymore, no] (61). The
farmer is proud of his talent to cultivate the land; he loves to create
nourishment out of practically barren terrain. In this sense, his refusal
to continue to be party to his own exploitation also takes on metaphorical associations (cultivate/culture) that refer to the artists protests against cultural exploitation.

This defiance then becomes linguistically focused, and at the
same time metaphorically generalized, into the major assertion of the
show:

Podem me prender
Podem me bater
Podem até deixar-me sem comer
Que eu não mudo de opinião.

[They can arrest me
They can beat me
They can even leave me without food
But I won't change my mind.] (62)

Thus far, the metaphor of protest has been mostly interpolated in opinions generated by socioeconomic conditions of the
Northeast. In and of themselves, these snatches of song refer to long-
standing problems that definitely predate the military coup of 1964.
These songs also point to conditions that the coup itself proposed to
ameliorate with its new economic programs. Up until now, it has been
the theatrical structuring of song with personal and historical statement that indicated the coup as the principal object of protest.

The moment is specified by Nara: "Eu não gostava de cantar

em público. Só resolvi mesmo ser cantora depois de abril de 1964" [I didn't like singing in public. I only really decided to be a singer after April 1964] (63). This leads into memories of the years directly preceding the coup on the part of all three. Rapid-fire mention of the cultural production of those years, especially of *cinema novo,* stands as judgment on "abril de 1964." As Nara sums up: "Foi cinema nôvo, foi bossa nova, foi o teatro que apresentou novos autores brasileiros. Teve uma coisa que eu descobri, que todo mundo descobriu—o Brasil era o que a gente fazia dêle" [It was "new cinema" [cinema novo], it was bossa nova, it was the theater that introduced new Brazilian authors. There was something I discovered, which everyone discovered—Brazil was what we made of it] (66). João balances this optimistic picture by removing himself, in memory, from the urban context back to his home: "Foi tudo bem, menos minha terra, que continuava a mesma depois de todo êsse tempo" [Everything was fine, except my home [region], which still was the same after all this time] (72).

The following long scene takes up the theme of the divisionary character of the unequal distribution of economic wealth. In it, cultural diversity is stressed and put in a context of freedom of choice of cultural voice. Freedom to sing becomes symbolic of political democracy. Nara wants to make a record of various types of Brazilian music and asks João to teach her a *baião.* The offstage voice interrupts her, questioning her choice. Nara retorts: "Por que? A constituição não permite cantar baião?" [Why? Doesn't the constitution allow *baião* singing?] (74). The voice scolds her: "Nara. Você é bossa nova. Tem voz de Copacabano, jeito de Copacabana" [Nara. You're bossa nova. You sound Copacabana, you look Copacabana] (74).

The voice sarcastically asks her if she intends to distribute her earnings from the record among the poor, if she thinks that music is Red Cross work. Nara insists on a role of cultural mediation: "Música é pra cantar. Cantar o que a gente acha que deve cantar. . . . Aquilo que a gente sente, canta" [Music is for singing. For singing what we think we ought to sing. . . . Whatever we feel, we sing] (77). The voice insists equally that cultural differences are determined, irrevocably, by economic differentiation: "Você não sente nada disso. . . . Você tem uma mesa de cabeceira de mármore que custou 180 contos, Nara. Você já viu um lavrador, Nara?" [You don't feel any of that. . . You have a marble bedside table that cost 180 *contos,* Nara. Have you ever seen a farmer, Nara?] (77). Nara refuses this categorization, rebutting: "Não. Mas todo dia vejo gente que vive à custa dêle" [No. But every day I see people who live at his expense] (77).

Again, the voice appeals to sociocultural realities, saying that Nara will lose her Copacabana audience; the farmer won't hear her because he doesn't even have a radio; the *morro* won't understand . . . In response, Nara sings the "Marcha da quarta feira de Cinzas" (Ash Wednesday March), which by that time had already become an anthem of collective contestation to the coup:

> E no entanto é preciso cantar
> Mais que nunca é preciso cantar
> É preciso cantar e alegrar a cidade
> A tristeza que a gente tem
> Qualquer dia vai se acabar
> Todos vão sorrir, voltou a esperança
> É o povo que dança, contente da vida
> Feliz a cantar.

> [And yet we must sing
> More than ever we must sing
> We must sing and gladden the city
> The sadness we feel
> Will end any day
> Everyone will smile, hope has returned
> The people are dancing, glad about life
> Happy to sing.] (78)

This metaphor of bad times and hope for good times becomes historicized in conjunction with the penultimate segment of the show, which follows into the reading of the death sentence for Tiradentes, hero of the first major uprising for democracy in Brazil. The song that accompanies this, "Tiradentes," tells of the rebellion of 1789, ending:

> Essa história bem verdadeira
> Foi a luta primeira que se deu no Brasil
> E depois tantas houveram *[sic]* que por fim fizeram
> Um Brasil mais decente, Um Brasil Independente.

> [This very true story
> Was the first struggle that took place in Brazil
> And after it came so many that at last
> A decent Independent Brazil was made.] (81)

The ironic tone in which this last phrase is sung leaves no doubt that, the heroism of Tiradentes's action notwithstanding, independence and democracy in Brazil is at the moment of the show very much a battle yet to be won.

Zé suggests the solution is to be found in the collective voice in the last song, "Cicatriz." Poetically, he equates the poor man's life *(vida = tristez = cicatriz).*[9] Personifying these elements of desperation into an *ela,* understood as she who could understand a metaphoric call to action, he sings:

> Mas é explicar a situação
> Dizer pra ela que
> Pobre não é um
> Pobre é mais de cem
> Muito mais de mil
> Mais de um milhão
> E vejam só
> Deus dando a paisagem
> Metade do céu já é meu.

> [But explaining the situation
> Telling her that
> The poor are not one
> The poor are more than one hundred
> Much more than a thousand
> More than a million
> And look
> God is making way
> Half of heaven is already mine.] (82)

The show ends with a reprise of verses that give most meaning to the opinions expressed throughout. Protest and affirmation are summed up:

> Mas plantar pra dividir
> Não faço mais isso, não.
> Podem me prender, podem me bater
> Que eu não mudo de opinião.

> [But planting to divide
> No, I won't do that anymore

They can arrest me, they can beat me
But I won't change my mind.] (82)

The collective voice of "Cicatriz" is affirmed by an additional verse of the song asserting that "O resto é só ter coragem" [For the rest, all you need is courage]. The courage that is needed is the courage to face the military government, as the explosively sung last symbol announces: "Carcará / Pega, mata e come!" (82).

Opinião can be considered a theatrical work made up of discrete and interlocking segments, or scenes, where a segment's boundaries are marked by stylistic change in music or a topical shift. Counting in this manner, part 1 of the show contains thirteen segments and part 2 fourteen, giving a sense of balance to the whole. Sometimes these changes are abrupt; at other times they flow into one another. However, the fragmentary nature of these segments is augmented by corresponding fragmentation in speech and verse. In this respect, a kind of metonymic code, in which one word evokes its larger linguistic and social context, is set up with the audience.

Fragmentation works on three purposeful levels. The syntactical cuts and scene shifts enunciate a style of crisis, transmitting the social confusion and anxiety to communicate that characterized the months following April 1964. But this aesthetic of fragmentation also is experienced as emblematic of the spontaneity of invention and association that the singers and authors find in popular culture. In terms of the structuring of thematic content, the juxtaposition of discrete segments of meaning is meant to build the social and political arguments behind the opinion expressed.

It should be clear that the textual analysis done here emphasizes the tight and complementary structuring of reference and metaphor. In terms of its content of social, economic, and political criticism, there are weaknesses that are contextually relevant. The economic and political notions that underlie the text share the same analytical shortcomings of the dependency theories of development that the ISEB was just beginning to delineate before the coup. Also, as will be discussed shortly, the ideological stance that the show takes regarding the *povo* is questionable. However, regardless of whether all the resonances and correspondences mentioned in this analysis were perceived by the show's audience, it was the *texture* of the allusions that created a truly histrionic relationship between the production and its audience. The show embodied a texture of moral recognition in a time of crisis.

The large public success of *Show Opinião* can be seen more clearly in conjunction with the proposals of the show. In the preface of the 1965 edition of the text, the authors specify two principal intentions. The first refers to the "espetáculo" itself and centers on the strength of opinion and unity the authors find in popular music:

> a música popular é tanto mais expressiva quanto mais tem uma opinião, quando se alia ao povo na captação de novos sentimentos e valores necessários para a evolução social; quando mantém vivas as tradições de unidade e integração nacionais. A música popular não pode ver o público como simples consumidor de música; êle é fonte e razão de música.

> [popular music is all the more expressive the more you have an opinion, when you join with the people in picking up the new feelings and values that are necessary for social evolution: when you keep alive traditions of national unity and integration. Popular music cannot regard the public as a mere consumer of music: it is the source and reason for music.] (Vianna Filho, Costa, and Pontes 7)

The second intention refers more generally to Brazilian theater. The authors see the theater in a particularly grave moment of crisis, where previous problems of lack of national repertory, importation of foreign commercial successes, and the subordination of the actor to the director—all conditions aggravated by the political crisis—have exacerbated the division between the reality recreated on stage and that of the public. In response, Opinião proposed to collaborate in the search for "saídas para o problema do repertório do teatro brasileiro" [solutions for the problem of Brazilian theatrical repertory] by creating an intense spontaneity between stage and public (9). Although the conventions of *Opinião* were relatively fixed by its focus on music, its loose structure left it open to textual changes as new performers entered and contextual references to modifications in the political situation.

Both intentions have to do with the construction of codes of identification between stage and audience, where theatricality is defined by that which is effectively testimonial. Within the dialogue of cultural mediation the show sets up, three interacting factors stand out: the ideological presuppositions behind the opinion expressed; the audience's reception of the show; and the theatrical innovations it presented.

In its ideological discourse, *Opinião* created an uneasy equation between popular and democratic. Throughout their testimonial statements the singers insisted on seeing themselves as representatives of the popular voice of the nation, accentuating the common ground of the Brazilian masses *(o povo)* over class divisions. The oppositional terms underlying protest were *povo* versus the military. As a social category *povo* was extremely comprehensive: any Brazilian who opted for democracy over military rule became *povo*, regardless of class background or economic interests. *Opinião*'s rhetorical appeal was directed to the formation of a united front against the coup, and the cultural democracy that the show wished to exemplify as already existent in Brazil was meant to stand in metaphoric contrast to lack of political democracy.

On the one hand, it is understandable that concepts such as democracy and popular should slide into one another without clear definition. *Opinião* was situational theater, and its rhetoric obeyed metaphorical necessities provoked by its political environment. On the other hand, this conceptual vagueness can not be attributed solely to circumstances. It can also be traced to the ideological formulations of the intellectual Left of the early 1960s.

Edélcio Mostaço puts the ideological stance of *Opinião* in direct relationship to the political praxis of the Brazilian Communist Party before the coup, citing the influence of Nelson Werneck Sodré, who was one of the most prominent theorists of the PCB and of the last phase of the ISEB (Mostaço, *Teatro e política* 75–88). In 1962, Sodré published a small book entitled *Quem é o povo no Brasil* (Who Are the People in Brazil) in which he essentially concluded that the *povo* was made up of all classes and social subgroups that, within their own spheres of influence, were working toward the social and economic development of the nation (22).

This broad categorization encompassed revolutionaries, progressives, liberals, and even nationalist conservatives. Clearly written and easily read, the book was also designed as a teaching device to reach the literate masses (working class and peasants) who might not have already articulated their perceptions about themselves as Brazilians-*povo* into a politicized framework.

Sodré did discuss class and power structure in Brazilian society, but the inclusiveness of *povo* effectively subsumed the rigorous class analysis one might have expected from a Marxist. However, as

Mostaço rightly points out, Sodré's analysis allowed him to fuse an essentially anthropological concept *(povo)* with a political one *(nação,* or nation) under a rhetorically generalized banner of national popular culture. Mostaço sees this fusion and paradigmatic confusion from the point of view of ideological strategy:

> Quando ajuntados, [the concepts of *povo* and *nação*] ainda mais sob a égide de uma "cultura", são dissipados os contornos históricos que formam a nível do real um e outro conceito restando a aparente harmonia de termos, que encobre, em realidade, uma estratégia ideológica, que é a suposição de um Estado indiviso.

> [When taken together, especially under the aegis of a "culture," the historical outlines that make up at the level of the real of one or the other concept is dissipated, only an apparent harmony of terms remaining, that, in truth, conceals an ideological strategy, which is the supposition of an undivided state.] (*Teatro e política* 78)

He then relates this ideological strategy to the political praxis of the PCB, referring to the PCB's theoretical papers of 1958 that called for a strengthening of the national bourgeoisie toward the growth of the internal market. According to Mostaço, the idea of *nação* described in these papers was nothing more than rhetoric of an anti-imperialist bourgeois revolution with little real intention to speak to the issues of the exploited sectors of the Brazilian masses (78).

Mostaço applies his analysis of what he calls the myth of the undivided state to the cultural scene of the 1960s in a series of points that underscore the contradictions of that myth. He reminds us that the conceptualization of the national and the popular, as put into practice by politically engaged artists, was based on the ISEB-and PCB-generated idea of *povo*, or based "na ratificação estética e sociológica dos compromissos assumidos com a *frente nacionalista* que, em última análise, correspondem à estratégia política do PCB quanto à prática das esquerdas" [on the aesthetic and sociological ratification of the obligations with the *nationalist front* that, in the final analysis, correspond to the political strategy of the PCB as to the practices of the Left] (86).

He then signals the political opportunism behind these concepts. He says that the determination of the *povo* and of students as primary agents of social transformation disguises the real debate (the political empowerment of the bourgeoisie), while at the same time conforming to popularized policy of the PCB. This policy was to boil down to a populist pact in the years preceding 1964 and to an antifascist front after the coup.

In line with this reasoning, Mostaço reduces *Opinião*'s message to one of mystifying catharsis that served to embroil its audience in "rituais cívico-esquerdizantes" [civic-leftist rituals] (86). This ritual enunciated two subtexts, with the more obvious one transmitting the notion that, to topple the government, it would be enough to express an opinion. In other words, the public catharsis generated amounted to a substitute for concrete struggle in the revolutionary realm. Mostaço views the second subtext as the more insidious: *Opinião* insinuated that behind the scenes a real revolutionary struggle was being organized. He ties this illusion to a general attitude that the PCB would take care of the "tasks of the revolution" (86). He remarks that history has proved that assumption to be incorrect, for even at the time the Left was far from united.

Despite this passing remark on dissident opinion in the Left, Mostaço insists on what he calls the "hegemonia cultural do PCB nos domínios da cultura brasileira" [cultural hegemony of the PCB in the domain of Brazilian culture] (86). This, he says, is not a question of specific adherence to the party but to a "determinada visão ideólogica" [particular ideological vision] that, overruling discordant voices, took over the cultural space and production of the 1964–69 period.

Mostaço concludes this series of points with two very important observations on the practical articulation of this ideological vision. The first has to do with the replacement of political practice by cultural practice. Speaking of the "determinada visão ideólogica," he observes:

> sua articulação ampla, difundida em praticamente todos os setores da criação cultural torna o quadro da cultura brasileira a partir desta época o grande terreno da prática política, impedida de ser exercida nos seus mecanismos próprios e coerentes.

> [its wide articulation, divulged in practically every sector of cultural creation, makes the whole of Brazilian culture as of this moment the great field of political practice, prevented from being carried out in its proper and coherent mechanisms.] (86)

Mostaço gives great importance to the fact that curtailment of dissident political activity led to a reformulation of the political voice into a consensually contestatory cultural practice. However, Mostaço offers no analysis here, leaving the wider social implications hanging.

His second statement, immediately linked to his comment on cultural hegemony, has to do with the predominance of theater in the 1964–68 period:

> Destaque-se de saída, nestes primeiros tempos, o disparado privilégio do teatro frente a outros setores de produção artística e intelectual, tanto pelo seu amplo poder de catalisação do público quanto de captação dos demais criadores culturais, constantemente chamados a integrar coletivos de trabalho nas produções teatrais do período.

> [Let us single out from the start, in these first times, the theater's overwhelming privilege in comparison with other sectors of artistic and intellectual production, as much for its wide ability to catalyze the public, as for its captivation of the other cultural creators, constantly called to integrate work collectives in the theatrical productions of the period.] (87)

What he says in terms of theater taking on the major role of cultural protest is essentially correct: theater had access to a wider public than did the other arts; it was more quickly producible than cinema or published works (which also suffered, at the time, different and more laborious processes of economic and political censorship); and theater, by nature, permits a more collective enterprise both in production and in audience relationship than other arts. This collective virtuality was well realized as cineasts, musicians, and other artists lent their talents to theater productions of that period.

However, Mostaço overly reduces the scope of the cultural mediation of theater to assumptions about its production, implying that the "disparado privilégio" of theater (I gather he is being ironic by calling this an "overwhelming privileged position") was a result of a rather mechanical theatrical implementation of PCB ideology. Seeing *Opinião* as the symbolic expression of PCB edicts, he considers its conventions mere iconic messages.

He equates artists and audience in a too tightly complicit act of production of meaning in this schema. It can not be argued that public participation in the theatrical events of the period was totally or even primarily filtered through the ideological prism in the manner that Mostaço suggests.

To return to the example of *Opinião,* Mostaço contends that it constituted a closed circuit of communication where "o *povo* do palco era o mesmo *povo* da platéia" [the *people* onstage were the same *people* in the audience] (77). His italics refer to the discrepancy between the class origins of the public and the *povo* idealized in the show as well as to the ritual of self-delusion *(povo* as *nação)* earlier described.

There is truth in this characterization, but it obscures the more complex social impact of the show. For one thing, the audience was larger and more varied in ideological disposition than the hegemonic circle Mostaço sees.

Who was the real audience? According to João das Neves, a member of Grupo Opinião and later its director, *Opinião* basically attracted students and people from the artistic world, although its public ran the gamut from student to upper middle class (interview by author). However, the number who saw the show gives a broader idea of its reception. Ross Butler reports that within weeks over twenty-five thousand people had seen it in Rio, and that in São Paulo and Porto Alegre (where it later played) more than one hundred thousand attended (78). The show also had a ripple effect: *Opinião* became emblematic of protest and solidarity for many others who didn't see the show but, having heard of it, bought the record.

Writing in 1975, Yan Michalski remembers the dynamic effect of *Opinião,* which he feels constituted an "authentic" moment of choice, an option for democratic values: "[*Opinião*] constituiu-se, em 1964, num autêntico divisor de águas: identificar-se com ele equivalia a optar por um certo sistema de valores que seriam depois defendidos por vários outros espetáculos" [*(Opinião)* became, in 1964, an authentic watershed: to identify with it was the equivalent of opting for a certain value system that would later be defended by other shows] ("De volta, *Opinião*" n.p.).

While Michalski remarks on the show as a generalized opportunity for defense of democratic values while the actual theme of the show was the demarcations of cultural space, Roberto Schwarz views it as a dynamic for a more politicized discourse. Schwarz, a literary critic whose essay on cultural hegemony and the PCB during the 1964–69 period offers a more balanced and dialectical perspective than Mostaço's, reflects on *Opinião*'s legacy. According to Schwarz, more than a site of ritual, *Opinião* provided an expanded arena of political debate. He emphasizes the importance of the show for the student movement, which "vivia o seu momento áureo, de vanguarda política do país" [was experiencing its golden moment as the country's political vanguard] ("Cultura e política" 81).

Like Mostaço, Schwarz notes the ideological complicity between audience and show. However, Schwarz also sees this complicity in terms of a theatrical form that generated debate and diversity: "Essa cumplicidade tem, é certo, um lado fácil e tautológico; mas cria o espaço teatral—que no Brasil o teatro comercial não havia conhecido—para o argumento ativo, livre de literice" [This complicity has, to be sure, an easy and tautological side; but it creates the theatrical space—which commercial theater in Brazil had not known—for free discussion, free from "literariness"] (81). In other words, *Opinião* cut through the theatrical distance of text-performance with a common language of spontaneous interaction. As Schwarz comments: "Em lugar de oferecer aos estudantes a profundidade insondável de um texto belo ou de um grande ator, o teatro oferecia-lhes uma coleção de argumentos e comportamentos bem pensados, para imitação, crítica ou rejeição" [Instead of offering students the unfathomable depth of a beautiful text or a great actor, the theater offered them a set of well-thought-out arguments and behaviors, for imitation, criticism, or rejection] (81).

Both the consensual attitude that Michalski mentions and the political debate that Schwarz stresses were elicited and sustained by theatrical conventions that were, to a large degree, innovative. As Schwarz affirms, the music of *Opinião* was both its primary attraction for the audience and its basic mode of communication. He also notes the Brechtian construction of the arguments of the text, where the case for or against points brought up was presented in contrapuntal style, with music (and lyrics) that distanced, commented on, and complemented textual arguments. Although neither musicals shows nor Brechtian technique were new to the Brazilian stage, *Opinião* had a novel way of weaving these two theatrical devices together.

In response to a question regarding the modifications or influences on theatrical structure that resulted from *Opinião*, João das Neves cites four innovations (interview by author): (1) it brought Brazilian music to the Rio stage; (2) it introduced a work based on the lives of the actual performers as the point of departure for the discussion of Brazilian reality; (3) it validated the spontaneous culture of the Brazilian people, leading to a different dialectic of identification between stage and audience; (4) it was the first truly collaborative work of the Brazilian stage; text and performance were elaborated by democratic participation within the group.

João das Neves sums up *Opinião*'s uniqueness by pointing to the hybrid mixture between the genres of show and theater these four elements produced: "É a primeira vez, o primeiro show que se pega à forma a letra, e com ela [letra] elabora um texto teatral, pegando o próprio texto da música como forma teatral" [This is the first time, the first show that seizes upon form and lyrics, and with them (lyrics) elaborates a theatrical text, making the text itself out of the music as a theatrical form] (interview by author).

Neves analyzes *Opinião* in terms of the approximation of theatrical technique with a certain dramatic structure. He acknowledges that the show did not have the elements of what one generally considers theater: sustained dialogue, conflicts, and plot development. However, he argues that the use of languages parallel to theater (music, cinematographic intercutting of the diverse elements of the show) in a manner that provoked, at each instant, a tension *(entrechoques)* gave show a high degree of drama.

The experience in *Opinião* with this pastiche or collage device was crucial to the development of Vianinha's work. Although the collaborative nature of the production makes it impossible to pinpoint his exact contribution, Vianinha often refers to the theatrical solutions that *Opinião* suggested to him. As will be more fully discussed later, this is especially applicable to *Rasga coração,* in which he manages to translate the collage technique into dramatic structure.

For Vianinha, the collage structure will come to offer distinct advantages in organizing perceptions of systems of representation, allowing him in his own theater to question traditions he considers false but operant and validate other traditions more pertinent to the growth of national theater. He will use the collage to cut through the canonic, or overly literary, authority of the text. It will be the vehicle of expression for his research into the songs, slang, publicity jargon, and so on that characterize personal and collective everyday experience of a specific period. It will permit him to fuse the two traditions he considers most important to the Brazilian stage, dramatic realism and the *revista,* into a national representation of the Brechtian concept of theatricalizing the shock between systems of values. Above all, it will give him a mode to incorporate history as a dramatic category.

Opinião was important to Vianinha's work in another aspect. It represented another step in the fusion of his ideological praxis and his more broadly philosophical ideas on value systems with his understanding of theatrical conventions. As an openly committed member of the PCB and a highly visible cultural activist, Vianinha received a great deal of criticism from an increasingly disgruntled Left.

Already in 1964 the PCB was attacked as being bourgeois, reformist, and culturally opportunistic. In this respect, the tone and focus of Mostaço's condemnation of *Opinião,* written in 1982, offers a continuation of this view notable for its exaggeration: after seventeen or eighteen years of repression and frustration, the PCB becomes a kind of scapegoat for much deeper rooted, albeit diffused, issues of authoritarianism that definitely predate the 1922 organization of the party. Inherent in the colonial structure, passed on through positivist ideals symbolized by the national motto Order and Progress (imprinted on the flag), personified by Getúlio Vargas, and endemic to the nationalist anti-imperialist discourse, authoritarian values are tightly woven into the fabric of Brazilian society and culture.

Vianinha had to contend with attitudes much like those expressed by Mostaço. In point of fact, rather than being directly dictated to by PCB policy, he created theater out of the antagonisms inherent in the hegemonic discourse. He had an essentially moral vision of the world that led him to continually question his own perceptions and analyses of political and social reality. This is revealed in his theory as a dialectical tension between readings of values and political pragmatism. This tension, plus his own battles with authoritarian values, underlie the dramatic conflicts and aesthetic of his plays from this point on.[10]

In an article he entitles "Perspectiva do teatro em 1965," Vianinha reveals a view of democracy that points to both its necessity and its contradictions. Always trying to understand infrastructure in terms of cultural values, he starts with a criticism of professional theater:

> O teatro de um tempo para cá, submetido a uma forte concorrência, quase sem força econômica, procura sobreviver como simples distração. A contradição, que tem origem na estrutura econômica do teatro brasileiro, passa para o plano cultural assim: o teatro—que, basicamente, não tem os elementos para distração que possuem o cinema e a televisão—dá ênfase à distração em detrimento de sua condição essencial de diversão.

> [For some time now, the theater, subjected to strong competition, almost without economic clout, seeks to survive as a mere amusement. The contradiction, which has its origin in the economic structure of the Brazilian theater, passes on to the cultural plane thus: the theater—which, basically, does not have those

elements for amusement that film and television possess—
emphasizes amusement to the detriment of its essential condition as entertainment.] (*Vianinha* 103)

He uses *distração* in the sense of amusement, connoting a
kind of fantasy that distracts *(distração)* people from reality. Although
both *distração* and *diversão* are kinds of audience reception (or the act
of engaging the audience's attention), the difference is not a matter
of degree but of distinct modes of perception. He uses *diversão* in the
most participatory meaning of entertainment:

> Distrair não exige compromisso do público; divertir, exige. E
> teatro, devido à presença física de ator e público, exige compro-
> misso do público. Um público que não se sente empenhado ao
> ver um espétaculo, que não se sente estimulado, controvertido,
> surpreso, revoltado—não se divertiu e, principalmente, não foi
> público—não atuou.

> [To amuse [distract] does not demand a commitment of the
> public; to entertain, does. And theater, because of the physical
> presence of both actors and public, demands a commitment of
> the audience. An audience that does not feel committed while
> watching a show, that does not feel stimulated, controverted,
> surprised, revolted—was not entertained and, particularly, was
> not an audience—it did not act.] (103)

These are very lucid terms of contrast that go to the heart of the social
role of theater as he conceives it: a live performance proposes to be an
active dialogue with its audience.

He then notes the impasse between the social role of theater
and political reality in 1965:

> A condição básica do teatro é essa—o público atua. Para que o
> teatro possa atuar, possa divertir—possa reunir um mundo de
> sensações novas, originais, recém-reveladas—a condição política
> básica é a existência da democracia; a liberdade de expressão e
> de manifestação do pensamento.

> [This is the basic condition of theater—the audience acts. In
> order for the theater to act, to entertain—to bring together a
> world of new, original, recently revealed sensations—the basic

political condition is the existence of democracy; freedom of expression and manifestation of thought.] (103)

Vianinha links economic development (the necessary precondition for
secure theatrical space and experimentation) to political democracy,
contending that only under democracy could Brazil undergo the self-
criticism necessary to defending and exploring its own economic, social, and cultural interests.

This statement is in line with the united front (and PCB)
position. However, Vianinha carries the value of democratic participation into an affirmation of an aesthetic of contemporaneousness in
theater, declaring: "Teatro participante é a paixão da descoberta do
espírito humano contemporâneo" [Participatory theater is the passion
of the discovery of the contemporary human spirit] (103). He expands on his concept of contemporaneousness in another brief article
written shortly thereafter, employing a pertinent definition of contemporaneousness as the "realização da sensibilidade social virtual" [real-
ization of virtual social sensibility] (107). By this he means to make
real and give force to a social sensibility, or consciousness, that is latent
or unorganized. Or in terms close to those discussed in the introduction to this study, he wished to politicize, or emphasize the political
content of, histrionic sensibility.

These statements are in response to criticisms made about the
circumstantiality of Grupo Opinião's work (both *Opinião* and *Liberdade, liberdade*). While Vianinha agrees that *Liberdade* is perhaps the
most circumstantial show in the history of Brazilian theater (its democratic message elaborated in direct opposition to the growing curtailment of political rights), he argues that it is not propagandistic. He
sees it as a theatrical dynamic of universal implications:

Para nós, ser artista significa ser contemporâneo. Ser contemporâneo significa um ato de cultura que—tornando existente o po-
tencial sensível da consciência social, dando-lhe objetividade,
formando o chamado espírito social objetivo—abre caminho
para o enfrentamento prático da existência, para a superação dos
problemas que entravam a realização universal do ser humano.

Ser contemporâneo significa formar sempre um novo
presente.

[For us, being artists signifies being contemporary. To be contemporary means an act of culture that—calling into being the

sensitive potential of social awareness, giving it objectivity, shaping the so-called objective social spirit—opens the way for the practical confrontation of existence; for the overcoming of problems that hamper the universal realization of the human being.

To be contemporary always means forming a new present.] (106)

The expansive nature of his sense of contemporaneousness is demonstrated in a handwritten note he added to the typed manuscript: "Uma arte feita nos limites da consciência social—é, portanto, propaganda. Uma arte feita para novos limites da consciência social—portanto, livre" [An art made at the limit of social consciousness—is, therefore, propaganda. An art made for new limits of social consciousness—therefore, is free] (109).

This intention to nonpropagandistically challenge the limits of social consciousness is central to his next play with Grupo Opinião, *Se correr o bicho pega, se ficar o bicho come,* written jointly with Ferreira Gullar and produced in 1966. The title comes from a northeastern expression that, loosely translated, means, "You're damned if you do, damned if you don't." Thematically, it treats the impasse of development and democracy. Stylistically, it falls neatly into Vianinha's category of "teatro de diversão," being a comedy—more precisely a farce—whose diverse techniques combine to question perceptions of reality and values.

Written in verse, *O bicho* draws heavily on the traditions of *literatura de cordel,* the small booklets of popular verse sold in weekly fairs throughout Brazil and most particularly in the Northeast. Treating varied themes—fantastic stories including moral lessons, current events, or natural phenomena (comets and the like), historical subjects (there is a cycle on Charlemagne)—these poems are often sung as well. A favorite theme of the *cordel* is the astute trickster, the social underdog who manages to manipulate events and people to his advantage through cleverness.

O bicho tells the story of such a trickster, Roque. As in much of *cordel* and folklore, Roque has a sidekick, Brás das Flores, who often acts as a straight man for Roque's pranks.[11] These pranks are ingenious strategies for survival whose comic elements serve to underscore the economic hardships suffered by the *povo* in the Northeast, but in conjunction with the blatant satire of regional politics the ensuing dramatic stalemate becomes emblematic of the political impasse of 1966.

Dramatic action in the three acts of the play proceeds chronologically, interspliced by fantastic scenes in a manner that pits the over-riding sense of closure (the impasse) against frequent attempts to enlarge that space through a frenetic energy of invention. In terms of dramatic conflicts, this rhythm of enclosure and rupture is established by Roque's struggle to consolidate his gains and cut his losses. Theat-rically, the rhythm is produced by a structured mix of *cordel* devices, Brechtian techniques of alienation, fantastic figures, and music. Dra-matic content and theatrical intent merge in the clearly metatheatrical end of the play: in response to the paralyzing implications of the im-passe *(o bicho)*, the actors propose three distinct endings as possibili-ties from which their audience can choose.

The verbal humor of the play is broad, constituted by the juxtaposition of scatological references, sexual innuendo, and political jabs. Correspondingly, stage movement is gesturally large and choreo-graphic, designed primarily by dances of beatings administered mainly to Roque and farcical entrances and escapes through doors according to sexual and political intrigue. The cast is big; the original production counted thirty-two actors, many of whom were on the stage at one time. The scenic space is small, adding to the sense of movement within the thematic ambience of stasis.

The play opens with all the actors entering. After they have greeted each other, all sing the theme song:

> Se corres, bicho te pega, amô.
> Se ficas, êle te come.
> Ai, que bicho será êsse, amô?
> Que tem braço e pé de homem?
> Com a mão direita êle rouba, amô,
> e com a esquerda êle entrega;
> janeiro te dá trabalho, amô,
> dezembro te desemprega;
> . . . .
> Será êsse bicho um homem, amô,
> ou muitos homens será?
>
> [If you run, the beast will get you, love
> If you stay, he will eat you.
> Ai, what beast is this, love?
> That has a man's arms and feet?
> He steals with the right hand, love,
> And gives back with the left;

January brings you work, love,
And in December, you're out of a job;
. . . .
Can this beast be one man, love,
Or would it be many?] (3)

The theme of the precariousness of life and the indeterminate nature of those or what is responsible for that precariousness thus set, the actors leave the stage.

Brás remains on stage. Drunk and morose, he laments his luck: he is being expelled from the plantation for having robbed cotton from the *patrão,* Coronel Honorato, to sell on the open market. His friend Roque, also an employee of the *coronel,* comes in sent by the boss to beat Brás up and see that he leaves. A capoeira-style dance follows. Blows are exchanged, and Roque wins. As in most of the fight scenes of the play, the choreographic element distances the stage action from the social critique implied (why Brás had to rob, etc.). The friendly formality of these dances—the combatants compliment each other on well-placed blows—adds to this Brechtian distancing at the same time it points to the basic law of survival: the opponents hold nothing personal against each other, but are following the boss's orders.

The *coronel* is meant to be prototypical of the contradictions of underdevelopment. Indeed, the "honorific" title of "colonel" refers to a regional political boss, whose entitlement to his land is often questionable in terms of how it was obtained (inheritance, violence, legitimately purchased?). The *colonel* complains: "Dinheiro tenho, mas onde aplicar? / Plantar êsse algodão? Perder dinheiro, / pois os seus preços só fazem baixar!" [I have money, but where to invest? / Plant cotton? Lose money, / those prices are only going down!] (20). His predicament, how to reinvest his capital, is lampooned by a "crisis" of social ostentation. Aping what he considers culturally de rigueur, the *coronel* has bought a bidet. However, since there is no bathroom or running water in the house, he is at a loss as to where to show it to best advantage. Asserting patriarchal authority, he orders:

Coronel (A Roque). Ponha o bidê lá na sala
num ponto bem situado.
Roque. Sim, senhor. Ponho de frente
ou um pouqinho de lado?

Coronel. De lado, naturalmente,
que fica mais caprichado.

[*Coronel (to Roque).* Put the bidet over in the living room,
where it'll look good.
Roque. Yes, sir. Shall I set it to the front
or a little to the side?
Coronel. Sideways, of course
it'll stand out more.] (26)

The love theme of the farce begins in a scene contrapuntal
to the political theme. Roque is smitten with the *coronel*'s daughter,
Mocinha, who is engaged to Furtado, the son of the senator and the
coronel's political "employee." Furtado and the *coronel* discuss alliances and problems of the upcoming election, their speeches intercut
by an impassioned duet between Roque and Mocinha that describes
the various manners in which animals and insects make love. These
conversations bounce off of and comment on each other with theatrical dexterity. For example:

Coronel. O Presidente não é
o nosso grande aliado?
Furtado. Ele é imparcial:
ajuda todos os lados.
Mocinha. Louva-Deus? . . .
Roque. Morre . . .
Mocinha. Coitado . . .
Furtado. Quem pode pois salvar?
Estou falando com êle!
O senhor e mais ninguém!
Quem foi que abriu o sertão
ao homem antes do trem?

[*Coronel.* Isn't the president
our great ally?
Furtado. He is impartial.
He helps all sides.
Mocinha. The praying mantis? . . .
Roque. Dies . . .
Mocinha. Poor thing . . .
Furtado. Who then can save (us)?
I'm speaking to him!

You, sir, and nobody else!
You, who opened the backland
to man before the train?] (33)

Fired by passion and knowing the hour when Mocinha goes
to the outhouse to take her nightly "pee" (*xixi* and *cacá* are words
often spoken in the play), Roque waits for her. The *coronel* arrives,
complicating their rendezvous. Roque hides behind Mocinha, and
after a number of scatological interchanges, they manage to back into
the outhouse, where they consummate their passion. (As the hero of
the play, Roque is the only man who actually gets to sleep with the
women—three women—although much of the action revolves
around all the characters' sexual intrigues.)

Unfortunately for him, Roque is incapable of hiding his passion. First he confides in two donkeys, a fantastic touch that lyrically
elevates his passion and delights the audience. Inevitably, the *coronel*
finds out, told by a hired hand seeking vengeance on the *coronel*, who
has exercised his *droits de seigneur* on the hand's wife. Roque flees.

We next see Roque and Brás in a market fair. Incognito, they
are both begging alms as blind men. This scene introduces a number
of refugees from the drought. Dressed pitiably, they are sobering figures. Their speeches detail their sufferings and point an accusatory
finger at the *coronel*, who has ceased production in order to raise prices
for his cotton. This seriousness is interrupted by the discovery of
Roque and Brás, who give themselves away by arguing over a wallet
dropped accidentally by the mayor. They dance around each other,
each claiming to have seen it first. Outraged by their deception, the
refugees give chase, and Roque and Brás escape amid a rain of blows.
As in other such scenes of frenetic movement, the commotion gives
the actors the opportunity to shift around or remove the few props
and elements of set design (chairs, doors, small tables) that demarcate
the space of the scenes.

The act ends with the confrontation between Roque and the
hired killer *(matador)* the *coronel* has sent after him. The dance of the
balas [bullets] begins, with the chorus singing "Rolou tiro, rolou
tiro / rolou tiro pra valer" [There's been a shooting, there's been a
shooting / There's been a lot of shooting] (67–69) as Roque rolls
around on the floor evading the matador's shots. Their dance is interrupted by a priest who informs them that it is Christmas and that even
in Vietnam no killing is allowed on this sacred day. In dramatic time,
this cease-fire lasts only long enough for the matador to explain why

he gave up being a cowboy to become a hired killer ("Porque ser matador dá mais dinheiro" [Because being a killer pays better] [71]). His bullets spent, the matador continues his fight with Roque, now with knives. Victorious, Roque learns from the other's dying words that he has killed his own father. Roque kisses his father, masters his tears, and philosophically exclaims: "Pô, papai . . . até que enfim!" [Gee, Dad . . . at long last!] (74).

The second act mainly takes place in the small center city of the region, at the hotel of Vespertina, former lover of both the political opposition, Nei Requião, and of the *coronel*. Ostensibly lodged there to protect their interests in the election, the occupants soon engage in a ballet of frustrated sexual encounters. With the stage lit by candles and flickering matches, doors open and slam. Tiptoeing through the hall, men bump into each other in front of the doors of their intended lovers, offering feeble excuses to each other, such as they were looking for the bathroom or a chamber pot. This movement is accompanied by the sung refrain, "Noite de verão / de verão, verão. / Noite de paixão, / de paixão, paixão" [Summer, summer, summer night / Night of passion, passionate, passionate, of passion].

In the general mayhem of frustrated reunions, Roque manages to bed both Mocinha and Zulmirinha, the wife of Requião. (Roque's and Brás's dramatic presence is explained by their jobs as porters.) The ballet halts abruptly as the *coronel* realizes that Roque is there. Roque saves himself by yelling that the train is coming, escaping from the *coronel* in the ensuing scramble for luggage. Again, stage movement stops as the participants exclaim—one by one—that they were not going anywhere. Just as abruptly, the amorous ballet recommences.

As a result of Roque's prodigious sexual feats and his renown as a fighter (he has killed the most feared gunman of the area), Zulmirinha gets her husband to hire Roque. At first he doesn't understand what the job involves: he is being asked to break the heads of the striking workers who have been blocking the entrance of refugees from the interior willing to work for food and rum. The pandemonium of the hotel ballet is transposed to Roque's meeting with the workers. Attacked by the workers, he protests "Sou o herói da peça. / Não me fica bem / apanhar à beça" [I am the hero of the play. / It doesn't look right for me to get beat up] (109). This metatheatrical warning insures enough time for Roque to sort out what is happening.

He goes back to Requião for an explanation for the violence. In sophisticated rhetoric, Requião explains that prices and production must be maintained at a certain level in order to compete with the economic dominance of São Paulo; that the strikers don't understand that wages must be lowered; and also that the other starving refugees (strikebreakers) must be given a chance to make a living.

Confused, Roque takes this message to the workers. Tales of their poverty convince him that Requião's solution is merely a justification for further exploitation. Roque then gathers the workers and the strike breakers together, organizing a march to break into the company store. This scene marks a significant change in the pattern of stage movement, which before had been configured in circular or crisscrossed directions. Now having a focus for their frustrations, movement is directionally motivated toward the store, symbol of the profits denied them from their labor.

Of course, the police come and people run. Urged by Brás to flee, Roque remains transfixed, contemplating the dilemma he has come to perceive:

> *Roque.* Fugir? Ninguém some.
> Se correr o bicho pega.
> *Brás das Flôres.* Se ficar, o bicho come.
> *Roque.* Se correr o bicho pega,
> se ficar o bicho come. . . ?
> É interessante o problema,
> vou meditar sôbre o tema.

> [*Roque.* Run away? No one disappears.
> If you run, the beast will get you.
> *Brás das Flores.* If you stay, he'll eat you.
> *Roque.* If you run the beast will get you,
> If you stay he'll eat you. . . ?
> That's an interesting problem,
> I'm going to meditate on that theme.] (121

Roque is literally caught in his meditations. The second act ends as he is carted off to jail.

The third act opens with the song of the cynical jailer:

> Como disse Marx, sou
> vítima da sociedade.
> Claro, dialècticamente,
> sou seu carrasco também.

Logo: inocente e culpado.
Sou, enfim, um alienado.

[As Marx said, I am
A victim of society.
Of course, dialectically,
I am also its hangman.
Therefore: innocent and guilty.
I am, in all, an alienated person.] (125)

The jailer breaks off his song to announce a visitor. The disconsolate Roque, who has been in jail a month, does not recognize the elegantly groomed Brás. Brás explains his good fortune. He has become a best-selling *cordel* author, recounting the exploits of his best friend, Roque Penaforte. The addition of the Penaforte ("strong in suffering"), Brás contends, is a literary license taken to emphasize Roque's suffering and resistance.

Roque's situation changes immediately. Now a hero of the people, he is approached by both sides for his support in the elections. The *coronel* wishes Roque's adherence to his candidate, the senator, and Requião also looks for Roque's help. Accepting offers from both, Roque is released from jail, to the dismay of the jailer's wife, who has fallen in love with him, and against the protest of Brás, who sees the end of Roque's martyrdom as the end of his thematic gold mine.

A political operetta in counterpart to the sexual ballet of the second act begins. Roque has been installed in a luxury suite of adjoining rooms by both parties, neither of which knows that the other has paid for part of the suite. The operetta has its prelude of sexual trysts. Hearing a knock at the door, Roque muses that it might be Mocinha, then reflects that it couldn't be, because no decent play would have the heroine enter just because "faz tempo que não aparece" [it's been awhile since she's appeared] (135). Of course, it is Mocinha, who escapes by the window when her father enters. All this followed by the entrance of Zulmirinha in the other room, who likewise jumps out the window when her husband comes in to talk politics with Roque.

In the separate rooms, the *coronel* and Requião declaim their political programs, trying to enlist Roque's support. The substance of their claims is identical to the extent that, giving the barest excuses (he has to brush his teeth), Roque can rush from one room to the other to attend to both his protectors, arriving in time to add his words of approbation to whomever is speaking. Several comic devices underscore the absurdity of these equal pretenses on the parts of the candidates to be the champion of the poor and the savior of the nation.

Often, as one speaks, the other silently mimics his gestures, emphasizing the rhetoric of the social gesture. At times they speak simultaneously, in a singsong rhythm. (Both of these devices are common Brechtian techniques to augment the impact of the social gesture.) In line with the traditions of exaggerated farce (and Brazilian *revista*), Roque resolves his dilemma by placing a chair in the doorway where he can most comfortably answer both politicians, who are much too absorbed in their own rhetoric to notice the other. Smiling directly at the audience about his genial invention, Roque terminates the interview by demanding a large sum of money from both the *coronel* and Requião. Passing by each other through the door, their view supposedly obscured by Roque, both present him with a check.

The theatrical crescendo of this scene begs for a truly ridiculous conclusion. It comes with another knock at the door. Roque comments that it can't be breakfast because the production is too poor to afford to feed the actors. Offhandedly, he observes that it wouldn't surprise him if Napoleon entered. Napoleon comes onstage to the sound of a French hymn, asking directions:

> Favor, podia informar
> onde fica Waterloo?
> Perguntei na portaria
> me indicaram o *water-close*.
> Eu pergunto Waterloo.
> *Ce n'est pas la même chose.*

> [Please, could you tell me
> Where Waterloo is?
> I asked the concierge
> and they showed me the water closet.
> *Ce n'est pas la même chose.*] (148)

Napoleon's Waterloo presages the political fortunes of both candidates and prefigures further outrageous complications in the plot.

Social reality, which up to this point has been interspersed in predominantly humorous form or by the brief appearances of the refugees, reenters with a directional movement that relates to the second-act sacking of the store. The *coronel* and Requião find themselves in the same room waiting for Roque's answer. Looking out the window, they observe a parade for the newly announced candidacy of Jesus Glicério while reading lines from a campaign pamphlet. Glicério's program is simple: "Terra a quem trabalha nela" [Land for who works it] (150). They joke about the people's candidate, making a linguistic connection between *povo* and worms: "Esse sujeito é boboca. / Quer dar terra pra minhoca?" [This guy's an idiot. / He wants to give land to worms?] (151).

Their laughter turns stale as they notice Roque in the midst of the crowd, raising his arm to them in an obscene gesture. Brás comes in to return their checks, saying that Roque was so impressed by Glicério's speech that he has renounced their money and joined Glicério's campaign. For his part in the demonstration, Roque is again imprisoned, charged with being an instigator and subversive.

Meanwhile, Requião and the *coronel* join forces. Requião reasons that if Roque were to remain in jail, his fame would grow, helping Glicério's cause. On the other hand, if he were freed, he would go about preaching subversion. Requião relates this dilemma to that of a play he had seen:

> Lembra no enrêdo e no nome
> a peça do Opinião
> "Se correr, o bicho pega,
> se ficar o bicho come."

> [It reminds me of a plot and name
> of a show by Opinião
> *Caught If You Run,*
> *Eaten If You Stay.*] (156)

This device, which draws attention to the theme of the play, expands the Catch-22 situation beyond the treatment of poverty and survival in the play's plot. Spoken by those with political power in a scene where the balance of power is tenuous, Requião's humorous theatrical allusion also suggests the precarious alliances of 1966 as well as the authors' (and players) hopes that such a person as Jesus Glicério might come to the forefront.

Unable to reach agreement as to how to defeat Glicério, Requião opts to jump on Glicério's bandwagon, taking advantage of the popular tide to destroy the *coronel*'s favorite and force him to accept a coalition candidate. The *coronel* remains true to the principles of the rural oligarchy, opposing Glicério with what riches he has left.

Again freed, Roque suffers two more beatings. Requião sends three toughs to insure that Roque stick with Glicério. The same three, delighted to have two jobs the same day, immediately turn around and pulverize Roque on orders from the *coronel*, who "suggests" that Roque leave town on the next train.

Under protest from Brás, who laments "Que vou escrever agora / se meu herói, Penaforte, largou Jesus, foi-se embora?" [What will I write now / if my hero, Penaforte, leaving Jesus, went away?], Roque decides to leave, acidly retorting: "Herói é quem não tem sorte / para escapar. Mas tenho / chance e aproveito a hora" [The hero is the one who doesn't have the luck / to escape. But I have / the chance and I'll take advantage of it] (166). Roque escapes, first followed by Brás and Mocinha, who abandon him as the killers hired by the *coronel* approach. After a shooting-dance (like that of act 1), Roque finally succumbs and dies. Brás runs offstage, proclaiming the glory he will achieve with this story.

The political plot is resolved in narrative as opposed to being scenically demonstrated: we learn that Requião's machinations have proved successful and the *desembargador* (judge) is now governor. However, onstage the romantic plot, following the dictates of farce, invents a novel ending. From his deathbed the *coronel* laments the death of Roque, to whom he had wished to leave his land. On the *coronel*'s cue ("É verdade que o [Roque] mataram?" [Is it true that they killed Roque?]), Roque enters, alleging purely dramatic license as reason for his resurrection:

> É certo, todos os tiros
> foram em lugar mortal.
> *(Ao público)* Mas o mocinho morrer
> no fim pega muito mal.

> [It's true, all the shots
> hit mortal targets.
> *(To the public)* But for the young lead to die
> in the end would be really bad.] (176)

The *coronel* then explains his ambivalence toward Roque. It seems that Roque is really his son and therefore cannot marry Mocinha. The *coronel*'s wife, Bizuza, saves the situation: Mocinha is really the daughter of the *desembargador* (the new governor). In this happy conclusion to the love complications, Roque gets the girl, the land, and the political parentage.

However, the resolution of the fable, or plot, of the play is not the termination of its theatrical intentions. Playing dramaticity against theatricality, Roque asserts that the play requires a real end and proposes a theatrical vote:

> Para a peça ter um fim,
> vamos mostrar três finais.
> Escolha o que achar mais certo,
> o que lhe falar mais perto
> ou da alma ou do nariz.
> Mande às favas os demais.
> Primeiro: final feliz!

> [For the play to have an ending,
> We will show three of them.
> Choose the one you like best,
> The one that speaks closest
> To your heart or to your nose.
> Send the rest off packing.
> First: the happy ending!] (178)

The happy end politicizes the amorous conclusion. Putting on a *coronel*'s hat and picking up a cigar, Roque hears Mocinha tell of the birth of their thirteenth baby. Brás enters saying that he has expelled two workers caught selling surplus cotton, just as the boss (Roque) had ordered. The "happy end" thus reproduces the cycle of the play itself (*O bicho* starts with the scene of Brás's expulsion) as well as indicting the circular movement of corruption and exploitation of the rural economy.

Roque declares the second ending to be the "final jurídico," which turns out to be an ironic play on the idea of justice. Roque tells Mocinha he has decided that the only just thing to do would be to divide the land with the tenant farmers. His justice is met with juridical force: Brás, now a judge, declares Roque to be insane and drags him off to reopen the case of subversion held against him earlier in the act.

Roque announces the third ending as the "Final brasileiro," and it is an ending whose weirdness can only be understood as a displaced metaphor for very recent (1960–66) Brazilian history. Mocinha tells Roque that she has heard the radio proclaim the victory of Jesus Glicério on a recount vote and that he, Roque, has been nominated to help in the new radical agrarian reform program.

On one level, the theatricalized reworking of a play within the play itself functions as a metatheatrical convention pointing to the inconsistencies (and wish fulfillments) of fictional reality. On the deeper thematic level of *O bicho*, it also serves as a displacement and symbolic correspondence to the hopes held for political change and agrarian reform in the early 1960s. Within this "final brasileiro," these hopes are countermanded by a bizarre and visually striking image: dressed as a medieval warrior, Brás enters to declare that under the name of "Dom Requião, o Gentil," the monarchy has been restored in Brazil (180). The play ends with these words.

Clearly, the last ending is the most important. Not only does it have the greatest visual impact, it supersedes the two previous ones and incorporates them in a sweeping historical allusion made up of incongruous images. The Brazilian monarchy (1815–21) came centuries after the Middle Ages, but many historians and economists point out that rural Brazil presents a neofeudal structure (Brás as medieval warrior). The "Brazilian" monarchy was in addition the period in which the Portuguese crown resided in Brazil in flight from Napoleon's armies. The theatrical restoration of the monarchy, transposed to the actual time of the play, makes subtle reference to the problematic relationship between national and imperializing interests. This anachronistic "final brasileiro" puts the immediate context of impasse in a broader historical view: as ten steps backward for every few steps forward.

The conception of theater exemplified by *O bicho* is explained in the prologue to the published play, entitled "O teatro, que bicho deve dar?" (The theater, what beast should it give [us]?"). Signed by Grupo Opinião, it comprises three sections of the reasons behind the production: "as razões políticas," "as razões artísticas," and "as razões ideológicas."

Contending that *O bicho* is "de alguma maneira, uma resposta política à situação em que vivemos" [in some way, a political response to the situation in which we live] (i), the group outlines what they see as the constituent elements of the political impasse. First, in clear reference to the military's justification for seizing power, they charge the government with practicing a moralistic concept of politics. By this they mean that the government has judged that only certain privileged sectors have the moral right to govern and has withheld electoral power from the *povo* by alleging that the masses are only capable of "Julgamentos políticos imediatistas e não é capaz de julgamentos político-morais" [Immediatist political judgments and not capable of political-moral judgments] (i).

They say that *O bicho* was born, in part, to contravene that position, pointing out that *all* the characters in the play are equally corrupt and corruptible, only approaching moral integrity to the extent that they almost reach an affirmation of its political principles. They add that since not one of the sectors of interest is able to implement their political program, then the moral compromises made become integral to the political existence portrayed.

As their second point, they accuse the government of confusing social order with quietism: "O Bicho, em segundo lugar, nasceu para ser contra o quietismo social. A existência dos personagens só é festiva, alegre, vital, quando pode se manifestar. Existir é manifestar, é objetivar a existência" [*The Beast,* in the second place, was born to confront social quietism. The existence of the characters only is festive, happy, vital, when they are allowed to "show" themselves. To exist is to show yourself, it is to make existence objective] (ii). They contend that real social order is born of a system that allows the means (manifestation and organization) of its own modification, which is, of course, the definition that Vianinha gives of democratic process.

Thirdly, they propose *O bicho* as a vote of confidence in the political discernment of the people. They base their faith in the ingenuity and invention of popular traditions, which leads them to their artistic reasons for elaborating *O bicho*. Although the artistic inspiration is drawn from popular literature, they give their aesthetic model as the film *Tom Jones* and cite Brecht as the theoretical font of their theatrical conventions.

In an interview with the author, Ferreira Gullar relates that he and Vianinha came up with the idea of a popular antihero after seeing *Tom Jones*. This is reaffirmed in the prologue to the play, where such characteristics as self-irony, antiasceticism, sensualism, virtue, an inevitable and sarcastic complacency, and, above all, a "fiel e maduro amor à objetividade" [faithful and mature love for objectivity] (iii) are given as the constantly shifting traits that relate the play to the movie.

Their linguistic amplification of the Brechtian concept of alienation (*distanciamento* in Portuguese) is, to my mind, very appropriate given the natural affinity that techniques of Brazilian popular theater, at its best, demonstrates with Brecht's ideas. They call it "encantamento," which they define in the following manner:

Com encantamento queremos dizer uma ação mais funda da sensibilidade do espectador que tem diante de si uma criação, uma invenção que entra em choque com os dados sensíveis que êle tem da realidade, mas que, ao mesmo tempo, lhe exprime intensamente essa realidade. O espectador passa alternativa-mente e dialèticamente da constatação do belo em si da criação à constatação da justeza da síntese proposta. Repõe no homem seu amor à ação, à intervenção, à criação. Abre o apetite para o humano. Em Brecht a forma não é mais tirada da natureza; é tirada da beleza, da necessidade de expressão do artista.

[By *enchantment* we mean to say a deeper action of the specta-tor's sensibility, who has before him a creation, an invention that collides against the sensitive data he has about reality, but that, at the same time, intensely expresses this reality to him. The spectator passes alternately and dialectically from the affirmation of the beautiful in and of itself to the affirmation of the justness of the proposed synthesis. It replaces in man his love for action, for intervention, for creation. It opens his appetite for what is human. In Brecht the form is no longer taken from nature; it is taken from beauty, from the artist's need for expression.] (iii–iv)

This is a term that has much in common with Vianinha's the-ory of "teatro de diversão," but it stresses the admixture of theatrical devices that make up the effect: "Versos, música, interpretação cons-tante dos diversos níveis de emoção, golpes de teatro, lirismo, comé-dia 'mad,' melodrama" [Verses, music, constant interpretation of the several levels of emotion, theatrical surprises, lyricism, "mad" com-edy, melodrama] (iv).

They link Brecht with what they find in their own popular literature, which they characterize as an "intuição da arte dramática como uma manifestação de encantamento, de invenção" [intuition of dramatic art as a manifestation of enchantment, of invention] (iv). This is not reality, nor is it a copy of reality, rather a "sentimento justo da realidade" [fair (or, exact) sense of reality] (iv), a way of knowing, or perceiving, reality.

Perhaps recognizing the possible pretentiousness of such cat-egorical statements, the group adds two caveats to their artistic rea-sons. First of all, they assert that they do not consider this theatrical mode to be the only path for Brazilian theater, but a step toward building a viable plurality for a strong national theater. Secondly, they admit that they may have erred in excess in some of the comic elements of *O bicho* but attribute any exaggeration to the need to respond to the political enclosure in which they find themselves.

Their ideological reasons encompass the political and the artistic. For them, *O bicho* is an attempt:

> ordenar, de desenhar o impasse entre o ser real e a vontade de ser das pessoas na realidade brasileira—cuja característica central é a celeridade de transformações no plano da consciência e a lentidão das transformações no plano institucional. . . . O impasse, na sua violência, chega à inércia. O "Bicho," usando a cômica, pacata e relaxa linguagem da inércia, tenta fixar os diversos tipos de impasse, suas diferentes tensões, fixando como raiz o impasse econômico.

> [to order, to draw the impasse between the real (inner) being and the people's desire to be in Brazilian reality—whose central characteristic is the swiftness of transformation on the conscious plane and the level of sluggishness of transformations at the institutional plane. . . .The impasse, in its violence, reaches inertia. *Bicho,* using the comical, placid, and relaxed language of inertia, attempts to establish the different types of impasse, their different tensions, establishing the economic impasse as root (of this).] (v)

This is, in essence, a dialectical vision of impasse, where cultural and social perception ("plano da consciência") may quickly comprehend events but remain—at least temporarily—suspended in a state of inertia, unable to find a way of influencing change on a institutional level. The language also wishes to incorporate this dialectical movement: the enunciatory function describes the impasse, the theatrical devices create the tension between the terms of the description, and the gestural tone that results is meant to signify that the impasse can be surpassed and not just endured.

O bicho was a box office success but was not without its critics. The most cogent criticism was written in 1966 by Luiz Carlos Maciel. His article, "O bicho que o bicho deu" (The Beast That the Beast Begat), responds to Grupo Opinião's idea of what "bicho o teatro deve dar." First of all, he disagrees with the group's assessment of popular traditions, finding most of commercial theater based on this literature to be picturesque, stressing quaint customs, easy moral lessons, and theatrical formulas, thereby flattening out any serious dialectical treatment of the social themes to which it might pretend.

In line with these comments, Maciel challenges their use of Brechtian technique, pointing out that in epic theater the action is multiplied and explicated, but not dispersed. Thus, while he approves of *O bicho*'s way of justifying its narrative by its content (as opposed to the picturesque popular theater he decries), he notes that the failings of the show "são produto da falta de rigor dêsse conteúdo" [are the product of its lack of rigor in content] (291).

He goes on to pick apart the political logic and ideological presuppositions that construct the artistic principles of *O bicho*. Referring to the revolutionary populism of the CPC, he asserts that the play only substitutes revolutionary romanticism with "the love for the picaresque" (291). He elaborates on this in his criticism of the play's hero: "Roque . . . não é nem um herói problemático, nem um herói positivo, num sentido realista para usar os têrmos de Georg Lukács. É apenas o herói positivo do romantismo revolucionário corrigido" [Roque . . . is neither a problematic hero nor a positive one in a realistic sense, to use Georg Lukács's terms. He is only the positive hero of corrected revolutionary romanticism] (291). In other words, the patina of conflict given to Roque, although meant to signify a deeper perception of reality in accord with the changes after 1964, does not modify or amplify Roque's essential dramatic unidimensionality.

Maciel considers the choice of *Tom Jones* emblematic of the ideological confusion of the romanticized characterization of the hero. He observes that Fielding's individualistic, anarchistic, yet practical character was born in the cultural context of Rousseauesque romanticism, in harmony with the times ("a expressão fiel da atmosfera espiritual da Europa" [the faithful expression of the spiritual atmosphere of Europe] [293]), adding that the novel was a realistic treatment of its epoch. He sees it inevitable that Tom Jones's boisterous self-confidence, transposed to Roque, would shrink to a romanticized portraiture of *malandragem* (roguish or scoundrel-like invention).

In part, Maciel sees this a sign of the times in Brazil, commenting, "para os nossos autores populares, a malandragem é além de tôda dúvida o máximo de consciência possível em nosso tempo" [for our popular authors, "conmanship" is, beyond any doubt, the highest level of consciousness possible in our time] (295). He criticizes the *alegria*, or sense of inventive joy that *O bicho* wishes to transmit in the same vein, commenting that when born of frustration, *alegria* rarely achieves a sense of proportion.

He relates this and the overuse of bathroom humor to the kind of catharsis the play provokes, which he says is "eficiente nos espectadores atingidos pela mesma frustração que a [the play] originou" [efficient in the spectators affected by the same frustration that (the play) created] (295). This, he thinks, is contrary to the authors' wishes since it is a catharsis that takes away the thirst for liberty. His judgment of the play in this respect is implacable precisely because of the little room for impact he ascribes to it: *O Bicho* "tem cumprido uma tarefa limitada mas importante: a de gratificar emocionalmente uma pequena burguesia democrática machucada pelo decepção e o sentimento de impotência" [O Bicho has accomplished a limited but important task, that of emotionally gratifying a small democratic bourgeoisie wounded by deception and the feeling of impotence] (295).

Obviously, in 1966 Maciel has a considerably more pessimistic view of the future and of the audience than Vianinha. In late 1965, Vianinha demonstrates a hope that the turn of events would be actually be beneficial to the reconstruction of a real democracy: "Não há que desanimar. A democracia foi destruída enquanto organização, mas não enquanto absoluta aspiração do povo e do artista brasileiro. A destruição dos valores democráticos custou também a destruição de vários mitos que enredavam a consciência social" [Not to get discouraged. Democracy was destroyed as an organization, but not as absolute aspiration of the people and the Brazilian artist. The destruction of democratic values also cost the destruction of several myths that entangled social consciousness] (103). This idealistic hope sets the tone for *O Bicho* and for the high jinks that were devised to demystify the myths of social, political, and cultural participation that were fallacious constructs in the pre-1964 democratic state.

As in the case of *Opinião*, it is difficult to say exactly what Vianinha's input into *O Bicho* was. His coauthor, the poet Ferreira Gullar, modestly claims that Vianinha was the major author while he, Gullar, acted mainly as "poetic advisor," helping to authenticate the popular verse forms (interview by author). The tone and the comic twists in the play are certainly characteristic of Vianinha's work after *Bilbao*.

More importantly, we see in *O Bicho* several partially resolved problems of dramatic construction and theatrical communication that, along with the collage technique of *Opinião*, will resurface in different modes from 1966–74. In brief, these are questions of language and the dramatic hero and how to juggle discrepancies (and the perception of them) between behavior and objective reality of dramatic characters in a way that will open up audience perception.

With the increasingly evident solidification of the authoritarian regime between 1966 and 1968, Vianinha's optimism seems to dim. In 1968, his theoretical stance reflects this closure. A closer look at "Um pouco de pessedismo não faz mal a ninguém," the article included in the special edition of *Revista Civilização Brasileira, Teatro e Realidade Brasileira*, will serve to summarize Vianinha's theoretical preoccupations and assessment of the cultural space available to theater of the 1964–68 era. This article also includes attempts to formulate his concepts of the hero and dramatic language within the context of the real audience of the period.

First of all, it responds to the general dissatisfaction about the problems and possibilities of Brazilian theater that characterizes the other critical articles of this volume. Vianinha particularly answers to what he sees as the alienation of the radical vanguard from the real economic problems of Brazilian theater.

The term *pessedismo* refers directly to the political philosophy of the leading political party at the time, the Partido Social Democrático, and was used in the most pejorative sense by the Left. However, the term also invokes other tendencies of the Brazilian political scene at the time. It is important to reiterate that, although he often questioned PCB analysis and policy, Vianinha held active membership in the PCB from the age of fourteen until his death. In this respect, the title of his article cleverly suggests another sense: in the pronunciation of *pessedismo,* the double consonant "ss" is almost indistinguishable from "c," which insinuates, by sonorous means, an association with PCB cultural and political strategy. For some readers, this was the analytical nexus of the article, a nexus that, by the ironic tone of Vianinha's title, pointed to a conciliation of left political theater with liberal policy.[12]

The points Vianinha makes in "Um pouco de pessedismo" were based on a mature and serious consideration of Brazilian socioeconomic reality as well as on an understanding of the complexities of cultural and ideological struggle in the theater, and they serve as the theoretical nucleus of his later work.[13] Several of his arguments bear discussion in this light.

Vianinha makes a reevaluation of recent Brazilian theatrical history in order to organize a cogent perspective on the problems of Brazilian theater in 1968. These views differ significantly from the politically radical assessment of professional theater he espoused in the early 1960s (see chaps. 2 and 3). He considers that most members of the "teatro engajado" [committed theater], in which he includes himself, have done a disservice to theory and practice in ascribing simplified monolithic powers, especially in the negative sense, to the middle class as culture builders.

He analyzes several "erros de apreciação histórica . . . que terminam em erros de perspectiva atuais" [errors of historical appreciation . . . that end in current errors of perspective] and contends that groups such as the Teatro Brasileiro de Comédia, which had been written off by many leftists as bourgeois, were instrumental in the creation of a theatrical tradition and should be historically seen as "sob o signo de participação e da luta. A luta da implantação da cultura e da complexidade" [under the sign of participation and struggle. The struggle for the implantation of culture and complexity] (72). To consign these groups, derisively, to a category of theater as "divertimento de bom gosto" [entertainment in good taste] was also to ignore their significance to the posterior, more socially oriented theater.

First of all, he points out that these groups were significant precisely because they had created a consistent theatergoing public that had a level of aesthetic expectation regarding text and performance, and these expectations had given rise to conventions that were now integral to theatrical tradition. Vianinha reminds the reader that the bourgeoisie of that decade (the 1950s) was a divided and contradictory class, whose cultural interests and political programs cannot be reduced to mercantilism or aestheticism. In effect, the nationalism that was expressed, for example, in the fight for state monopolization of oil or in Kubitschek's term of office was also the attitude that provided much of the enthusiastic response to Arena's innovative earlier repertory of national authors who spoke to working-class, or marginal-class, problems (most notably, Guarnieri's *Eles não usam blacktie* and his own *Chapetuba Futebol Clube*).

Vianinha discusses the ideological isolationism of the left professional theater, attributing Arena's later financial failure to a misreading both of the theater's real audience and of its target and thematic audience, the working class:

> Em têrmos de dramaturgia, rapidamente se constata que o filão descoberto era cândido e comovido demais para enfrentar um público cujos problemas e valôres eram mais complexos e ricos. Daí ao isolacionismo, foi um passo. Como sói acontecer, o revolucionário que ainda não consegue um tática adequada à sua

estratégia, procura, no primeiro impulso, o isolamento, como forma de se instalar, ainda que abstratamente, na proximidade do mundo social que almeja.

[In terms of dramaturgy, one may quickly verify that the discovered vein was too candid and emotional to confront a public whose problems and values were richer and more complex. It was only a step from there to isolationism. As is usually the case, the revolutionary who still has not obtained a tactic adequate to his strategy seeks, at first impulse, isolation, as a way of establishing himself, albeit abstractly, in the proximity of the social world to which he aspires.] (73–74)

It must be remembered that, as a professional theater, Arena competed for much the same audience as other commercial theater. Left within a dwindling framework of support, a small audience of like-minded persons who accepted the plays on ideological grounds, Arena also found itself without many of its most radical participants, who had left in reaction to what they considered Arena's petit bourgeois elitism.

From this rereading of history Vianinha draws the lesson that the positioning of these two types of theater, the political and aesthetic, in antagonistic battle had falsified the issues. As he states, these tendencies, both of them with their respective riches, have always existed in Brazilian theater, but are not its principal contradiction:

Com êste paralelismo a luta artística assume um primeiro plano, a luta entre duas posições no interior do teatro. Não é êste o centro do problema. Na verdade, a contradição principal é a do teatro, como um todo, contra a política de cultura dos govêrnos nos países subdesenvolvidos.

[With this parallelism, the artistic struggle comes to the foreground, (becoming) the struggle between two positions in the interior of the theater. This is not the center of the problem. In truth, the main contradiction is that of theater, as a whole, against the cultural politics of the governments of underdeveloped countries.] (74)

The debate regarding who represented the aesthetic and ideological vanguard and what part commercial theater played in perpetuating what was deemed by some as reactionary values had, by 1968, clouded reflection within the Left about the lack of a viable economic basis for creating theater. To give his point of view, Vianinha makes a brief statistical overview of the most blatant infrastructural problems besetting Brazilian theater—lack of theatrical space and financing for production—to solidify his main point: the basic survival of Brazilian theater is what was in question; what seemed irreconcilable cultural positions were rather the "fruto do pequeno espaço econômico em que vive a cultura no país" [fruit of the small economic space that culture inhabits in the country] (74).

He feels that in order for Brazilian theater to survive and grow, given the economic instability and the censorship and repression of the period after 1964, the only realistic policy would be the creation of a united front within the theater class where debate on directions could take place within a general consensus of communality of interests. He applauds efforts on the part of some theater class members to unionize theater workers and form an association of impresarios as necessary steps to the formation of a base for a cultural movement that could function as a forum for political representation and pressure.

Vianinha was attacked by many people for this inclusiveness of tendencies and interests, and his "pluralism" was seen as concession to a spurious idea of national theater—which denoted all theater produced, including Shakespeare and, for example, Feydeau, in the Brazilian season—at the expense of the strengthening of national dramaturgy. Although Vianinha responds directly to the problems of the national author only parenthetically in this article, his case for the refusal of the dichotomy national theater versus national dramaturgy, developed in other writings, is well implied here: a strong national theater is a prerequisite for the development and solidification of a national dramaturgy.

Vianinha stresses that only with the creation of a secure theatrical infrastructure—that is, a consistent audience and economic opportunity for artistic growth and experimentation—could the theater start to explore the conventions that are, and would be, specific to Brazilian theater. In other words, such an infrastructure would be necessary to provide a cultural space within which playwrights could fulfill their potentials.

The major theoretical importance of "Um pouco de pessedismo" was its insistence on a realistic look at the economic structure of Brazilian theater as substantiated by its well-considered indications of the relationship between structure and artistic product made in the historical analysis of recent Brazilian theater. Other than a repeated emphasis on the necessity of incorporating cultural complexities into national drama, little is said on how to incorporate these complexities. Two key theatrical elements necessary to the structuring of conventions adequate to the kind of national theater he wished to vitalize are mentioned, however, toward the end of the article: language and characterization.

Both statements are made within the context of critical commentaries that minimized the work of Grupo Opinião as, among other things, political reductionism. He counters that it went beyond political affirmation: "o Grupo Opinião tenha dado boa contribução para deslindar o mistério da linguagem do autor teatral brasileiro" [the Opinião Group has made a good contribution toward solving the mystery of the language of the Brazilian theatrical author] (75). And, although he doesn't specify, I assume that the theatrical devices and linguistic contributions that Vianinha defends center on Opinião's use of collage and the musical show for a testimonial protest *(Opinião; Liberdade, liberdade)*, and on the neo-Brechtian techniques employed in *Se correr o bicho pega, se ficar o bicho come.*

Vianinha asserts that in its capacity to "syntonize," or tune into, reality lies the potential of this particularized, or Brazilian, theatrical language:

> linguagem que surgirá, plena, apta a perceber conteúdos mais ricos, mais cedo ou tarde, mas que fatalmente terá que sintonizar a característica básica do poder perceptivo do homem brasileiro submetido às mais instantâneas e contraditórias modificações conjunturais, sôbre uma estrutura rígida. Uma linguagem que grite e se despedace e se recomponha e se serenize, tão vertiginosamente, que se torne a imagem viva da sensibilidade do espectador.

> [language that shall emerge, complete, prepared to perceive richer contents, sooner or later, but that will inevitably have to tune into the basic characteristic of the Brazilian man's power of perception, up on a rigid structure, submitted to the most instantaneous and contradictory conjunctural modifications of the political moment. A language that screams and is shattered and recomposes itself and calms itself, so vertiginously that it becomes the living image of the spectator's sensibility.] *(77)*

This brief statement is an assertion that underlies other theoretical elaborations in his work. From around 1960, Vianinha had been preoccupied with developing a theater and theory of "comprehension." The idea of comprehension is Brechtian, adapted to a tradition of realism that has characterized Brazilian social theater. Comprehension involves dual senses of inclusiveness and understanding, where a dramatic treatment is inclusive of reality in its constituent social constructs in such a way that the play produces an audience response in keeping with (though capable of questioning) the "basic characteristic of the perceptive power of the Brazilian." As should be apparent in the following discussion, I understand the nominal phrase "característica básica do poder perceptivo" to refer to a *dynamic* of perception, (i.e., to systems of representation), and not to a specific characteristic, (i.e., sharpness or delusion, etc.).

In spite of the fact that Vianinha's ideas on language, or the subsequent one to be discussed on characterization, are not developed in "Um pouco de pessedismo" and present us with some rather vague terms, the idea of the transmission of reality into theatrical forms found in Vianinha's earlier articles here achieves a sharper emphasis. Involved is a change away from an emphasis on the representation of ideological conflict, or of cultural attitudes, as a direct manifestation of opposing economic interests, an approach that dominated left theatrical representations of the late 1950s and early 1960s.

In an important sense, the dramatic stress now is on perception rather than on action. This is achieved by understanding that behavior is not directly caused by socioeconomic conditions but is mediated by cultural and ideological values of divergent class origins and orientations. The goal was achieving a dramatic presentation of social conditions and consequences in such a way as to engage and modify an audience's perceptual field. Language would be a major force of mediation in this process, but perhaps even more important would be the portrayal of dramatic personae, and most especially, of the dramatic hero whose situation, understanding, and action would be shown as conditioned by socioeconomic circumstances but could not necessarily nor easily be reduced to them in a way that was unrealistic and unconvincing to the potential audience. The full scope of this dimension of Vianinha's orientation is not directly stated in "Um pouco de pessedismo," but the matter is implied.

Right after his statement of language, Vianinha adds: "O herói afirmativo que Hélio Pellegrino vê aparecer na literatura brasileira com *Quarup* e *Pesach,* só pode avançar e afirmar com plena consciência de suas contradições, sem voluntarismo—e só poderá ser expresso na linguagem de contradição" [The affirmative hero that Hélio Pellegrino sees appear in Brazilian literature with *Quarup* and *Pesach* can only move forward and affirm (himself) with full awareness of his contradictions, without (voluntaristic reaction)—and shall be expressed only in the language of contradiction]. This problematic hero—obviously treated differently in each of the books mentioned— portrays the confusions, conscientization, contradictions, and political impulses of 1960s political activists in their attempts to integrate some collectivized form of revolutionary struggle.

Vianinha's reference to voluntarism in the context of contra- dictions returns us, and may best be understood in relation to, his earlier, apparently enigmatic statement about powers of perception being submitted to the "contradictórias modificações conjunturais, sôbre uma estrutura rígida." Once explicated, the relationships in- volved take us to the core of the theater he would later envision and attempt to actualize.

The reference to a "rigid structure" focuses us on the very situation that was causing him to reconceptualize the problematic of a social theater in Brazil. After so many surface conjunctural contra- dictions and crises, after so many "objective" bases for social transfor- mation and revolution, the same rigid and stubborn social structure has persisted. According to Vianinha, a theater genuinely concerned with the deepest and most lasting kind of social change had to respond to this circumstance, and in effect had to deal with and move beyond the constant, almost daily mutations of Brazilian economic and politi- cal life and yet place them in relation to the structural field to which they responded and could not seem to transcend. (This is the in- tended emphasis in *O bicho*.) In the face of the persistence of the social structure through the many vicissitudes of recent years, the question became how social groups and the individuals representing them could act in such ways that would break with the structure and gener- ate a new one.

In terms of dramatic structure, the problematic presents sev- eral partial resolutions that, although often used, are not acceptable to Vianinha. If characters responded in deterministically reflexive ways to the existing order whose primary mode of action was self-reproduc- tion, then there could be no convincing escape from the circle. And indeed, the characters would be perceived as mechanistic, narrowly conceived, and unreal. If characters were portrayed as relatively free and readily able to transcend their social specificity toward something else, the result would be an impression of incoherent motivation and causality, a vision of voluntarism and virtual anarchy, without any determinate resolution.

For Vianinha, the goal for the new theater had to be one that both acknowledged Brazilian society's structural rigidity and nevertheless sought roads beyond it through the portrayal of characters who embodied a struggle between social conditioning and relative autonomy. Above all, the new social hero Vianinha would seek to develop (later personified in *Rasga coração*) would be a prototype for characters freed enough by their political and personal perspective to contribute to progressive social processes in the midst of difficult objective conditions. Only the portrayal of such figures active in the midst of a rigid social structure could begin to find acceptance by an audience that was itself immersed in the structures portrayed.

The above argument is largely implicit, or germinal, in "Um pouco de pessedismo" and applies to what is essentially a theater of identification, an illusionistic theater. In fact, in the search to synthesize his ideas in the context of his real audience (the middle class), Vianinha's works from 1968 on will rely heavily on the psychological study of a central protagonist, portraying political tensions from the viewpoint of the contradictions between voluntarism and authoritarianism found in the protagonist's sense of social alienation.

5

Consolidation of Authoritarian Control and Theater

Historical Overview: Institutional Act No. 5 and Closure of Cultural Space

In an article written in 1973, Thomas E. Skidmore maintains that the real discontinuity in the Brazilian political process was the democratic period of 1945–64. He argues: "In historical perspective, the 'democratic' era from 1945 to 1964 now appears as an interlude between authoritarian governments—between the Estado Nôvo (1937–45) and the 'revolutionary' regime of Castello Branco, Costa e Silva, and Garrastazú Médici" ("Politics" 3).

The adjectival qualification signaled by quotation marks ("democratic") indicates Skidmore's main hypothesis, that the authoritarian policies instituted by Vargas—which remained operant throughout the 1945–64 period, even if various statutes were not used—served as the basis for the institutional and juridical reformulations of the military regime.[1] Skidmore emphasizes the institutional continuity from the administrative structure created by Vargas, whose most important feature in his opinion was its network of state corporations and regulatory agencies (32). He basically agrees with other analysts (Linz, Stepan, Ianni) that 1964–68 signified a period of political and economic stabilization. He also contends that the economic growth after 1968 ("the Brazilian miracle") resulted from the fact that, no longer constricted by any real threat of popular complaint, the military and its economic technocrats (his word) could use these corporations and agencies to set up a series of inflationary measures and controls, implement taxation, and utilize foreign capital to advantage.

While Skidmore's analysis centers on the relatively neat juncture between economic policy and authoritarian structure, he remarks briefly that there were several ideological inconsistencies that perturbed the coup's otherwise smooth implementation of its policies. He notes both internal and external pressures. On the one hand, energy was consumed in observance of democratic form in matters of congressional procedure during the first years of the coup, measures that led to continuous "revamping [of] the old constitutional forms in order to 'legalize' the growing powers of the executive" (18). On the other hand, Skidmore finds it ironic that the hard-line anticommunist military policies that had brought international approval (mainly from the United States) had, in a sense, boomeranged. He posits that, in view of the repressions of the era after 1968, it was very possibly fear of the disapproval of international opinion that kept the military from openly proclaiming and directing a "straight-forwardly authoritarian regime" (45).

These inconsistencies, and several others, are the crux of Juan Linz's argument that Brazil constituted an authoritarian situation rather than an authoritarian regime. Writing in 1973, Linz submits that the full political institutionalization of authoritarian power had been hampered by the failure of the military to "civilianize" their rule, to go beyond the limited and elite alliance between the military, supportive technocrats, and a few businessmen (235). He repeatedly makes the distinction between the consolidation of authoritarian power (which he feels has been successful in Brazil) and the legitimization of that power by a consensually accepted political structure.[2]

Following Linz's basic argument, Velasco e Cruz and Martins trace the expansion of authoritarian control in terms of the varying tensions between the military and the civilian sectors.[3] Their analysis is particularly useful to reflection on cultural activity at the time in that it stresses the importance of the images of nationhood generated by the successive realignments of power.[4] Whether questioned, refuted, or assimilated, these images will be interpolated into aesthetic form.

According to Velasco e Cruz and Martins, the "slogan" of humanization colored the policies of the Castello Branco presidency (31), affording a communicative margin of cultural contestation taken by such groups as Opinião. They also see Institutional Act 5 in the light of the testing of that slogan. Among the factors that they see as converging to cause the military to suspend the 1967 constitution and declare a state of siege with Institutional Act 5 are the political front that allied rightist politicians (headed by Carlos Lacerda) and leftist members of the opposition party (MDB) in a play to propose a civilian candidate; the rise of serious and sometimes violent protests in the student movement; the Archbishop d. Helder Câmara's mobilization for agrarian reform in the Northeast; and public proclamations of guerilla warfare made by PCB dissident Carlos Marighela, which, published in a major newspaper (*Jornal do Brasil,* September 1968), claimed responsibility for various bank robberies. During this time, Congress continued to meet, despite the fact that many of its members had had their political rights revoked. The final stimulus came from within the Congress itself. Accusing the deputy Márcio Moreira Alves of having made public speeches prejudicial to the honor of the military, the executive demanded that Congress start a process against Alves. Nine members of the commission appointed to the case had to be substituted, and the Congress also rebelled. At the end of the day of the vote, December 13, 1968, the constitution was suspended and Institutional Act 5 implemented.

Armed opposition to the regime met with little success. Contrary to Marighela's prediction, the masses did not adhere to the guerilla struggle as the repression increased. In fact, President Medici enjoyed a high level of popularity as a result of the "economic miracle" that, as Velasco e Cruz and Martins put it, ran parallel to the revolutionary activities (39).

Looking back at the restructuring of power that occurred between the time the three-member junta took over from Costa e Silva (who left the presidency because of illness) and Medici's term of office, Velasco e Cruz and Martins remark that a horizontalization of power replaced the vertical hierarchy of the 1964–68 period. A result of a shifting of bureaucratic coalitions and functions, this relative dispersal of power gave rise to a new concept of government called *o sistema.* The authors underline the importance of this articulation:

surge em 69 o termo "sistema," até então inusitado no vocabulário político corrente. A introdução daquela novidade terminológica correspondia à necessidade de designar uma realidade que, tendo acabado de emergir, ainda não tinha um nome. O novo pacto—ou, mais precisamente, a nova estrutura de poder que estabelecia as relações entre os setores componentes da coalizão dominante passou a ser chamado de "o sistema."

[in 1969 there appears the term *system,* until then unusual in the political vocabulary of the time. The introduction of that terminological novelty corresponded to the need to designate a reality that, having just emerged, did not yet have a name. The new pact—or, more precisely, the new power structure that established the relationships between the component sectors of the dominant coalition, came to be called "the system."] (39–40)

They observe that the term *sistema* not only represented "a conciliação finalmente lograda entre os interesses dominantes" [the conciliation finally achieved among the dominant interests] but also carried the idea of harmonious unity among diverse elements where, even if its parts were differentiated, the functioning of the whole more than compensated any loss concerning a particular element.

One can see that such an image would bestow considerable advantages. It helped calm the political waters and smooth over the waves created by policies that taken singly would have caused much greater consternation and protest (like some of the taxes implemented). The sense of bureaucratic security implied by the phrase helped to diffuse anxieties in the civilian sector, which, for the most part, welcomed the stability of a functioning "system."

Although the extent to which the term system itself was recognized or utilized throughout the civilian sector is doubtful, the idea of order it invokes certainly filtered down. This somewhat staid sense of progress took a turn toward popular national delirium when Brazil won the World Soccer Cup in 1970. Velasco e Cruz and Martins see this as a subtle turning point in the nation's image of itself. Spurred on by the championship, which they feel was perceived as a "trophy of development," and inspired by an anonymous popular *marchinha* that had animated the team's triumph ("São 90 milhões em ação, prá frente Brasil, salve a seleção" [90 million in action, onward Brazil, hail the team]), Brazilians began to identify with a common goal of fulfilling Brazil's destiny of "grandeza e glória" (42).

This image was verbalized as "O Brasil Grande" and became

the symbol of government propaganda from 1970 to 1973, being aggressively applied to the high-visibility programs or agencies of social reform that were being promoted.[5] Velasco e Cruz and Martins comment that first of all this was an image for internal consumption: "Um país forte, dinâmico, seguro, em paz consigo mesmo. Essa a fachada que o regime procurava exibir, sobretudo para efeito de consumo interno" [A strong, dynamic, secure country, at peace with itself. This was the front that the regime sought to exhibit, above all for internal consumption] (42). However, the image also helped to assuage international doubts about what might be happening underneath this surface of progress that could possibly damage foreign investment.

Although it had no effect on international relations at the time, there was a lot going on beneath the *fachada* that had immediate and posterior repercussions on the political and cultural life of the country. Protected from public view by ubiquitous censorship and its image of order and progress, the regime carried out increasingly severe measures of repression.

At first aimed primarily at eradicating guerilla warfare, imprisonments and torture grew as a method of securing information and punishing suspects.[6] In addition, there was considerable arbitrariness in arrests and persecutions, due, at least in part, to the relative autonomy that the police arms of repression (DOPS, DOI-CODI [Destacamento de Operações-Centro de Operações de Defesa Interna/ Information Operations Detachments-Center for Internal Defense Operations]) enjoyed from direct juridical accountability. Cause for arrest went far beyond acts of political subversion, or rather, "morally reprehensible" acts (drugs, sexual activities, strange dress) were assumed under the rubric of suspicious political activity. Attempts to mobilize opposition or questioning within the nominally still existent political parties of the suspended Congress were quashed by further revocations of political mandates.

Hopes for reform or liberalization were fanned by rumors and governmental doublespeak. Treading a tenuous ground between "institutional order" and "constitutional order," and harkening back to Medici's inauguration promise to restore democracy during his presidency, rumors regarding a possible *descompressão,* or decompression—a term used to signify cautious redemocratization—were spread as early as 1972.

These rumors led to a kind of qualified optimism centering on the partial or full revocation of Institutional Act 5. Most informed opinion, however, doubted that there would be any significant changes before the next president was to inaugurated in 1974.[7] Furthermore, change was a specious concept, since the presidential candidate was chosen by the military presidential cabinet and advisers, the pro forma election by the electoral college amounting to a rarely contested ratification of the former president's choice.

In June 1973, Médici announced General Ernesto Geisel as the next president. Geisel talked about "normalization" in his speeches, but it was clear that each step toward reinstituting participatory political process would be taken to the extent that the regime managed to guard its prerogatives by constitutional measures of exceptional cause. Velasco e Cruz and Martins quote Geisel on his justification of exceptional measures and their institutionalization, measures that would remain in vigor "até que sejam superados pela imaginação política criadora, capaz de instituir, quando for oportuno, salvaguardas eficazes dentro do contexto constitucional" [until they are surpassed by the creative political imagination, able to institute, when appropriate, effective safeguards within the constitutional context] (46).

Taking office in March 1974, Geisel's presidency was characterized by the strategy of *distensão* (the loosening of political restrictions seen as a prelude to redemocratization). Officially, this meant that the government began giving dates for further modifications in electoral process while still holding a tight rein on practical policies. Speeches and manifestoes were made, one of the most instructive in terms of the institutionalization of convenient nationalist images being the "cultural plan" drawn up by the designated minister of culture, Ney Braga. The cultural politics of this "Plano de Ação Cultural" detailed the institutional reorganization of various cultural organs guided by a specified ideology of the promotion and commercialization of Brazilian popular culture.[8]

By this time, there was very little danger that support for popular culture would encourage protest. The popular sector, or its supporters, was absent in the streets and in the Congress. Although it did not filter down to the disadvantaged groups and classes, the Brazilian economy continued to expand, creating, on this level, a secure base for political "normalization." On the other hand, Geisel's announced policy of liberalization created a distinct reaction in the military extreme Right who, fearing the curtailment of their autonomy, conducted or authorized a most intense year and a half (from the end of 1973 to the beginning of 1975) of torture and "disappearances."

How did theater fit into this context of political enclosure and economic expansion? Vianinha's dream of building a strong infrastructure for national theater was clearly not destined to be one of the beneficiaries of economic growth at this time, especially since theater was well known to be the prime cultural troublemaker of this turbulent period.

Velasco e Cruz and Martins make an observation on the demarcations of the space of general oppositional activity from 1967 until the late 1970s worth quoting here:

Hoje [late 1970s] a oposição é bastante bem-comportada: contida, no que diz e no que faz, ela avança nos espaços deixados abertos pelo poder, procurando expandi-los apenas incrementalmente. "Ocupar os espaços"; "forçar os limites do possível," assim se expressa a sua sabedoria. Em 67–68, ao contrário, valorizava-se o exercício da insurgência, a invasão dos espaços vedados, a ação que ignorava limites.

[The opposition today (late 1970s) is quite well behaved: contained, in what is says and does, it advances in the spaces left open by power, searching to expand them only incrementally. "To occupy the spaces," "to force the limits of the possible," is thus the way wisdom expresses itself. In 1967–68, on the contrary, it was the exercise of insurgence, the invasion of forbidden spaces, the action that ignored limits that was prized.] (36)

Due to its high profile of political protest, these restrictions were levied against theatrical activity somewhat earlier.

By the end of the Médici regime most of the groups that had been important in the search for political and aesthetic expression of national themes (Arena, Oficina, Opinião) had either been disbanded because of political persecution and the imprisonment or exile of its members, or rendered ineffective, as political protest, by the problems of economic survival caused by censorship. For example: Boal (Arena) and Zé Celso (Oficina) went into exile in the early 1970s; Vianinha, who left Opinião in 1968 mostly because of financial reasons, died of cancer in July 1974.

Impresarios who had previously been committed to staging Brazilian texts could no longer afford to produce national playwrights, nor even foreign plays, with anything a censor could pounce on. Because of limitations, the tendency was toward small plays (those using few actors, which if prohibited, would not be so economically damaging), toward plays that expressed political questions in metaphors, or back to social theater in the broadest sense of the word (plays on existential-psychological conflict).

As for the playwrights, persecution led to a process of self-censorship that, although impossible to assess statistically, is still considered in today's critical postmortem to have been crippling to the course of Brazilian dramatic literature.

Another influence on the shaping of theater was the rising popularity of the television *novela* (soap operas). An inevitable part of the rise of television as mass media, this new popularity of the *telenovela* (a form on the air since the early 1960s) was also a result of the crisis in theater. Stage actors went to television as a means of economic survival and became media stars. The media star system was self-perpetuating, the actors going from novela to novela. The influx of theater actors, usually well trained, also improved the quality of these novelas. Besides all the other problems besetting theater at the time, productions begin to suffer an unevenness in acting as actors returned from television to stage. However, hiring prominent novela actors was about the only way to insure an economic return for a stage production. The problems generated by this system remain unsolved.[9]

Playwrights also went to television, among them such figures as central to the development of a national, politically oriented theater as Dias Gomes, Jorge Andrade, Vianinha, and Paulo Pontes. Claiming economic survival as one motive, these writers also maintained that television was the only way to reach an audience, and they placed hope in using the media to increase social consciousness. Other playwrights (like Nelson Rodrigues, censored on moral grounds) returned to other remunerative activities, with only occasional forays into the theatrical world. Guarnieri wrote some for television but mainly continued with the stage, writing plays of metaphoric contestation (e.g., *Um grito parado no ar* [A Cry Suspended in the Air], 1973). Plínio Marcos, the only major playwright who maintained a consistent style—that of social protest by realistic dramas of the marginal aspects of urban life—won by this persistence the distinction of being the most censored playwright in the history of Brazilian dramatic literature.

When we take a closer look at the aesthetic tendencies that informed theatrical conventions in the 1968–74 period, we see the rift between an *estética da palavra* (aesthetic of the word) and an *estética de agressão* (aesthetic of aggression) that predominated on the eve of Institutional Act 5 taking on more subtle characteristics in relationship to the stultifying enclosure of the bureaucratic authoritarianism of the political system. In early 1968, both tendencies made their appeals through concepts of scenic innovation and reformulations of audience-actor communication. As stated in chapter 4, Oficina's openly aggressive challenge to audience perception relied heavily on the actor's craft of gesture, suggestive props or sets, and a surprising (at that time) use of stage space, often extending the action into the audience itself. Language was secondary to, or subservient to, or sometimes bludgeoned by, these techniques.

As Tânia Brandão rightly points out, signaling a conservative element of the *estética da palavra* by referring to it as the *estáctica,* giving the term two meanings of paralysis and noise that interferes with communication, the *estética da palavra* had its first major formulation in the work of Arena in the 1950s (15–17). The double political commitment of that group to social change and to laying the base for a national dramaturgy was expressed in a textual politics of verbal exegesis: dialogue had to be explicit regarding the social conditions it was transmitting. This did not really change after 1964. However, as discussed in the work of Opinião and in Boal's experiments with the *coringa*/joker system in Arena, the emphasis on the textual word conjoined with new antirealistic theatrical techniques.

After 1968, scenic innovation became increasingly formulaic, or conventions tended to revert to previous forms of illusionist theater. This was not just a result of the physical disbandment of these core groups or the exile of key persons that had influenced experimentation in the 1964–68 period. Rather, it expressed a sense of exile and individualism understandable under the circumstances.

In the early 1970s the political facts of exile and of censorship had produced a kind of internalization of exterior fact. Speaking about the cultural ambience as a whole, the literary critic Antônio Cândido remarks that the very limited choice of adhering to the regime or keeping quiet resulted in an interior exile: "A pessoa não emigra nem para fora de sua cidade nem para fora de seu país, mas para dentro de si mesma, fechando-se totalmente para o mundo e apresentando uma máscara de conformismo" [A person does not emigrate out of his city nor out of his country, but into himself, completely closing himself out of the world and presenting a mask of conformity] (qtd. in Ianni, "Estado" 234).

The sense of interior exile predominated in the themes and tone of the poetry and novels of this period. In theater it became symptomatic of formalism. The thoughts of Paulo Pontes, a staunch defender of the textual aesthetic, indicate the consequences of this sense of exile to theatrical trends:

Na nova fase [after 1968] já não se podia falar abertamente, e uma das conseqüências disto foi o surgimento de trabalhos voltados para o formalismo e o individualismo. Dentro deste formalismo os artistas continuam com uma visão do mundo, continuam querendo indagar sobre isto ou aquilo mas existem inúmeras barreiras entre eles e o público. A censura era apenas uma delas. Para romper este muro, foram procurados novos caminhos que visavam ludibriar a censura. Como conseqüência, a palavra, instrumento do pensamento organizado, centro da dramaturgia e da encenação teatral e chave do fenômeno dramático, passa para segundo plano em detrimento da forma e dos estímulos formais.

[In the new phase (after 1968) one could no longer speak openly, and one of the consequences of this was the appearance of works directed toward formalism and individualism. Within this formalism artists proceed with a world vision, continue wanting to inquire about this or that, but countless barriers exist between them and the public. Censorship is only one of them. In order to break down this wall, new paths that intended to outwit censorship were sought. Consequently, the word, instrument of organized thought, center of dramaturgy and theatrical staging and key to the dramatic phenomenon, moves, to its detriment, into the background in regards to form and formal stimuli.] (Qtd. in Ianni, "Estado" 238–39)

The formalism that Pontes decries was, first and foremost, a heritage of Oficina's experiments with theater of aggression. Starting with relatively tame productions of *O rei da vela* and Chico Buarque's more audacious *Roda viva,* directed by Zé Celso although not produced by Oficina, and influenced by their abortive attempt to collaborate with the Living Theater and Argentina's Los Lobos, by their 1972 collective creation of *Gracias Señor,* Oficina's tropicalist aesthetic in their most experimental pieces had become so esoteric or fragmented that they reached a very reduced and often extremely critical public. In a sense, what had started as a fiercely lively theatrical investigation of the symbols of Brazilian culture had, by 1974 (when

Zé Celso went into exile in Lisbon), become an often incoherent scream of experimentalist frustration.

However, by the early 1970s the tropicalist aesthetic that had originated with Oficina had already taken a more generalized turn from aggression to *curtição* (then-current slang for the ecstatic high produced by drugs, meditation, sex, or whatever else a person could pleasurably immerse themselves in—preferably to the point of ignoring unpleasant social realities).

An expression of the *desbunde* (dropout) phenomenon, *curtição* was an individualistic, or do-your-own-thing, response to social alienation that organized collectively in theatrical rites or happenings. The spontaneity and enthusiasm that accompanied these events was formalized by the ritualistic aspects of the theatrical communication. In addition, music, mainly rock, assumed the major role of structuring theatrical form.[10] Much akin to countercultures in the United States and Europe in the late 1960s, discursive or analytic thought became subsumed by, or encoded in, linguistic circumlocutions or expletives. This generation's mistrust of words is understandable, given the climate of verbal obfuscation of the authoritarian situation in which they came of age.[11]

But Pontes is not just referring to theatrical tropicalism. He is also talking about the problems of theater that, until recently, had given primary importance to the "word." In this respect, the formalism he mentions is both linguistic and theatrical. As already pointed out in this study, in both cases it is structured by metaphor.

The aesthetic impasse as Pontes describes it is, of course, configured by his belief that *a palavra* is the key to effective dramaticity and theatricality. His analysis, made in 1977, demonstrates little hope for any resolution or way out. In contrast, Vianinha, who shared Pontes's views on theatrical priorities and who up until *O Bicho* had looked for a way out of the impasse, paradoxically returned to look for a way in from 1968 until 1974. Largely eschewing metaphor, he went back to traditional forms to try to explicate social alienation and answer legitimate questions raised by the aesthetics of aggression and *curtição*.

Vianinha: Professional Theater and Conventions of Identification

At the time of writing "Pessedismo," Vianinha was still collaborating on musical reviews and writing light comedies and television pieces, which he continued to do until his death. For the purposes of this study, however, I wish to limit discussion to those plays that sought a cultural insertion within the parameters of mainstream professional theater, with the political intention of opening up these parameters to both build an audience and change its perceptions.

Between 1969 and 1972 he wrote and had staged three full-length plays.[12] All three dealt with protagonists in some way linked to the communications industry. The first of these, *A longa noite de Cristal* (Cristal's Long Night), written in 1969 and staged in 1970, was meant to be a thought-provoking study of an on-the-skids telejournalist as he succeeds, albeit in an entertainingly frantic way, in alienating himself from his friends and work; is saved from a suicide attempt by his former boss and former wife and ends his dramatic time as a radio announcer on an all-night show. Questions of social consciousness and ethics are raised in the context of the reified atmosphere of consumer-oriented television as Cristal, the protagonist, enters into abrasive conflict with his environment. Cristal's attempts to maintain some degree of moral coherence degenerate into voluntaristic behavior as he continually cedes to the limelight of the cheap joke. His process of social isolation is accentuated by the staging, a large-cast production that revolves around the congested ambience of the television studio and the festive-leftist bar scene.

The second of these plays, *Corpo a corpo* (Hand-to-Hand Combat), written in 1970, first staged in 1971, is a monologue, although at the beginning of the play there is some offstage dialogue between the protagonist, Vivaqua, and his fiancée. This time the character is a director of advertising films who dreams of becoming a Fellini, but who is, as we see him, immobilized by a sense of the futility of trying to change himself within the demeaning framework of his job and relationships. His interpersonal encounters are characterized by large and small betrayals. The dramatic impetus of his revolt is nominally the firm's impending dismissal of his old master, whom Vivaqua sells out at the end of the play.

In his long night of despair and desperate telephone calls, Vivaqua reveals at times a tenacious lucidity about his own situation and expounds eloquently on the commodification of human communications that is required of him in his job as a publicist. These moments notwithstanding, he rapidly sinks into the conflicts of his own alienation, striking out at whomever he can get to listen to his incoherent calls. The primary modality of his conflict is his incapacity to stick by decisions pertaining to his perceived moral responsibility.

Vivaqua is temporarily saved from his self-destructive voluntarism by a call from the agency's owner, who is in the United States
negotiating a deal of international cooperation to gain control over
advertising in the hinterlands of Brazil. The cultural sponsor of this
campaign is the Fulbright Commission, who has been so impressed
by a thirty-second spot commercial on floor wax that they insist that
Vivaqua take charge of the artistic direction of the project. Vivaqua is
thus reincorporated into the social structure—the publicist as high-
tech ideologue—although he characteristically retains illusions of
using his Fulbright connection as a stepping stone to artistic freedom.

Both *Cristal* and *Corpo a corpo* are in the mode of the urban
existential drama, although both incorporate strong comic elements
to underscore social structure and the *vivência*, or lived experience, of
the protagonists' anguish. These plays were both well received although they presented problems (to be discussed shortly), in characterization and audience response. The third play of this grouping,
Alegro Desbum, subtitled *Se Martins Pena fosse vivo* (If Martins Pena
Were Alive), written and produced in 1972, was a partial farce, conceived in the spirit of Martins Pena and within the parameters of boulevard comedy. The main character, Buja, is an advertising writer who
tries, by living the dropout life in Copacabana, to submerge himself
into the electronic world of television and stereo (preferring old Dalva
Oliveira recordings), refusing as much as possible to participate in the
world of economic and social connections by making himself a zom-
bie with products of secondary, displaced communications. He loses
his girl and his job, and at the end of the play is left in the company
of a lovesick drag queen.

Vianinha was attacked by many leftist critics and theater people for this play. They considered it socially irresponsible, a farce pandering to glitter entertainment. For Vianinha, it represented another
experiment in approximating Brazilian theatrical conventions (the audience appeal of ribald farce) with a character who, although clownish,
would embody some of the most essential conflicts of his social environment. In this sense, he also considered this work important as exploration and perfecting of his "theatrical carpentry," the term he
used to denote the architectural structuring of theatrical devices
within the mechanisms of playwriting.[13]

As seen in previous chapters of this analysis, characters able
to give a living sense of their predicaments in a way that elucidated
social conditions is an integral part of Vianinha's socially committed
plays. As always, this practice related to his reading of the ongoing

formation of dramatic and theatrical conventions. These three plays all respond, in varying degrees, to the aesthetics of aggression, *curti-ção,* and the metaphorical displacement of the early 1970s. While he recognized these aesthetics to be emblematic of reaction to bankrupt social values and expressive of the search for contestatory values, Vianinha dedicated much theoretical energy to analyzing the shortcoming of this theater as a viable vehicle for provoking consequential thought on the part of the audience. He stressed that the times called for a theater of words, a form that could question the ideological assumptions of bourgeois conventions without violating the valuable structures of communication already established by those conventions.

Viewed thus in the light of his dedication to clarity of expression, the explicated and self-explicating characters of these three plays become particularly important. Even so, the dramatic characterization of the protagonists presents a problem commonly intrinsic to the dramatic structure of this kind of play, one often exacerbated by directorial license in production: an overidentification with the alienated hero. This problematic of playwriting, direction, and audience reception can best be seen in the polemic that surrounded the production of *Cristal,* an interpretation with which its own author completely disagreed. The nexus of scenic misinterpretation would seem to reside in the fact that Cristal, as a dramatic character, lends himself to the mode of the glamorized depiction of alienated antiheroes that has proliferated in mainstream theater since the late 1950s.

After seeing *Cristal,* directed by Celso Nunes in São Paulo in 1970) Vianinha synthesized the clash between his intentions and the scenic interpretation of the play in this manner:

> a peça é sobre um pequeno drama de um indivíduo e sobre a urgente necessidade de não soçobrarmos em pequenos dramas; fizeram-na um drama diluviano, quase alegórico, que vale a pena ser vivido, porque todo grande drama vale a pena ser vivido; o personagem "Cristal" é um personagem que se desatarraxou da vida e ainda assim é tratado por todos na ponta dos dedos; a encenação faz de Cristal um tresloucado homem superior que é tratado a pontapés por todos; a peça tenta amarrar os comport-amentos às situações objetivas, grudá-los com cola-tudo às situações objetivas; o espetáculo é voluntarista—as pessoas agem de tal ou qual modo porque querem. Estas três inversões de con-

cepção e não de estilo (que terminam resultando uma inversão de estilo) tornaram-me irreconhecível a peça.

[the play is about a small drama of an individual and about the urgent need of not going under in small dramas; they made it a diluvian drama, almost allegorical, worth living because every great drama is worth being lived; the character Cristal is a character who has disconnected himself from life and, even so, is treated with kid gloves by all around him; the staging makes Cristal a crazed superior man who is horribly treated by everyone; the play tries to link his behavior to objective situations, glue them with all-purpose glue to objective situations; the staging is voluntaristic—people act in this or that manner just because they feel like it. These three inversions of conception and not of style (which end up as an inversion of style) rendered the play unrecognizable to me.] (*Vianinha* 131)

Vianinha charged that the play had been turned into moralist theater of individual behavior. He categorically denied any such intention: "Não posso conceber nenhuma solução que só sirva a indivíduos isolados ou a categorias sociais privilegiadas" [I cannot conceive of any solution that will serve only isolated individuals or privileged social categories]. Such dramatic solutions have nothing to do with the social sectors he wanted eventually to reach, an audience that would embrace the majority of Brazilians:

A estes setores da população não interessam as atitudes voluntaristas—não estão interessados numa mudança de comportamentos mas na mudança de relações objetivas. E, para isso, como nunca, mais que nunca, precisam ter presentes estas relações, conhecê-las a fundo, investigá-las, dominá-las. Eles precisam de um teatro de encadeamento, do rigor de observação, da precisão de lâmina, de funda complexidade.

[Voluntaristic attitudes do not interest these sectors of the population—they are not interested in a change of behaviors but rather in the change of objective relations. And, for this, as never before, more than ever, they must have present these relations, know them thoroughly, investigate them, master them. They need a theater of interlocking chains, of rigorous observation, of bladelike precision, of deep complexity.] (133)

Evidently, his comments about the staging of *Cristal* amount to a restating of earlier manifestoes for socially committed theater, and he ends this interview with the following call to action:

> Estamos atrás de um teatro dos países subdesenvolvidos em luta por sua libertação e pela afirmação autônoma de sua capacidade criadora. Esta é a minha posição. Um teatro que sirva à luta consciente, paciente, determinada, irreversível, contida, disciplinada, final do mundo subdesenvolvido.

> [We are after a theater of the underdeveloped countries in their struggle for their liberty and for autonomous affirmation of their creative capacity. This is my position. A theater that serves the conscious, patient, determined, irreversible, contained, disciplined struggle, the end of the underdeveloped world.] (133)

It is clear from his reactions to the staging of *Cristal* that Vianinha does *not* consider that his plays subscribe to middle-class ideology inasmuch as that ideology promotes an individualistic perspective on society. However, it is also clear that for purposes of communication, given the constitutive reality of the Brazilian playgoing audience, the plays are configured by conventions marked by that ideology, and that given the habits of perception of that audience, it is indeed difficult to stage characters such as Cristal, Vivaqua, and Buja in such a way that allows for the distancing necessary to promote a critical vision.

The author's intention is clearly seen through the dialogue of the texts, which is carefully structured to provide a dialectic of approximation and distance. However, in *Cristal* the critical intention of the dialogue is confused or often refuted by theatrical and dramatic conventions indicated in the text itself.

Cristal is a two-act play with seventeen characters. In the stage directions, the author notes that with the exception of Cristal and Lise (Cristal's wife), actors may take on double or multiple roles. This doubling, according to Vianinha, is not just an economic consideration but, more importantly, has the objective of adding pace, vitality, and interest to the play. It can also be inferred that he hoped to provide a kind of distancing with this technique. However, given the mimetic focus of the characterization, it is difficult to imagine that roles could be doubled without damaging the dramatic referentiality of at least four others important to our vision of Cristal: Celso (his son); Fernandinho (his boss); Murilo (his friend and broadcast director of the news); and Flávia (his coanchor).

Although designated for a proscenium stage, Vianinha's instructions call for a "collage" set. These minisets include a corner of Cristal's apartment, a piece of the television studio where he works, the bar frequented by him and his coworkers; Fernandinho's office; and some visual indication of the doctor's office. Vianinha specifies that the sets are to remain at least semifixed during the production since dramatic action changes rapidly from one place to the other. Besides facilitating the tempo of the play, this scenic arrangement is also meant to break empathic identification that would come from a uniform locale.

References in the dialogue tell us that Cristal's crisis transpires during six months of the year in which the play was written and produced (1970). Dramatic time passes quickly back and forth between the present and the past. However, *Cristal* presents an interesting kind of temporal relativity that corresponds to the ambiguity of the protagonist's moral character: his past is not a fixed point of reference but surges forward in relation to the chronological movement of his present. Both temporal planes, or movements, take advantage of the various sets. Flashbacks (and what the author calls the "geography" of the play) are differentiated from present time by lighting; the present is illuminated by a bright, almost overexposed light.

The thematic point of the first act is to register Cristal's disintegration, self-indulgence, and voluntaristic behavior within a social context of alienation and displacement. Scenes treating the reification of human emotion and its transformation into marketable mass appeal frame the act: the play begins with voice-over dialogue from an exotically melodramatic *telenovela* and ends with Cristal calling in the applicants for the station's "oldest living person" contest. The overall tone of the act is humorous since Cristal still maintains a shaky control, defending himself with his quick wit. The encounters between Cristal and the unprofessional doctor he goes to see to cure his sexual impotence are also funny, yet it is evident that his impotence is the only sign of "purity" in his character, a negative statement born of frustration and refusal.

In line with his intention to describe an individual of doubtful character caught in his incapacity to overcome problems largely of his own making ("um pequeno drama de um indivíduo e sobre a urgente necessidade de não soçobrarmos em pequenos dramas" [a small drama of an individual and about the urgent need of not going under (drowning) in small dramas]), Vianinha makes it very clear in the first act that Cristal's battle is, first of all, with himself by surrounding him with people who generously and genuinely care for him. Even Cristal is aware of the emotional injustice of his situation, as he tells Lise: "Pára de me tratar como se não houvesse nada, Lise. . . . Você devia ir embora, já disse" [Stop treating me as if nothing were going on, Lise. . . . I already said that you ought to leave] (11).

Vianinha uses the close relationship between Cristal and his eighteen-year-old son, Celso, to differentiate subjectively indulgent reactions to objective situations from the moral responsibility to objectify personal reactions by analysis of the elements that condition that subjectivity. The contrast is heightened by the fact that at eighteen Celso is emotionally mature, cares deeply for his father, and sees him clearly enough to claim the positive moral heritage Cristal has given him (Cristal's best moments of courage and lucidity).

This is seen in the middle of the first act. Cristal wonders about Celso's preoccupation with the university political structure and analysis of the job market when, as far as he, Cristal, can see, Celso should be concentrating on his subject matter, chemistry. Linking academic material with the base elements of his father's trade (the half-truths of television news), Celso chides his father, saying: "você devia estudar o problema de televisão em vez de ser especialista em dizer meias verdades só" [you should study the problem of television instead of only being a specialist in saying half-truths] (13). In other words, and following Vianinha's Marxist analysis (implicit here), the means of production deform both the product and condition a situation of social alienation.

This interpretation is verified in the manner in which theatrical device designs the pattern of meaning of the next scene, the crucial moment of the first act. The dramatic conflict is simple: Cristal inserts an item in the news broadcast. On the way to the studio he saw a woman forced to give birth in the park in front of the hospital to which she had just been denied entrance (obvious reason: poverty; given reason: she was crazy).

While he is reading this item, slides show scenes from his domestic life: Lise crying, Celso laughing, the doctor talking. Normally in the play, the slides complement rather than contrast what is happening in the news broadcasts. This projection of the emotional reality of Cristal's private life is set up in a disturbingly qualitative correspondence with the objective realities of poverty and class that condition humiliation and despair (the woman's story). There is a spatial relationship of displacement and approximation in this scene that functions very well, producing a "U" effect: on one side and behind, the visual impact of the slides; placed on the other side and behind by narrative distance, the woman's story; Cristal front and center at his broadcaster's desk "reading news" (displacement) while seeking attachment (visual and verbal signs) to the significance of the events connected to him.

The second act begins on a serious note and ends with a tone of pathos, or calmer resignation. The act is framed by encounters between Cristal and Fernandinho. Cristal begins by defending his broadcast against Fernandinho's demand that he make a public retraction. Fernandinho explains that there will be political repercussions as a result of the story that will cause both Cristal's and Murilo's dismissals and damage his own position. Cristal retorts that it was the truth and therefore news. Fernandinho points out the inconsistencies of Cristal's dedication to the truth. For Cristal's journalistic triumphs are well in the past—he cites his excellent coverage of Vargas's suicide in 1954—and, besides, the news broadcast that Cristal anchors is in jeopardy because of its low ratings. Cristal's era is over, partly because of market demands in the media, but it is equally evident that Cristal has played a large role in his own demise. (Again, Vianinha wishes to juggle external forces with internal impulsions.)

Cristal's confusion and lack of clarity in choosing defensible issues stems from an alienation from the values that had previously sustained his convictions, as seen in the scenic juxtaposition of his public and private lives. When Lise leaves him, he pleads with her to stay. Without accusing him, she comments that for over a year he has not even wished to sleep with her. He tries to explain his impotence as a consequence of the absurdity and alienation of his work: "é a insipidez, Lise . . . é horrível, perdi qualquer noção do que vale a pena, do que não vale" [it's the insipidness, Lise . . . it's awful, I've lost all sense of what's worthwhile and what isn't] (32). Going out the door, she verbalizes his real problem (intellectual and emotional indulgence): "você quer que a insipidez vire filosofia . . . de todo mundo. Fica sozinho, desiste sozinho" [you want insipidness to become philosophy . . . for everybody. Stay alone, give up alone] (32). Cristal's alienation may be an explanation, but it is not a justification.

The lack of coherence in Cristal's character is further theatricalized by the proxemic relationships of a dual scene that follows. Cristal, in center focus, plays against Fernandinho on one side and against Celso on the other. Fernandinho again begs Cristal to reconsider, even though he concedes that Cristal, in theory, is right. On the home front, Cristal is asking Celso to turn a group of students out of the house that are meeting to plan a protest. The contradiction is apparent as Cristal turns directly around to apply Fernandinho's reasoning about the impulsiveness of the broadcast to his appeal to Celso. For example:

> *Fernandinho.* . . . mesmo que fosse verdadeira, eu não daria [the woman's story] . . . mas já foi dada . . . você tem de me ajudar, Cristal, por favor.
> *Cristal* [now directed to Celso]. . . . concordo, viu Celso, a reunião é importante mesmo, viu, mas na minha casa, não . . .
> *Fernandinho.* . . . não é por minha causa, Cristal . . . isso aqui é uma emprêsa . . . por mim . . .
> *Cristal* [again to Celso]. . . . por mim você podia reunir até desmaiar . . . mas eu sou conhecido . . . não quero, na minha casa, não . . .

> [*Fernandinho.* . . . even if it were true, I wouldn't give it (the woman's story) . . . but it's already done . . . you have to help me, Cristal, please.
> *Cristal* (now directed to Celso). . . . I agree, see Celso, the meeting is really important, see, but not in my house, no . . .
> *Fernandinho.* . . . it's not for my sake, Cristal . . . this is a business. . . . as far as I . . .
> *Cristal* (again to Celso). . . . as far as I'm concerned, you can meet until you drop . . . but I'm known . . . I don't want, in my house, no . . .] (34–35)

Fernandinho's logic reveals a consistent appraisal of reality, and the contrapuntal scene suggests that, although Fernandinho may subscribe to equally indefensible attitudes about social change, Cristal's moral inconsistency undermines his occasional virtuous act.

Celso's judgment of his father's abdication of responsibility prefigures Cristal's act of self-destructive affirmation. Speaking about people like his father, Celso proclaims: "eles desistem aos gritos, convidando todos para um grande torneio de impotência, fascinados e superiores com a estranha sensação de não precisar mais viver" [they give up screaming, inviting everybody to a grand tournament of impotence, fascinated with and superior to the strange sensation of no longer needing to live] (39). In the next scene, instead of retracting,

Cristal cuts into his coanchor's retraction of the item, categorically stating that the tragedy at the hospital did occur exactly as he had first announced it.

Not only does Cristal's gesture cause him his job, but it also gets Murilo fired. Murilo had nothing to do with the story and had always stood by Cristal. Throughout the play, Cristal's friends blame themselves for their inability to help him or cure him. Considering Cristal's behavior, it is somewhat difficult to understand his friends' fierce loyalty. Both Lise and Fernandinho get spiritual "shocks" or premonitions (quite a dramatic license on Vianinha's part) of his suicide attempt and rush to rescue him. The play ends as Cristal adjusts himself to his losses, with Fernandinho's visit to him, and the narrative wrap-up (told by Fernandinho) of how Cristal is still loved by those who are no longer physically by his side.

When we look at the play in the light of Vianinha's intentions, we see that the first act is structured to present Cristal as an unreliable witness, his self-indulgence pitted against the greater coherence of those who treat him as a friend, even in their questioning of his actions and motives. Occurring so abruptly at the end of the first act, his decision to present the truth (the woman's story) is ambiguous, coming off as much as an impulsive gesture as an act of moral courage.

In the second act, Vianinha presents a problem of moral relativism in Cristal's act of defiance: why should Cristal now be seen as a hero? The author wishes us to identify with the act but question the motives behind it. Without denying the importance of Cristal's refusal, all previous symbols (his sexual impotence) and interpersonal encounters indicate that it is an ambiguous gesture that is generated more from impotence and rage than from conviction. Vianinha makes it clear that moral and political responsibility is not a question of purity, but of clearheadedly assessing consequences and priorities. This is ironically shown as Cristal realizes that in his sensationalist defense of the news item he has killed the chance to responsibly report and comment on other news of social and political importance (for example, a segment on pollution on which he was to report).

Despite the care that Vianinha takes to portray Cristal, it is not too difficult to see how Vianinha's critical intentions could go awry in production. For one thing, Cristal is by much too far the most interesting character in the play, and it is hard not to overidentify with him. Other characters are more coherent in their struggles (Celso, Murilo, Lise, and even Fernandinho), but their integrity, or struggles for same, exists dramatically as illumination on Cristal's basic (or temporary) lack of character. Since Cristal is always figuratively center stage, and since the others are so dedicated to him, it would be difficult not to have their integrity reflect back on Cristal in a manner that promoted him as a hero.

Even in the text we can see that this is also a problem of positioning in stage space, where spatial oppositions, proxemic relationships, and movement all go to aggrandize Cristal's predicament. The most notable exception to this is the instance of the "U" effect, where although he is center stage, the referential devices (slides, gestures) of his interior life versus external reality are truly beyond his control. As a rule, the force of acted confrontations—actor against actor—allows him to modify or manipulate audience reaction. In brief, although one can read Vianinha's intention in the text, the very conventions he indicates in the text work to defeat the clarity of his vision on stage.

There is a slight possibility that Vianinha may have taken into consideration his analysis of the problems in *Cristal*'s staging as he wrote his next play, since *Cristal* was put on in 1970 and *Corpo a corpo* in 1971. In any case, the later work demonstrates a theatrically more felicitous rendition of many of the same themes. Whereas *Cristal* enters into dialogue more obliquely with theatrical trends of its time—its realism is more directly positioned against the climate of enclosure and alienation of the political moment, per se—*Corpo a corpo* was written expressly as a praxis in clarification of Vianinha's theoretical assessment of the conventions of contestatory theater in the early 1970s.

The title of the preface to the published play, "O meu corpo a corpo," alludes to the confrontation he invites between theatrical ideas. He begins by describing the theater of aggression:

Quem vê o teatro de hoje, feito à bofetada, aos urros, desgrenhado, desdenhando a platéia, julgando o público, desafiando o espectador com repelões, invectivas, meneios e nudez e sensualidade; quem vê êsses espetáculos retorcidos, intransigentes, escarnededores, niilistas, elitistas; quem vê este teatro e passa ao largo e trata-o como modismo passageiro, quem não se abala, se inquieta, se amendronta com este teatro—não sabe o que está perdendo como conhecimento bruto de sua época, de sua realidade.

[Whoever sees the theater of today, put together with slaps, howls, disgruntled, disdaining the audience, passing judgment on the public, challenging the spectator with shoving, invective, jiggling and nudity and sensuality; whoever sees these twisted, intransigent, contemptuous, nihilistic, elitist shows; whoever sees this theater and gives it a wide berth and treats it as a passing fad, who is not jolted, disquieted, frightened by this theater— does not know what he is missing as brute knowledge of his time, of his reality.] (29)

After this litany countering the abrasive intentions and communicative transactions of the theater of aggression, Vianinha turns around to use the same rhetorical devices to underscore the symptomatic nature of these conventions:

Quem não vê neste teatro, principalmente a revolta funda e humana, quem não vê neste teatro a profunda solidariedade humana—perdeu a perspectiva de que as coisas não acontecem como nós queremos—principalmente nos momentos em que a história dá nós para prosseguir nos seus trilhos inúteis mas os únicos conhecidos socialmente.

[Whoever does not see in this theater especially the deep and human revolt, whoever does not see in this theater the deep human solidarity—has lost sight of the fact that things do not happen as we wish—especially at moments when history ties knots in order to proceed along its useless tracks that are nonetheless the only ones socially known.] (29)

Vianinha's refutation doesn't deny the frustration at the base of aggressive techniques, as he says above, "things did not happen as we had wished." His qualified admiration for the aggressive mode rests on his basic feelings of solidarity with its practitioners: he knows that these are serious, committed theater people, but he questions their tactics. To his mind, this aesthetic (which he calls an abstraction) amounts to an abdication of social responsibility, presenting theater as a "happening" or refuge from life.

He elaborates on this, poking fun at the image he knows he has gained as being a political anachronism:

Não aceito, neste tipo de teatro, a sua sofreguidão pequeno bur-
guesa (a palavra pequeno burguês está fora de moda, mas fica
ela mesmo), a sua visão deformada do teatro—não mais como
um componente de nossa vida espiritual mais como um mundo
separado, livre, aberto; não mas um meio de fazer viver, mas um
"habitat," um lugar, não de trabalho, mas de vida.

[I do not accept, in this type of theater, its petit bourgeois impa-
tience (the term petit bourgeois is out of fashion, but I've said
it), its vision of the theater—no longer as a component of our
spiritual life, but as a separate world, free, open; not as a means
of bringing to life, but a "habitat," a place, not of work, but of
life.] (29)

Although he states that this theater, this idea of theater as a
countercultural habitat, does not interest him as an author, he admits
being attracted by its insistence in articulating the reality it perceives
and in provoking audience response:

Mas não posso deixar de tentar incorporar ao meu teatro esta
sêde de riqueza, de criatividade humana que êste outro teatro
reivindica fortemente—o lugar da capacidade criadora do
homem! Interessa-me muito neste outro teatro a imperiosa necessidade de resposta que ele impõe.

[But I cannot refrain from trying to incorporate into my theater
this thirst for richness, for human creativity that this other theater so loudly demands—the place for the creative capacity of
man! I am very interested in the imperious need for answers that
this other theater imposes.] (29)

Corpo a corpo is his response to the abstraction he describes,
a frontally direct and concrete dramatization of the frustrations and
anxieties that inform the aesthetic of aggression. He analyzes Vivaqua's conflict in that vein, contending that his character's anxiety and
hostile behavior result from that fact that the only weapons that he
has to impose himself on life are those of a game he detests.

As a dramatic character, Vivaqua demonstrates an interiority
conventional to illusionistic theater that Vianinha takes particular care
to contextualize as a desperate sense of self-exile. For Vianinha, this

treatment put Vivaqua and *Corpo a corpo* into the very traditions of Brazilian theater he values:

> Vivaqua, porém não está no teatro de "vanguarda" onde as coisas só existem nos seus limites abstratos—ele está no teatro brasileiro—que longamente tem perseguido a percepção dessas mediações, os claros escuros da realidade—e nesse campo, Vivaqua decide, muda de opinião, decide de novo, redecide, revoluteia, pensa, pensa, pensa.

> [Vivaqua, however, is not part of the "vanguard" theater where things exist only at their limits—he is in Brazilian theater— which has long pursued the perception of these midterms, the chiaroscuros of reality—and in this field, Vivaqua decides, changes his mind, decides once again, redecides, revolves, thinks, thinks, thinks.] (30)

Vianinha emphasizes that *Corpo a corpo* is not any kind of important experiment in Brazilian theater. To the contrary, it is a restatement of past traditions of social theater that take into consideration its precarious fight for survival in the present. In a sense, Vivaqua's crisis of survival-co-optation-possible rebirth forms a holding pattern that is referential to, if not fully metaphoric of, Brazilian theater at the moment. This connection can be surmised by the affirmation with which Vianinha ends his article:

> As novas formas [of theater] têm que surgir, não de nossas fugas, de nossos sentimentos de culpa, de nossa urgência, de nossos desapontamentos com o povo—têm que surgir de nossa necessidade de sobreviver e, portanto, de transformar as coordenadas que nos atrelam historicamente ao subdesenvolvimento, à pobreza, à miséria. Têm que surgir de nossa luta, não de nossa demissão ou abstenção.

> [The new forms (of theater) must emerge, not from our flight, from our feelings of guilt, from our urgency, from our disappointments with the people—it must emerge from our need to survive and, therefore, of transforming the coordinates that historically tie us to underdevelopment, to poverty, to misery. They must emerge from our struggle, not from our resignation or abstention.] (30)

How well does this work? Vivaqua's scream of despair is an attempt to articulate motives behind the theater of aggression in a form that Vianinha felt would be more theatrically productive, that would question cultural values directly in their own context without abstraction. While we see that this is also part of his intention in *Cristal,* unlike Cristal it is difficult for the audience to establish any "positive" overidentification with Vivaqua as a hero.

Vivaqua is the only character on stage. Paradoxically, the use of the monologue form serves to distance the audience from Vivaqua's crisis. There is no other explicit presence with whom he can interact, to whom he can justify himself or by whom he can be corroborated. In short, the actor-character has no way of distracting the audience from forming a clear vision of him. In his lashing out at the world, Vivaqua is often beyond the point of trying to justify himself. Although he does give sporadic explanations of his behavior, these explanations come across as manipulative acts. Almost like balloons of dialogue, they hang in the air—stuck above his head as he tries to explain himself to himself, or hung in the communicative space between himself and others. Assuming a certain quality of physical presence (the balloon effect), these statements constitute a kind of inverse deixis: all the semantic indicators of person and place point to the lack of real connection in dialogue, while at the same time they work very well to place Vivaqua in his social and historical context. (How this functions can be seen in the examples of dialogue given in the next segment of this analysis.)

However, Vivaqua is not totally alone in the scenic space. A series of disembodied voices provides further distancing, giving a critical contrast to Vivaqua's interpretation or representation of himself. This is structured by the absence-"presence" of other characters as well as by the modes of communication that Vivaqua chooses.

There are two offstage presences: Suely (his fiancée) and his neighbors. The play starts with an argument between Vivaqua and Suely. She is on the other side of the door (offstage), and Vivaqua refuses to let her in. He yells through the door: "Você sufoca, Suely! Todos sufocam; não quero ver gente e as suas gravatas, . . . Me diz como é que podem fazer isso com o Aureliano? Querem botar ele na rua assim vai, vai, vai" [You suffocate, Suely! Everybody suffocates; I don't want to see people and their ties. . . . Tell me, how can they do this to Aureliano? They want to kick him out into the street just like that? Out, out, out] (31). In the beginning, Suely is the symbol of his revolt and recipient of his moral indignation regarding the agency's perfidious treatment of his former mentor. At the end she signifies his capitulation and co-optation.

Vivaqua's nausea in this first dialogue is real, and the audience is thereby led to sympathize with him. Toward the middle of the play, though, we too tend to lose patience with him and empathize with the exasperated cries of his neighbors ("Cala a bôca!—Não dá prá ficar desesperado ao meio dia, ô meu?" [Shut up!—Can't you try and freak out at noon, fellow?] [35]). These outside voices are a nice theatrical touch by which we know that Vivaqua is creating a tremendous racket without this racket having to be reproduced, decibel by decibel, onstage. This also can be seen as Vianinha's solution and modification of the direct and earsplitting anger of the theater of aggression.

The telephone becomes a fetishized object referring to Vivaqua's alienation, and is accordingly the prop that most consistently draws attention. Sometimes he hangs up on people, sometimes they on him. Often he stares at it or refuses to answer. Then he grabs it again to give vent to his frustrations. We learn a lot about Vivaqua's faulty commitments from these "conversations." His estrangement from reality is accentuated by the repeated gesture of snorting cocaine that punctuates the series of phone calls.

His objectifying treatment of women is constantly registered, although it is somewhat softened by his real anguish to reestablish some affective link. He calls a former lover, begging *her* come over *there* and sleep with *him* (the strong deictic function of these calls). But the affective distance is too great and, when she refuses in no uncertain terms, Vivaqua tries to wheedle sympathy from her, promoting himself as a victim of a society that objectifies all human relationships.

Vivaqua's feeling of victimization extends to his relationships in the sphere of political activity as well. We learn that Vivaqua has had some sort of connection with leftist activism by another call. This one is to Lourenço, who we are given to understand is a movie director involved in community or working-class organization. Infuriated that Lourenço would question his commitment (he never goes to meetings), Vivaqua accuses Lourenço of self-righteousness and political impotence:

> Parece missa, não é missa? tudo igual, igual, igual . . . missa pelo menos tem órgão, tem mulher, nas reuniões de vocês nem cinzeiro tem . . . espera, Lourenço, vai desligar por que? Não pode ouvir crítica construtiva? O proletariado também tem suas

vaidades? Quer que eu diga que está ótimo? . . . O que é que a gente deve fazer, isso que é bom, vocês não dizem! Eu sei que você não é Deus, porra; não estou cobrando de você o destino da pátria.

[Sounds like a mass, doesn't it? all the same, same, same . . . at least the mass has an organ, and women, your meetings don't even have ashtrays . . . wait a minute, Lourenço, why are you hanging up? Can't take constructive criticism? The proletariat got some vanity of its own? You want me to say that's fine? . . . What we ought to do, which is what you ought to say, you never say! Shit! I know you're not God; I'm not asking you to answer for the future of the country.] (35)

On one level, Vivaqua is trying to find assurance that political commitment has meaning. However, his own impotence and social abdication is reflected in the advice he gives Lourenço: "Se irritou porque? Que defensiva é essa? Toma calmante, Lourenço; pó, toma pó, estou numa onda fortíssima, estou na Apolo 30!" [Why are you so bent out of shape? How come you're so defensive? Take a tranquilizer, Lourenço; coke, snort some coke, I'm high as a kite, I'm on Apollo 30!] (35).

Vivaqua's complete regression into infantility is theatricalized by a series of mildly obscene and childish prank calls, set off by an incomplete attempt to call his mother. Picking names out of the phone book, he invents questions suggested by the names (example: Pereira, to whom he asks the price of a dozen pears).

The fact that throughout these various types of calls we hear only Vivaqua's insistent voice and less-than-credible rephrasing of what is being said to him creates an effective theatrical tension. Twice he has refused to accept a call from the United States, implying that it would define his future one way or the other. When he finally takes the call, happily accepting the job offer even though he knows that it means Aureliano's dismissal, his obsequious tone and the consequences of his capitulation are emphasized by the auditory absence of the authoritative voice at the other end.

While other calls show Vivaqua's lack of decision and abdication, this one clearly marks the direction his life will take, affirmed by his last two calls in which he receives Suely's forgiveness and lies to Aureliano about his new position. That there will be no turning back in this realignment of his life is epitomized in two staccato interchanges with the national airlines: when he first realizes that his mother is probably dying, he calls to book the next flight to Aracajú; after he accepts the job offer, he cancels his flight, sending a pathetically self-delusory telegram saying he will come for a long visit when he returns from the States.

As a scenic object of approximation to and distance from a world outside of his subjectivity, the telephone operates on the plane of Vivaqua's verbalized and directed despair. Two other more subtle instances involving modes of communication indicate his deeper shame and the superficiality of his interchange with a captive audience (phone). Calling his uncle to find his mother, he is asked why he has not answered his mother's letter or his uncle's telegram telling him of his mother's impending operation. Rummaging through the mess in his room, Vivaqua finally finds both the letter and the telegram, which he "reads" to himself (and to the audience), repeating key phrases. Obviously, refusal to read—much less answer—mail is a means of guarding control of communication. The affective family ties are negated first by his previous denial of their existence and secondly by his incapacity to respond accordingly.

It is significant that the only truly two-way communication in the play—both in terms of his listening and the audience's hearing another voice responding directly to Vivaqua—comes through the mediation of the amateur ham radio. Although the radio is second to the telephone in its placement as a scenic object, thematically it reaches an equal importance by the contrast it provides. The anonymity of this mediation serves two important functions. First, it points to the displacement of Vivaqua's alienation in that the only real connection he achieves is with an anonymous correspondent. Secondly, it functions to synthesize and "syntonize" Vianinha's belief in continental solidarity.

Still early in the play, Vivaqua is desperate to express his revolt. Frantically trying to make contact, he tries Portuguese and English: "alô, alô, quero dizer coisas inteligentes . . . hello, hello everybody. I have a statement to do. . . , a very, very, very important statement" (34). Receiving no answer for the moment, he rushes to the window to shout his message: "Vou embora! Porque não sou cúmplice. Vocês pagam bem a cumplicidade, mas aqui, ó! . . . Dez por cento do que vocês ganham é prá publicidade deste mundo tal como é, tal e qual talll e qualll!" [I'm leaving! Because I'm not an accomplice. You pay well for complicity, but fuck you! . . . Ten percent of what you earn goes toward publicity for this world such as it is, such assss it izzzzz!] (34).

But of course he is an accomplice, both to the maintenance of the status quo in his own country and to underdevelopment in Latin America, according to the author's view. Vivaqua finally makes calls with a retired Bolivian who enjoys his free time making radio contact in the late-night hours. Speaking in Spanish, the Bolivian expresses alarm at Vivaqua's tone, obviously worried about his seemingly suicidal state of mind. Learning that the Bolivian lives alone, his three children gone from the house, Vivaqua persists in knowing why they have left. The Bolivian attributes their restlessness to youthful anxiety, to the fact that La Paz holds no attractions for them, but principally to the fact that they are ashamed to be known collectively as Indians, of mixed race, chewers of coca leaves, quaint folkloric figures, and so on. Affected by his own revelation, the Bolivian asks to talk about more pleasant things, but Vivaqua has already tuned out.

Vivaqua does not use the radio again. But Vianinha's point is made: Vivaqua loses human and political contact with Latin American reality. Or more explicitly, he sells his birthright, as we see in Vivaqua's last words. Dancing around as he tears into little pieces a message for a friend to send him his salary to his mother's house, and letting the pieces float out the window, he sings a snatch of song:

> Take back your samba, and your rumba, and your conga ai ai ai
> . . . . .
> South America, take it away. (43)

While these theatrical techniques (phone, radio, voices) structure the play, mediating Vivaqua's discontent and giving form to Vianinha's counterstatement on aggression, the core theme that opens up to an imagistic analysis of political subtlety is Vianinha's treatment of the world of publicity. This happens on three levels: one that refers to the co-optation of artists and intellectuals; a second that stresses the continuity between democracy and dictatorship in a criticism of capitalism; and a third that indicates publicity as a metaphor for theatrical practice.

The majority of Vianinha's plays after *O Bicho* (which was coauthored) treat publicity or the media in some significant way. In part, this reflects an astute recognition of the diffused yet omnipresent authoritarian voice. As discussed in the historical section of this chapter, the media—mainly television and the press—presented and confirmed the legitimizing images of the regime ("the system," "O Brasil Grande"). Paradoxically, while it also promoted the national myth, or mystification, advertising also undercut it with images that exacerbated a sense of national inferiority in its attention to foreign products, lifestyles, and advertising techniques. Vivaqua is well aware of this, as we see in his paean to Aureliano's integrity: "transformou filme de publicidade nesse país . . . foi o primeiro que falou que publicidade estrangeira tem que ser controlada" [he transformed commercials in this country . . . he was the first person who said that foreign commercials have to be controlled] (32).

Vivaqua's initial desire to enter advertising as a way of gaining technical knowledge and making inroads in mass communications with the objective of reaching and molding public perceptions toward social change constitutes more than a dramatic device on Vianinha's part. In reality, many liberal or leftist intellectuals and artists went into publicity with this in mind. However, the interest in publicity does not reflect just an ideological intent. It also combined with the economic realities of the job market. Unable to support themselves solely by their writing and art or film work, many people chose publicity or jobs as functionaries in government agencies of the arts as a way of retaining some active practice in their fields while earning a living. This pattern became even more common after 1968 as a result of the censorship that affected many artists' livelihoods.

Instances of public relations used as a dramatic framework to investigate the co-optation of ideals abound in contemporary drama, but Vianinha takes particular pains to specify this theme in the context of underdevelopment. As Vivaqua comments at the beginning of the play:

> propaganda é isso [meaning advertising and "propaganda"], uma corrida desesperada de todo mundo prá vender cenários e humilhação . . . sou pago prá não tomar conhecimento do povo, jogar luxo nos olhos . . . sou pago prá provar prá ele que uma geladeira é um ser superior que uma loja é um templo onde se dá a multiplicação dos liquidificadores.

> [that's what advertising is (meaning advertising and "propaganda"), everybody's desperate race to sell scenery and humiliation . . . I'm paid to ignore the people; to throw luxury in their faces . . . I'm paid to prove to them that a refrigerator is a superior being, that a store is a temple where the multiplying of the blenders takes place.] (32)

Significantly, Vivaqua does not mention items of great consumer prestige (fancy cars, yachts, or even homes) but refers to as luxuries *(luxo)* the basic products of domestic comfort almost uniformly taken for granted in more developed economies.

Vivaqua is conscious that he has reneged on his initial ideals, sucked into spending his energies on things of little importance to him: "estou correndo feito um desesperado prá conseguir fazer filme de cebola . . . e faz três anos . . . eu tinha gana de lutar . . . regulamentar esses estrangeiros" [I'm running around like a maniac trying to make an onion movie . . . and three years ago . . . I really wanted to fight . . . regulate those foreigners] (36). This consciousness, nonetheless, is transformed into a fear of being proletarianized himself:

> não quero ser povo . . . eles não têm telefone, só têm televisão prá ver, andam nas ruas, ruas estão muito cheias . . . quero minhas regalias . . . ar refrigerado . . . ar refrigerado é decisivo . . . não quero ser povo, não . . . já não tenho idade para sacrifícios e esperanças.

> [I don't want to be "people" . . . they don't have telephones, only have television to look at, they walk the streets, the streets are very crowded . . . I want my perks . . . air conditioning . . . air conditioning is crucial . . . I don't want to be part of the people . . . I'm too old for sacrifice and hope.] (36)

He is funny, pathetic, but most of all childish in his self-affirmation, differentiating himself from the *povo* who can only receive images (the television), while he at least still maintains the prerogative to express himself (the telephone). Even so, self-expression does not constitute identity for him. Incapable of anchoring any sense of self-worth in actions to which he would give value, Vivaqua feels legitimate only when he receives approbation from those he purportedly despises. His own persona (image) is validated by the phone call from his boss about the Fulbright position. Shouting out the window, obviously to the entire of Brazil, he ironically, but desperately proclaims: "Vou abandonar vocês, acabo de ser nomeado pessoa por eles, acabo de ser proclamado ser humano . . . vou embora, vou largar vocês, não vou triste, não!" [I'm leaving you, they've just named me a person, I've just been proclaimed a human being . . . I'm going away, I'm leaving you and I'm not unhappy about it, no!] (41).

Vivaqua has bought (and paid dearly for) the whole package,

turning himself precisely into the image he had previously wished to fight in advertising. Thus we doubt his integrity when, right after, he swears that he will turn that image around to Brazil's benefit: "Mas juro que levo essa nossa gana de aparecer no mundo . . . vocês não podem me xingar, é publicidade, é a única coisa que eu sei fazer" [But I swear that I'm going with a huge desire to get out in the world . . . you can't curse me, it's advertising, it's the only thing I know how to do]. That, he protests, will be his way of fighting: he will do his part to change Brazil's image in the developed world. As for those remaining in the country, he has ironic counsel: "não reclama de mim não . . . aprendam primeiro a ser povo, a acreditar na gente cegamente, a apostar na gente . . . vocês ainda acreditam no jogo de cada um prá si" [Don't complain about me . . . first learn to be the people, to trust ourselves blindly (here, Vivaqua switches to an inclusive pronoun), to back ourselves up . . . you still believe in that every-man-for-himself game] (41).

This latter statement is obviously Vianinha's message, where the author takes advantage of his character's momentary euphoria both to make a statement and imply the difficulty, if not impossibility, of carrying out the battle on the terrain that Vivaqua chooses. Vianinha leaves no doubt that the social responsibility that Vivaqua evades is that of finding a significant, as opposed to illusory, link with the *povo* in a concentrated fight to change the situation. Talking to himself in the mirror (another prop symbolic of his alienation), Vivaqua experiences a moment of identity with the times: "puxa, que tarefa arranjaram prá tua geração, garoto . . . se juntar com o povo que eu não vejo, que eu não entendo, que tem um ritmo tão ralentado . . . e a minha geração podia decidir, depende dela" [gee, that's some job they found for your generation, kid . . . to align myself with the people that I don't see, that I don't understand, that have such a (diluted) rhythm . . . and my generation could decide, it depends on us]. Then he sadly adds the most insightful and least self-justificatory words that signal his capitulation: "mas a minha cabeça entende, mas a minha alma é outra, é outra rotação" [but my head understands, but my soul is different, at another speed] (39).

Other than this dialogue, there are few specific references to the authoritarian situation that we can assume is the dramatic time of the play. Also, this reference could just as easily apply to the political strategies and tactics of the Left during the late 1950s and early 1960s as to the enclosure of the military regime. Another statement—"o povo cada mais vez de cabeça baixa . . . sem acreditar nele mesmo . . .

só acreditando em geladeria . . . é uma selva; publicidade não tem censura" [the people more and more downcast . . . not believing in themselves . . . believing only in refrigerators . . . it's a jungle; there's no censorship in advertising] (32)—signifies the free-market license of advertising as much as it alludes to censorship after 1964. In other words, this statement poses a veiled contrast between the "liberty" of publicity and the "repression" of artistic expression then extant in Brazil.

This lack of specific reference is, I believe, not simply a ploy on Vianinha's part to pass the play by the censor. It opens up the dramatic focus of the play from a possibly narrow portrait of one person's incapacity to rise to the historical moment. In his treatment of publicity, Vianinha is careful to balance the specificity of Vivaqua's co-optation with a larger picture of how he, Vianinha, feels it functions in capitalist societies.

Although I have noted earlier that Vianinha contextualizes publicity by choosing images (refrigerators and the like) referential to underdevelopment, his statements on the dynamic of advertising give a scope of continuity and internationality. In an important sense, in Vianinha's analysis, there is little difference between authoritarian rule and democracy, since the negative aspects of democratic ideology justify the exploitative elements of consumer-oriented capitalism. He refers to dreams of upward mobility and the validation of self by objects. We hear Vivaqua exclaim: "que propaganda, pelo amor de Deus? propaganda prás pessoas serem o que não podem ser? O que não têm jeito de ser e ficarem se roendo, os olhos amarelos de inveja? Passar a vida vendo se o vizinho tem geladeira de quantos pés?" [What advertising, for Christ's sake? propaganda for people to be what they can't be? What they aren't cut out for, eating themselves up, their eyes green with envy? To spend their lives checking to see what kind of refrigerator the neighbors have?] (31–32).

Advertising stimulates, at the same time and contradictorily, an elevating and a leveling effect. This movement is exemplified in a comment Vivaqua makes toward the end of the play:

> Publicidade tem lances bonitos! Aquele achado que plá eriça as pessoas por dentro, bem achado—plá! a poesia do dia a dia é a publicidade, pomba! É! É todo mundo, faz a gente virar todo mundo . . . pomba, meu Deus, a luta de séculos pro homem conseguir ter hábitos parecidos.

[There's some beautiful stuff in publicity! The discovery that-bingo-turns people on inside, well thought-bingo! Yeah! It's everybody, it turns you into everybody . . . Jesus, God, man's century's old struggle to have the very same habits (as everyone else).] (39)

In his short but amply illustrated treatise on advertising, *Ways of Seeing,* John Berger discusses how it interfaces with democratic ideology in an analysis with which Vianinha would heartily agree.[14] In his closing chapter Berger summarizes how publicity functions: "Publicity is the culture of the consumer society. It propagates through images that society's belief in itself" (139). Or, in Vianinha's words, publicity is "a poesia do dia a dia" [the poetry of everyday life].

Berger holds that "the purpose of publicity is to make the spectator marginally dissatisfied with his present way of life. Not with the way of life of society, but with his own within it. It suggests that if he buy what it is offering, his life will become better. It offers him an improved alternative to what he is" (142). The degree of dissatisfaction is important, since it should lead to anxiety and not to revolt: "All publicity works upon anxiety. The sum of everything is money, to get money is to overcome anxiety" (143).

Contending that the ideal of individual fulfillment within democracy as presently instituted is inevitably contradictory, Berger reasons:

The pursuit of happiness has been acknowledged as a universal right. Yet the existing social conditions make the individual feel powerless. He lives in the contradiction between what he is and what he would like to be. Either he then becomes fully conscious of the contradiction and its causes, and so joins the political struggle for a full democracy which entails, amongst other things, the overthrow of capitalism; or compounded with his sense of powerlessness, dissolves into recurrent daydreams. (148)

This merits extensive quoting for the distinction it posits between a real ("full") democracy and the illusion of democratic participation. The distinction is crucial to Vianinha's theory of democracy.

Furthermore, publicity turns the basic tenant of democratic participation inside out, proffering passive selection as a substitute for active election. As Berger notes: "Publicity turns consumption into a substitute for democracy. The choice of what one eats (or wears or drives) takes the place of significant political choice. Publicity helps to mask and compensate for all that is undemocratic within society. And it also masks what is happening in the rest of the world" (149). He also remarks on its power of co-optation of the imagistic attraction of historical struggles that would supplant capitalism, citing ads that "translate even revolution into its own terms" (151).[15]

In effect, Berger believes that publicity obliterates historical perspective, as we see in the following quote: "Publicity is essentially *eventless*. It extends just as far as nothing else is happening. For publicity all real events are exceptional and happen only to strangers" (153). This is precisely the stultifying effect that Vivaqua frequently denounces. But, as Vianinha has said, Vivaqua is caught up in the game he also manipulates and invests with authority. As an objectified and reified character, Vivaqua is emblematic of the limbo that Berger's describes: "Publicity, situated in a future continually deferred, excludes the present and so eliminates all becoming, all development. Experience is impossible within it" (153).

Berger closes his study with a statement that not only echoes Vianinha's analysis but also encapsulates Vivaqua's illusion and predicament:

> Capitalism survives by forcing the majority, whom it exploits, to define their own interests as narrowly as possible. This was once achieved by extensive deprivation. Today in the developed countries it is being achieved by imposing a false standard of what is and what is not desirable. (154)

In *Corpo a corpo*, we see that Vivaqua and Brazil are caught up in the midterm of Berger's assertion. As pointed out in the historical section of this study, "savage capitalism" is a term that has been used to describe the deprivation and authoritarian measures that accompanied the rapid economic development of the "Brazilian miracle." Through Vivaqua's torment Vianinha has wished to show the images of the underside of this development: the frenetic shock of a culture still molded by deprivation but bombarded by standards clearly inaccessible to the majority; a society in which creativity is brutal and co-optation is a particularly savage process.

Vianinha's dramatic treatment of co-optation and ideology in conjunction with the theatrical techniques he employs works to postulate publicity as a metaphor for the pitfalls of theatrical practice. It is interesting, in this respect, that in Portuguese specific acts of publicity (ads, television spots, etc.) are most often referred to as *propaganda,* and the same word is used for overt ideological pronouncements. (The field of publicity or an advertising project is called *publicidade.*)

George Szanto, in his study *Theater and Propaganda,* links theater and propaganda through the acts of communication particular to theater. Positing that "propaganda is a specific form of activated ideology," he argues that because of the communicative pattern of theater (which he describes as the line of ideology → propaganda → theater piece → production → audience) and its way of "signing" reality, theater will inevitably have characteristics of propaganda. He further classifies theater into two functional modes: integration propaganda and agitation propaganda. Integration propaganda "attempts to render its audience and society passive" or to get them to accept a problematic situation as "the way it is." Agitation propaganda "attempts to rouse its audience and society to active ends."[16]

While integrational theater does not always imply acceptance of the status quo, its predominant message—whether interpolated by theatrical form, dramatic content, or some mixture of the two—serves to nullify whatever contestatory concepts or images it might wish to transmit. Vianinha considers the theater of aggression in a similar light. According to him, as a result of its abstraction from specific social context, the agitational purpose behind its theatrical protest converts into propaganda for one of the most cherished symbols of bourgeois ideology: the artist as alienated individual. In addition, the nullification of agitational intent that occurs in the theatrical act itself tends to suffer a further modification in audience reception. For its images of protest are highly co-optable, and what was originally structured as gestures of rage are easily transformed into self-indulgent voluntarism or subsumed in the expressive energy of *curtição.*

Corpo a corpo is a mostly successful tour de force that conceptualizes these notions by presenting a character who dramatically incorporates the agitational-integrational contradictions of the vanguard.[17] In metatheatrical terms, it is a confrontation of the *estética da palavra* with gestural, nonverbal theater. Revolt, guilt, and capitulation are made intelligible through objects of verbal mediation (phone, radio, letters) whose use structures the discursive meaning of the play.

Even though these are his intentions, Vianinha treads a thin line in his characterization of Vivaqua, and his insistence on the power of the word is problematic. For the rhetoric of revolution, as well as the gestural rhetoric of revolt, is also highly co-optable, which is one of the points Vianinha makes in the play. (Even the military regime promoted itself as revolutionary.) In this respect, although the monologue form works well in establishing distance to see Vivaqua's particular personal crisis in relation to his social and cultural context, it is not quite sufficient to give reliable testimony that would lead to a more profound analysis of that context. Since Vivaqua's lucid statements about Brazilian reality are made so strongly in the context of his battle with his own co-optation, they effectively leave that reality uncontested and therefore on a unidimensional dramatic plane. In other words, the political and historical perspective that Vianinha wishes to transmit runs the risk of being too easily subsumed in the contemplation of Vivaqua's predicament. There is always an element of "co-optability" when a playwright uses conventions tightly intertwined with a given mode of seeing, and Vianinha has not yet learned to use the conventions of illusionistic theater in a way adequate to his critical purposes.

Vianinha started writing about the necessity of incorporating history as a category of representation in theater within the same time span of *Corpo a corpo*'s genesis and production (1970–71). Whether these postulations guided him in writing the play is hard to tell, as he had not yet found the conventions commensurate to his theory. In any case, the lessons learned with *Cristal*, the successes of *Corpo a corpo* and his continued experience with the *revista* comedy *(Alegro Desbum)* of this period surely jelled to help him implement this theory into practice with his last play, *Rasga coração*.

Rasga coração

Portrayal of the Anonymous Revolutionary Hero

If Vianinha's work to this point may be seen as a search for a theater where objective social relations are not subsumed in the dramatic treatment of personal lives, where drama of the characters illuminates social conditions, then his work really culminates in *Rasga coração* (Rend Your Heart).[1] The first act of this play was completed in 1973, by which time he already knew he was seriously ill. The second act, understandably not as polished as the first, was written with full consciousness of his terminal illness and completed only a few months before his death. It is a highly autobiographical work, concerned with generational conflict, political activism, and historical fact.[2]

In the preface to *Rasga coração*, Vianinha states his two primary intentions in writing the play and mentions what he considers the salient thematic and structural elements that convey those reasons. The first reason is to pay homage "ao lutador anônimo político, aos campeões das lutas populares; preito de gratidão à 'Velha Guarda,' à geração que me antecedeu, que foi a que politizou em profundidade a consciência do país" [to the anonymous political fighter, to the champions of the popular struggles; a token of gratitude to the "Old Guard," to the generation that preceded me, the one that deeply politicized the country's consciousness] (13).

The dramatic character who embodies this anonymous political perseverance is Custódio Manhães Jr. This adept custodian of the revolutionary tradition is generally referred to as Manguari Pistolão, in deference to his straight gunning against social injustice, as well as to his political influence, which, although limited to party connections, is not inconsiderable.

Manguari's forty years of political activism span the revolutionary pyrotechnics of the Communist insurrection and the Vargas years, the years of conciliations to nationalist interests (from Kubitschek until 1964), and the quiet drudge work of revindication of working conditions within the union organization and editorial writing that characterized much of the PCB's work from 1964 until 1974. The dramatic time of the play is 1972, the height of the repression of the Médici government, and Manguari is a minor functionary whose aspirations of advancement are nullified by his insistence on writing, whenever he can, letters and editorials calling for social justice.

The play, thus, presents a specific chronological reference. Its dramatic structure, however, is constituted by flashbacks into this historical span, creating a collage of historical moments as lived by the characters, even though, as Vianinha stated in an interview in 1973, he wanted to create a collage that focused on the explication of one person, one dramatic unit: "essa colagem pertence a um único movimento dramático, a um único personagem. . . . Quer dizer, esse processo de colagem ser a história do próprio personagem" [this collage belongs to a single dramatic movement, to a single character. . . . That is, this collage process is the story of the character himself] (171).

Obviously, the historical facts, although selected by this criterion, are filtered through Manguari's memory and must be bound by the dramatic parameters of the character. If this were the only element that dictated dramatic structure, it would indicate a closed reading of history. However, what opens the field of perception—both the characters' and the audience's—is the interweaving of the conflict between Manguari and his son, Luca, into the dramatic structure. This conflict provokes Manguari's flashbacks and provides the often antagonistic sounding-board for Manguari's painful process of autocriticism.

The scene of the quotidian conflict is set by a series of small interchanges between Manguari and Luca: Luca consumes only mac-robiotic foods, whereas Manguari relates food value to exploitation of food workers; Manguari blames personal alienation on capitalism and on the socialist countries' struggle to survive, but Luca pins it on the existential, the "fear of living." These conflicts of values center on the problematic stress between environmentalist concerns and un- or underemployment that, as Manguari sees it, is concomitant with un-derdevelopment and capitalism. The dramatic tension arises from the passion with which the father and son defend their positions, as well as from the pathos of their desire to be understood and to understand the other's position.

The dramatic action begins with Luca's dismissal from school because of his long hair. Luca decides to fight, and Manguari enlists as adviser and organizer of an editorial campaign to reclaim individual rights. It should be noted here that, although this issue of long hair may seem slight provocation for dramatic conflict from a contempo-rary point of view, or even if placed in a North American context of the early 1970s, it signified considerably more in the Brazil of the late 1960s and early 1970s, given the acts of repression—such as torture and "disappearances"—practiced by the military government. It is also important to note that the counterculture movement, best exem-plified by *tropicália,* did mobilize a significant portion of young peo-ple to voice protest and cannot be reduced to a dropout movement.[3]

Luca becomes increasingly ambivalent about his father's methods and accuses him of being outmoded in his political approach. Along with a group of students, Luca invades the school. After the "rebellion" is quashed, Luca drops out completely, getting into drugs and Eastern mysticism. The expelled students are offered the chance to complete their year's study in the *colégio* of a group of sympathetic friars. Manguari is ecstatic because Luca would have a chance to finish his *vestibular* (i.e., exams; Luca had planned to become a doctor in the interior) and because of the solidarity of the friars. When Luca refuses to return to school, maintaining that the educational system had nothing to teach him, Manguari expels him from the apartment. They part on good terms, however, with the mutual respect for each other's principled stand. The final curtain falls as Manguari calls com-rades to remind them of a meeting to discuss pension payments to urban sanitation workers. Thus, the play ends as Manguari returns to the quotidian business of his convictions.

The generational conflict grounds the second of the play-wright's intentions: "Em segundo lugar, quis fazer uma peça que estudasse as diferenças que existem entre o 'novo' e o 'revolucionário.' O 'revolucionário' nem sempre é novo absolutamente e o novo nem sempre é revolucionário" [In the second place, I wanted to make a play that would study the differences that exist between the "new" and the "revolutionary." The "revolutionary" isn't always absolutely new, and the new isn't always revolutionary]. Further along, Vianinha offers his own assessment of this question: "No final, no frigir dos ovos, o revolucionário para mim, o novo, é o velho Manguari. Revolucionário seria a luta contra o cotidiano, feita de cotidiano. A descoberta do mecanismo mais secreto do cotidiano, que só sua vivência pode revelar" [In the end, when all's said and done, what is revolutionary for me, what's new, is old Manguari. The struggle against everyday life, made of everyday life, is revolutionary. The discovery of the most secret mechanism of everyday life, which only his own lived experience can reveal] (12).

As we have seen, a primary goal of Vianinha's work has been to challenge perceptions about society and social relations in such a way that would lead people to question the precepts of social practice. So it is fitting that the functional definition of "revolutionary" in *Rasga coração* evolves through clashes of modalities of perception. The anguish of Manguari's autocriticism revolves around understanding what his son's values mean to Manguari's own commitment, which has deprived Manguari of much enrichment, affective as well as monetary, of his personal life.

The median ground of this self-questioning, and the play's central message, is transmitted by a school colleague of Luca's, Camargo Moço. Camargo Moço represents a synthesis of Manguari's experience and doubts with Luca's experiential search. It is Camargo Moço who validates Manguari as the anonymous hero, although Luca early on also characterizes his father as a "herói popular anônimo."

In the scene that provokes Luca's expulsion from the house, Luca sums up his father's life as wasted, naming symptoms of his father alienation:

> Você é que pensa que é revolucionário, . . . mas você é um funcionário público, você trabalha para o governo! . . . Anda de ônibus 415 com dinheiro trocado para não brigar com o cobrador e que de noite fica na janela, vendo uma senhora de peruca tirar a roupa e ficar nua!

[You think you're a revolutionary, . . . but what you are is a public servant, you work for the government! . . . You take the 415 bus always with correct change so the bus driver won't hassle you and at night you lean out your window, watching some lady in a wig take her cloths off and get naked!]

He ends his attack by proclaiming that he is being kicked out because "meu pai tem que descarregar em alguém ele ter vivido sem ter deixado marca de sua presença" [my father has to take it out on someone that he lived a life without ever having left his mark on the world].

Camargo Moço retorts with his own summary of Manguari's contribution:

teu pai não deixou marca? Mas cada vez que começa uma assembléia num sindicato, a luz baça, teu pai está lá, cada vez que um operário, chapéu na mão, entra na Justiça do Trabalho, teu pai está lá, cada vez que, em vez de dizer países essencialmente agrícolas, dizem países subdesenvolvidos, teu pai está lá, cada vez que dizem imperialismo, em vez de países altamente industrializados, teu pai está lá, cada vez que fecham um barril de petróleo na Bahia, teu pai está lá . . . teu pai é um revolucionário, sim.

[your father didn't leave his mark? But every time a union meeting begins, and the lights go down, every time a worker, hat in hand, enters the Worker's Hall of Justice, your father is there, every time they say underdeveloped nations instead of essentially agricultural countries, your father is there, every time they say imperialism instead of highly industrialized nations, your father is there, every time they put the lid on a barrel of oil in Bahia, your father is there . . . your father is a revolutionary, yes.] (76)

Thus Camargo Moço acts as the implicit receptor within the play, the dramatic link between play and audience.[4] He integrates the essential meaning of the play's action and reinterprets it to us. Symbolic of the next generation of activists, he points out the direction of the struggle and delivers the message of hope designed to open the structures of perception, to expand the dramatic ending of the play. Earlier, when Manguari asks Camargo Moço to explain Luca to him, Luca responds:

Pra mim, o importante não é conflito de gerações, é a luta que
cada geração trava dentro de si mesma . . . vocês [Manguari's
generation] descobriram uma verdade luminosa, a luta de
classes, e pronto, pensam que ela basta para explicar tudo . . . a
tarefa nossa não é esperar que uma verdade aconteça, nossa tarefa é descobrir novas verdades, todos os dias . . . acho que vocês
perderam a arma principal: a dúvida.

[What's important to me isn't the generation gap, it's the struggle of each generation inside itself . . . you (Manguari's generation) discovered a shining truth, the class struggle, and right
away, you think it's enough to explain everything . . . our job
isn't to wait for a truth to happen, our job is to discover new
truths every day . . . I think you lost the most important weapon:
doubt.] (67)

The importance of doubt as a perceptual weapon in conscious
and patient struggle is emphasized by Manguari's immediate response
to Camargo Moço. Speaking as much to himself as to Camargo, he
wonders, "a dúvida, menino? . . . a nossa principal arma, a dúvida? . . .
(Novo silêncio) . . . nunca tinha pensado nisso . . . *(Silêncio. Manguari
imerso em si mesmo)*" [doubt, boy? . . . our most important weapon,
doubt? . . . *(More silence)* . . . I never had thought of that . . . *(Silence.
Manguari is immersed in himself)*]. The stage directions leave no
doubt as to the importance of this interchange.

The Manguari Pistolão that Camargo Moço describes, validates, and transmits to the audience has his theatrical genealogy already inscribed in the theory of "Um pouco de pessedismo não faz
mal a ninguém." Subject to the tumult of the conjunctural modifications of Brazilian socioeconomic reality, Manguari struggles to ac-
knowledge his own contradictions, continually revising and
questioning his perceptions on the underlying social reality that structures these perceptions. Constantly searching for the tactics adequate
to a strategy of nonisolationism—tactics that would be denigrated by
many on the left as being reformist—he is seen as an affirmative hero
precisely because of his nonvoluntaristic commitment to the revolutionary struggle. He is a party man, a collectivist, willing to listen to
the *pessedistas*—the voice of the middle-class liberal—and incorporate
it into his political vision.

In these respects the original irony of Vianinha's title, "Um
pouco de pessedismo não faz mal a ninguém," takes on a very human

body: Manguari suffers the contradictions, constrictions, and conciliations of his own determined stance, and not only emotionally. He has
recurrent attacks of arthritis; this somatic symbol of internal conflict
and of the very real pain (i.e., price) of his practice situates his idealism
within the structures of daily life.

In brief conclusion to this introductory discussion of the play,
we might pose several questions regarding identification with this protagonist that suggest further study about the possibilities of audience
building in socially committed professional theater. In terms of audience identification, the foremost question would be: What are the
points of commonality between this petit bourgeois functionary, this
anonymous organizer for a workers' revolution, and the conventional
hero of the middle-class Brazilian theater, a commonality that promotes identification and questioning within that audience? First of all,
it seems clear that the professional theater audience would be very
sympathetic to a social statement that allowed entry to the humanitar-
ian principles of liberalism. Manguari's sense of ethics is the quintes-
sence of bourgeois ethics: liberty, justice, opportunity, and fraternity.
In other words, what gives him his "heroic" quality—his activism,
commitment, and perseverance—also sets up a process of identification with these commonly held ideals. Manguari is a very sympathetic
protagonist whose personal predicament of family strife, loneliness,
and review of personal memories invites identification. In this sense,
Manguari fits in perfectly with the tradition of the dramatic hero—as
differentiated from the epic or tragic hero—that characterizes contemporary Western theater of the illusionist mode.

What expands this reading is the manner in which the issues
of a leftist interpretation of Brazilian history are posed by this sympathetic hero's life. History as lived by Manguari raises continual questions for the playgoing public, in a manner that history as fact and
interpretation foregrounds the politicization of the quotidian.

Historical Reference and Dramatic Characters

Although Manguari's dramatized memories center on the
Vargas period, the play's historical references demonstrate what Vianinha meant by postulating "history as a category of representation."
These references are interpolated into dramatic structure and given
perspective by theatrical techniques. My discussion here follows his-

torical chronology,[5] although the play does not always observe linear chronology in the interventions of the past into the present (the action on the plane memory does proceed almost exclusively chronologically from 1930 until 1945). The kinds of allusions to history differ: some are to historical fact, others to political history, others to ambience, or social history.

In an inclusive sweep of "historical space," historical fact begins with this century, with Manguari's father's memories of Osvaldo Cruz's sanitation campaign in 1903 to wipe out yellow fever in Rio de Janeiro. The years of the government of Francisco de Paula Rodrigues Alves (1902–6) were ones of financial growth, support for the arts, and national reform programs. However, the compulsory vaccination program, headed by Cruz, was met with strong political opposition and fierce and sometimes violent popular resistance. Manguari's father, called 666 because of his serial number as a member of Cruz's army of sanitation workers, thus sets the precedence for political and social commitment.[6]

Dramatized history begins in the 1920s, although historical fact is not specified. Rather, this period reference sets the locale and the contrast between place in memory and in actuality. We see Manguari, at about the age of ten, delighted to accompany his father to Copacabana on a sanitation job.[7] Copacabana in the 1920s was a resort area, clean and great for picnics, as Manguari remembers, in contrast to the dirty, overpopulated, violent high-rise neighborhood of the 1970s.

Although not dramatized, the political turbulence of the 1920s should be noted. The early years of the decade saw a series of rebellions that prepared the ground for the revolution of 1930. These rebellions congealed the aspirations of the ascending middle class against the rigid oligarchical system that held political power, largely through the latter's complete control—on the Brazilian side—of the most important economic factor of the period, coffee production and trade. The surge of nationalism that accompanied the move toward industrialization took cultural form in the Semana de Arte Moderna, in São Paulo in 1922. This was also the year of the formation of the Brazilian Communist Party.[8]

The rebellions linked discontent in the military with that in the private sector. This discontent was prefigured already in the presidency of Epitácio Pessoa, who made the mistake (from the military's point of view) of appointing civilian heads of the war and navy ministries in 1919. The year 1922 also marked the beginning of the *tenen-*

tista movement, so called because it was lead by young officers (mostly lieutenants). Their revolt was against the central government and against the military old guard that sustained it. The first episode was the armed rebellion at Ft. Copacabana, in which seventeen soldiers and one civilian refused to accept the general surrender and fought it out on the beach. Most were killed.

In 1924, a group of officers who had been conspiring against President Arthur Bernardes—a nationwide movement but densest in São Paulo—managed to hold the city for almost all of July before being defeated by federal troops. Many of the insurgents fled south to join the insurgent *tenentista* group lead by Luís Carlos Prestes. Known as the Coluna Prestes, this group carried on an exhaustive guerilla campaign through the interior of Brazil (traveling almost 360,000 kilometers) looking for popular support in their war against the Bernardes government. They disbanded three months after Bernardes stepped down, but Prestes went on to join, and later become the most influential leader of, the PCB.

The end of the presidency of Washington Luís (1926–30) saw a battle for succession that culminated in the 1930 revolution. The opposition had united, forming the Aliança Liberal and proposed the candidacies of Getúlio Vargas and João Pessoa (as president and vice president) against the government's candidate, Júlio Prestes. Supported by the government's political machinery and the favoritism and forced votes of the *coronel* system, Prestes easily won, despite general dissatisfaction in the country, exacerbated by the worldwide depression, and charges by the middle class that the government was not paying necessary attention to industrial development.

The opposition immediately declared fraud in the electoral process, but the crisis took on the character of active revolt as a result of public outrage against the assassination of João Pessoa on July 26. The revolution started in the Northeast, the military joined it, and it quickly spread throughout the country. In 1930, after an interim junta, Vargas took over as provisional president of the Republic.

Vargas's regime was constantly tested by conflict originating in the deposed agricultural oligarchy and in the growing ideological radicalization of both the Left and the Right. A worldwide occurrence during the 1930s, this radicalism took on Brazilian expression in the highly organized opposition of the PCB and the not-so-organized but powerful Ação Integralista, the Brazilian right-wing nationalist party whose fascist tendencies and organization most closely approximated that of Mussolini in Italy.[9]

Among the most important political events of these years for this study are the following. First, there was a limited uprising, called the Revolution Constitucionalista de 1932, provoked by the oligarchy under the pretext of the lack of a constitution. In 1934, a liberal constitution was approved that accepted all political groups, reformulated the electoral process, institutionalized state intervention in the economic realm, and affirmed workers' rights (minimum salary, union representation in Congress). Vargas was also officially elected president in that year.

In the process of right-left polarization, the Integralists initially supported Vargas, particularly approving his authoritarian stance. Left and liberal forces united in the Aliança Nacional Libertadora. The ANL, under the leadership of Luís Carlos Prestes and radicalized by the PCB presence, continued to conspire against the government, much along the lines of the *tenentista* movement. Alarmed by the ANL's agitation and support from former political companions of the 1930 revolution, Vargas outlawed the organization and jailed some of its members. This resulted in the Intentona Comunista of November 1935, which aimed at bringing the ANL to power. The revolt centered in Rio, Natal, and Recife and was squelched in a matter of days. Supporters of the oligarchy tried unsuccessfully to take advantage of the upheaval as well.

Vargas's solution to the problem was to cancel the 1938 elections. A climate of fear was created by rumors of a supposed communist takeover. This intention was corroborated by the "discovery" of an obviously fraudulent, detailed plan for the coup, called the Cohen plan, which Vargas used to legitimize his own internal coup of 1937. On November 10, 1937, he proclaimed the constitution of 1936 operant and inaugurated the Estado Novo, which continued until 1945. This constitution gave the president full power over the legislative and judiciary branches of government.

Vargas outlawed all political parties, including the Ação Integralista, which had, up to this point, supported him. On May 11, 1938, members of this party invaded the Guanabara Palace (the government headquarters) to kidnap Vargas, but the *revolta integralista* was defeated, in part due to its disorganization.

The Estado Novo suffered from the energies lost in these struggles and from its own police violence, but this was assuaged by the pressures of World War II. In 1939, Vargas had declared neutrality, but Brazil declared war on Germany in 1942, at least in part as recognition of large U.S. investments in Brazil in 1941. After the war and the defeat of Nazi fascism, there was a new call for democracy. Elections were slated for 1945, but the military, fearing the force of the popular movement for another Vargas term—a movement called *queremismo,* from the slogan "Queremos Getúlio"—deposed him.

Vargas then supported the presidency of Eurico Gaspar Dutra. During the latter's term the PCB was declared illegal (1947) and diplomatic relations with the Soviet Union were severed (1948). In 1951, Vargas was again elected president. He became much more radical in his nationalism, creating Petrobrás (the national oil company) and nationalizing electricity (Electrobrás). He looked for support among the unions, but was increasingly politically isolated. Implicated in an attempt on the opposition leader Carlos Lacerda's life, Vargas found himself literally surrounded in the presidential palace by the armed forces, who pressured him to step down. On August 24, 1954, he reacted by committing suicide, leaving a note that blamed the enemies of the nation.[10]

Vargas derived much of his support from his populist programs, known as *trabalhismo,* which, although not really based in the working class, made a loose call to alliances of workers and classes in an urban framework.[11] He created the Ministry of Work, Industry, and Commerce (Ministério de Trabalho, Indústria e Comércio), under which he did such things as fix work hours, insure medical assistance for workers, implement retirement acts and job security measures, and provide for paid vacations. He also reorganized the unions, creating a channel for popular revindication of worker's complaints. This measure also created a legal dependence of the unions on the state. On the whole, his programs gained support from the masses, allowing a participation of heretofore marginalized groups, at the same time he instituted ways of controlling them. His nationalist orientation also was appealing to some non-working-class sectors.

Historical events from 1954 on will not be discussed here, partly because they have been presented in chapters 3–5, but also, and more importantly, because references to specific historical events from 1945 on in *Rasga coração* are made obliquely. Undoubtedly, the ever present possibility of censorship had some effect on Vianinha's reticence to treat this period with specific fact, preferring to focus the present through Luca's battle with academic authority.[12]

Whatever the case, the limitation of action on the plane of memory to the first Vargas years makes for a clear and powerful dramatic analogy. The dramatized segments that point to how Vargas came to power, his persecution of the PCB, and the antagonisms between Right and Left during the Estado Novo parallel very neatly Vianinha's conception of events from the early 1960s on. In addition (as discussed in the previous chapter), there was a continuity between the Estado Novo and the period after 1964, in which the institutional structure bequeathed by Vargas was again taken up by technocrats.

In this regard, an interesting twist in a pattern of hope, defeat, and dogged determination can be seen in two of Vianinha's epigraphs. The first is from Oswaldo Aranha, one of the *tenentista* leaders of the 1930 revolution, and later minister of foreign affairs in Vargas's wartime presidency. The quotes are placed in this manner:

> "não queremos, não aceitamos nada, absolutamente nada do que aí está. Temos que reformar tudo, da cabeça aos pés"
> Oswaldo Aranha—antes da revolução de 30
> "não se faz o que se deseja mas o que é possível"
> Getúlio Vargas—depois da revolução de 30

> "we want nothing, we accept nothing, absolutely nothing of what is here. We must reform everything, from top to bottom."
> Oswaldo Aranha—before the revolution of 1930
> "one does not do what one wants, but rather what is possible"
> Getúlio Vargas—after the revolution of 1930

Dated before and after the revolution, Aranha's statement remembers the feeling of 1962–64, whereas Vargas's implies the realistic determination of Vianinha, and so many others, faced by the enclosure that came with the 1964 revolution.

The twist is not only in implied reference but also in characterization in the play. Although he never appears in the text as a character onstage, Vargas is the very nonanonymous antihero around whose absence-presence questions of political and cultural authority and authoritarianism are posed. In this respect, it is important to note that Vargas *need* not appear in the play to cast an omnipresent shadow. His dramaticity is well established by historical fact, and he himself participated heartily in the creation of the legends that survived him.

As in history, the personalized (and fictitious) characters in Manguari's memory are polarized on either side of the figure of Vargas. On the Left and in the PCB, we have Manguari and Camargo Velho, the full-time militant and party ideologue. On the Right, we see the figure of Castro Cott, an Integralist who, once Manguari's friend, becomes his dramatic nemesis. Within this scene of polarization, Manguari is humanized by his friendship with Lorde Bundinha, a hedonistic Bohemian who serves as a sounding board for Manguari's moments of ambivalence and posits the value of friendship, often in direct conflict with political commitment. Nena is also a humanizing element in the plane of memory, where we see Manguari's and her courtship.

Lorde Bundinha's story coincides with the political markers of 1930–42, when Brazil entered World War II, and Manguari's flashbacks stop with Bundinha's death from tuberculosis in 1942, although figures from the past continue to provide brief commentaries in the two short scenes that remain in the play. Continuity from plane to plane is provided by Nena and by Cott, who is, in the dramatic present, the principal of Luca's school.[13] There is also a specific parallel of characters that links the planes of memory and the present. Camargo Moço, who is Camargo Velho's nephew, takes on his uncle's visionary role. There is a specified approximation between the figure of Luca and that of Lorde Bundinha. Milena, Luca's girlfriend and privileged (upper-class) radical, has some reference to the young Manguari in her impulsiveness (which shows in her character as voluntarism) but serves mainly as a counterpart to Nena, the loyal housewife.[14] The parallels are established onstage according by means of the connections in Manguari's flashbacks. There are also a number of background roles: soldiers, Integralists, students, and *povo*.

Most characters have multiple functions, and this is particularly true of Manguari. In the first act, he functions primarily as a father, husband, social reformer, and son. In the second act, where the play's themes are dramatically foregrounded over the wrap-up of the plot, he is presented as testifier to history, as the creator and upholder of conventions, and as the giver of faith.

Historical Reference and Dramatic Structure

Before analyzing how historicity as fact and personal experience is structured in the play, it should be noted that music is extremely important in *Rasga coração*, both as a structuring device and in its power of reference to the popular culture and personal lives of the time covered. The play is framed by the singing of a beautifully plaintive verse by a northeastern poet-songwriter, Catullo da Paixão Cearense. *Rasga coração* takes its name from the verse, which goes:

Rasga coração

Se tu queres ver a imensidão do céu e mar
refletindo a prismatização da luz solar
rasga o coração, vem te debruçar
sobre a imensidão do meu penar.

[If thou wouldst see the vastness of sky and sea
Reflecting the solar light with prismatic effect
Let your heart break, come and lean out
Over the vastness of my sorrow.]

Especially as sung at the beginning of the play, this eloquently encapsulates Manguari's interior landscape. The meaning of his life is illuminated *(luz solar)* by the prism of history, which scatters it in spots of color whose significance is apprehended in its totality only to the degree to which we, along with him, rend our hearts to commune with his suffering. The pathos of the images is mitigated by quality of light and the sense of expansion by the repetition of immensity *(imensidão)*. At the end of the play, the resinging signifies a kind of personification of history, referring to the intrinsic relationship between Manguari's personal pain and the pain of the historical era.

Rasga coração has two acts, traditionally structured. It has an open ending of partially resolved dramatic conflict, not uncommon in contemporary illusionist drama. The first act develops the characters, the conflicts, and the historical framework from the several years preceding the 1930 revolution until Getúlio Vargas's election in 1934. The second act elaborates these conflicts, taking the historical time from 1935 until 1945, and is largely an exposition of the significance of the themes. The first act "names" Manguari, identifying him as the anonymous hero, whereas the second act reveals the significance of the terms *anonymous* and *hero*. Although the play ends without a resolution of the conflicts (Luca's expulsion is a structural resolution), care is taken to present this ending in the most positive light, as an interim point of resolve in Manguari's—and by extension Brazil's—perseverance in the struggle for integrity.

The acts, of approximately equal length as staged, are divided into scenes. The four scenes of the first act are relatively long, the distribution of dramatic time relatively even among them. The act begins and ends stressing theatricality (Vianinha's theatrical carpentry) over dramaticity. All the characters are onstage and lights dim as the curtain goes up. The theme verse is sung. As dramatic focus shifts to Manguari and Nena (dramatic reality), the flashback characters present themselves, giving names and historical identification, then offering snatches of their motif songs. These presentations have no connection with Manguari's conscious memory, although they theatricalize the themes of his subconscious.

The act ends partly focused on Manguari and Lorde Bundinha, who are caught in respective postures of pain, Bundinha coughing up blood and Manguari alleviating an arthritis attack with the voyeuristic pleasure of watching a neighbor woman undress (his theater). With the contrasting exception of Manguari and Lorde Bundinha, all the characters and the chorus of extras are transformed into performers in an abbreviated *revista* sketch whose revealing motif is "Oi que terra boa pra se farrear" [What a terrific country to raise hell in] (49). This allusion to Brazil as the land of the festive spree, the inverse of Manguari's and Bundinha's pain, sets up a double correspondence to Vargas. On the thematic level, it gives a connotation of "sacking" to the spree, following a theme of the first act that treats Vargas's sellout from Manguari's point of view. This is reinforced on the level of theatrical conventions, since the *revista* was not just the favorite theatrical form of the 1930s, but Vargas's favorite entertainment as well.[15]

The second act contains six scenes (numbered 5–10). These are shorter, choppier, and less regular in length than those of the first act.[16] This act's framing emphasizes dramaticity, beginning with Manguari's arthritic pain and ending on the same note. The musical sequence of the beginning of the play is reversed. The historical figures, as if competing with each other for Manguari's attention, sing their motifs louder and louder until, exhausted, they abruptly stop. Then they and the chorus softly take up the theme song as the curtain falls on Manguari.

Each scene of the play presents a different thematic emphasis, according to conflict, the tone of the encounters, or the theatrical conventions and devices used. The marking of the scenes varies throughout, although they are mainly designated either by music or change in focus or brightness of stage light. Furthermore, the scenes are divided into segments. The structuring of segments generally follows shifts between the planes or the rhythm of intercutting between planes. Within this segmental structure, we find three different proxemic or kinesthetic variations that transmit a sense of space and movement in the mind of the beholder, if not on the stage space itself. There are segments that establish an alternating pattern between the planes of memory and the present; segments that intercut and overlap rapidly; and segments that occur simultaneously, although action on one plane may be represented by gesture only.

In contrast to the dreamlike presentation of the historical figures at the opening of the play, the first dialogues of the present plane specifically set time and place. This plane begins with Manguari's question and answer: "Que dia é hoje? 30 de abril de 1972" [What day is today? April 30, 1972] (19). He and Nena are going over the household budget, which indicates the generation gap, as Manguari questions Luca's expenditures on expensive macrobiotic foods. This scene is dense with signs of the quotidian as they imply social structure, and within three pages of the text we know their standard of living, what they eat, what their rented apartment is like, and the discrepancies between them and their child in consumer tastes.

These elements of a normal middle-class household are juxtaposed with a forceful image that links private space (the apartment) with public space. Looking out the window, Manguari notices a dead man on the pavement, covered with newspapers. We are given to understand that this is not an uncommon occurrence, as Manguari comments: "aquilo é o que vale a vida humana, coberto com classificados" [that's what human life is worth, covered in classifieds] (20).

Contrast between the old and new Copacabana provokes Manguari's memories of his father's resistance to his life choices, and Manguari resolves to respect Luca's path. The generational issue is emphasized in that Manguari is seventeen years old as the dramatized past begins and Luca seventeen in the present. 666 and Camargo appear on either side of Manguari as he murmurs "meu pai não me deixava fazer a minha [vida]" [my father didn't let me lead my own (life)] (22), making it clear that Manguari's path was political activism. Historical time is specified as Camargo joyously announces Washington Luís's fall, proclaiming, "Viva Getúlio Vargas! Oswaldo Aranha!" (23)—a link with Vianinha's epigraphs)—and as 666 protests that Getúlio lost the election.

Political reality and cultural ambience conflict on both planes as Luca enters to contest his father's vision of life. His father, as much as the capitalists he criticizes, is stuck in alienating power plays. A flashback shows Manguari and Bundinha dancing as if with partners in a waltz contest. Manguari wishes to win to get money for his political work. Bundinha reminds him that life is short. The frenetic spirit of competition of the contest ends the scene as planes intercut between the dance and the home discussion.

In the first scene, the planes alternate, directed through Manguari's memory. In scene 2, rapid intercuts between the planes take up most of scene, shifting the perspective from Manguari's memory to that of the other persons. Obviously, it is Manguari's memory that brings these characters to life. However, Vianinha takes some dramatic license with this effect, often giving the other characters dialogue, feelings, or action of which Manguari could have no knowledge in order to let us see Manguari outside of his own interpretation. This distancing of perspective is heightened by an effect like a triple camera: we see him (framed in his apartment) focusing through his window (another frame) into the window of the undressing neighbor.

Luca discovers Manguari in this compromising position, which leads to a discussion of generational values (sex versus justice). Luca, citing his father's voyeurism as proof, exclaims: "Diz que todas as gerações só pensam em sexo! Só que umas não querem encarar isso!" [They say all generations think of nothing but sex! Only some of them won't face up to it]. To which Manguari replies: "Todas as gerações só pensam em justiça, só que umas não querem encarar isso" [All generations think of nothing but justice, only some of them won't face up to it] (30).

After a segment of intercuts in which quick appearances of 666, Cott, Camargo, and Bundinha—set in the framework of the rise of the integralists—transform Manguari's personal doubts into the memory of ambivalence over political strategy, the scene ends as Luca comes back, providing an exterior perspective on his father's life. Asking his forgiveness for doubting him, Luca confirms Manguari, saying: "você é um . . . como é? . . . herói popular anônimo" [you're a . . . what is it? . . . anonymous popular hero] (34).

The long alternating segments of act 1, scene 3 elaborate on the conflict between sexual-affective values and political values. The plane of memory is stimulated by Nena's discovery that Luca and Milena are locked up in the bedroom, making love. A flashback to Manguari and Nena in a similar situation leads Nena to flash forward to the present, incriminating Manguari for using the political as an excuse for evading the personal:

> Se não é político, você não sabe como fazer. . . . Só pensa em política, você. . . . Seis anos para casar, casamos em 1940, Luca nasceu em 1954 . . . legalidade, manifesto da paz, Coréia, Petrobrás. . . . "Não posso ter filho, Nena, o petróleo é

importante . . ." eu fiz um . . . dois . . . cinco . . . abôrtos . . .
você só pensou em política.

[If it's not about politics, you don't know what to do. . . . You
only think about politics. . . . It took us six years to get married,
we got married in 1940, Luca was born in 1954 . . . legality,
peace treaty, Korea, Petrobrás. . . . "I can't have children, Nena,
oil's important . . ." I had one . . . two . . . five . . . abortions. . .
all you thought about was politics.] (37)

The irony here is that several brief interruptions on the memory plane have Camargo accusing Manguari of letting the personal
interfere with the political. Perspective is further relativized as Camargo and Bundinha vie for Manguari's attention, Camargo with examples of Vargas's sellout of the workers (29), and Bundinha gleefully
firing off a volley of advertising slogans for products to fight venereal
diseases, punctuating his remarks with obscene gestures.

Remembering that his father threw him out of the house
when he found him and Nena making love, Manguari resolves not to
interfere with Luca's private life. Nevertheless, he cannot resist coun-
seling him on his political life. When Luca and Milena come out of
the room, Manguari starts discussing the strategy for the students'
resistance. He deludes himself about Luca's intentions, proclaiming
to Nena: "Chegou a vez dele, Nena!" [It's his turn, Nena!] (38).

The sense of illusion is poignantly reinforced by Manguari's
memory, at first elated, of his days as a singer. To Nena he sings "Fascination," whose words in Portuguese are particularly relevant to
Manguari's cycles of doubt, frustration, and hope: "Os sonhos mais
lindos, sonhei / de quimeras mil, um castelo ergui" [I dreamt the
most beautiful dreams / Out of a thousand chimeras, I built a castle]
(40). Dreaming while awake in the present, Manguari crashes down
to perceive himself through Luca's eyes and to enter into Nena's
world of personal fears:

O, Nena, também estou muito espantado . . . não reconheço as
coisas . . . não queria me espantar, mas . . . queimei minha vida
na solidariedade. Nena . . . Luca me olha como se eu não pas-
sasse de um masoquista . . . uma pessoa que pensa nos outros,
porque tem medo de si mesmo, medo de viver.

[Oh, Nena, I'm scared, too . . . I don't recognize things . . . I didn't want to be scared, but . . . I burnt my life in solidarity. Nena . . . Luca looks at me as if I were just a masochist . . . a person who thinks of others because he's afraid of himself, afraid of living.] (40)

The last scene of the act has a very chaotic segmental rhythm in which the theme of Manguari's present pain *(dores)* is verbalized by Bundinha's reference to illusion in the political agitation of the early 1930s: "Vocês estão fervendo o caldo demais, mon choux, o povinho não vai acompanhar" [You overcooking the stew, *mon choux,* the little people won't follow you]. Illusion and reality about the historical past are immediately affirmed by Camargo's insistence that the time for revolution has come (42).

The spatial relationships onstage that split Manguari's loyalties in the past—Bundinha on one side, Camargo on the other— reformulate in the present as Manguari finds himself in a sense contradicting his past by partially taking Bundinha's position in the present. This occurs through the same theatrical device we have seen in *Cristal.* From the plane of the past, Bundinha begs Manguari to compromise his principles and help him get money for his medical treatment by joining him in a *revista* sketch. (Paid for by the state tourist bureau, it would be entitled *Cadê o Gegê* [Where's Gegê (Getúlio)], a "joke" on Getúlio Vargas.) Turning around to face Luca on the present plane, Manguari applies Bundinha's reasoning to Luca's case. He has talked to Cott, who has told Manguari that Luca could continue to wear long hair if he would sign a statement that he was a member of a rock group. Manguari begs Luca to consider the proposal, knowing that as a scholarship student his son will have little chance for an education if he doesn't compromise.

The past-present contradiction is in the affective realm of choices and loyalties versus principles. This establishes a sort of horizontal pattern of muddled feeling in the affective realm—indicated by the proxemic stance of Bundinha and Luca, who are both in intimate relationships to Manguari in stage space—which is counterposed to the vertical pattern of Manguari's insistence for strategic clarity, an insistence that gives a direct continuity from past to present.

Luca challenges his father: "É o famoso Manguari Pistolão que está me propondo isso?" [Is this the famous Manguari Pistolão who's proposing this to me?]. Manguari responds, speaking both to Bundinha and Luca: "Porque tem coisa inevitável e que tem coisa evitável. Não pode confundir as duas, se não vira destino. *(A Luca)* Eu sei que não é a melhor solução, companheiro. Mas de quinhentos alunos, só quarenta resistem" [Because some things are inevitable and others aren't. You can't mix them up, if not it becomes destiny. *(To Luca)* I know it's not the best solution, kid. But there's only forty students left out of five hundred] (47).

Manguari maintains that the symbol (long hair) is not worth the fight, since the students have no organizational base (a union, or even wide support) to justify their battle. Luca retorts that it is not a question of strategy, but one of integrity as opposed to alienation. As he has explained somewhat earlier in the scene to his mother: "Vocês não gostam de vocês, mãe. Podem gostar de sua missão, filhos, viagens . . . mas não gostam de si mesmos. Eu gosto" [You don't like yourselves, Mother. You may like your mission, children, traveling . . . but you don't like yourselves. I do] (44).

Manguari's reasoning, doubts, and present conflicts turn into the theatricalized free-for-all of the *revista* segment that ends the act (discussed earlier in the structural analysis of the acts), stimulated by Camargo's reappearance to announce Vargas's election.

The first scene of the second act (scene 5) tinges the theme of hope with pathos. It begins with Manguari stretched out on the table, almost paralyzed with arthritis. By sheer willpower, he manages an effort to put together the pieces of his political and personal lives (left in fragments in act 1), an act of self-investigation. He complains to God about his physical state and the state of the world: "vou fazer autocrítica, Senhor. . . . O Senhor também podia fazer a sua [I'm going to do my autocriticism, Lord. . . . You could do some too, Lord] (51).

The beginning of this segment is interspliced with dialogue between Cott and 666 about the future of Brazil from the Integralist point of view. It is a rosy and vague call to youth, implied to be anachronistic because of the ridiculous figure 666 cuts as an Integralist. The Integralist hope versus Vianinha's concept of their reality is emphasized by text's call for slides of the regiment of Integralists that Cott is directing.[17]

The next segment has parallel actions whose separateness and mutual explication is emphasized by the fact that Manguari, absent from the past presented, could have no memory of it. In one section of the stage we see Nena nursing Bundinha, both waiting for Manguari's return. In the present (which is almost always portrayed in the apartment), Manguari is dancing, having understood that the crux of his (mental) paralysis was his refusal to validate Luca's path to struggle. He calls out: "Como é que um pai que se preza pede a um filho que ele se proteja, se cuide, se poupe, que não lute, se despedace cicatrizes, gilvazes fraturas punhaladas rasga o coração na ponta de todas as dores" [How can a father who thinks anything of himself ask a son to protect himself, not to fight, to fall to pieces, scars, gashes, fractures, stabs, rip his heart at the tip of every pain] (52). Fired by his own battle cry, one that links internal and external forces in the imperative sense of the title of the play, Manguari sits down to write a plan of action for Luca.

Obviously, Manguari does not perceive the disjunction that marks what he sees as his contribution to the lives of those dear to him from their deeper need of him. The other action of this segment, as mentioned, has Bundinha and Nena waiting, Bundinha depending on his help. Cutting back to the present, where Nena's physical absence constitutes an accusatory presence, Manguari calls to her: "O Nena, como é que eu pude deixar o menino sozinho assim: Nunca abandonei ninguém, nem meu amigo Lorde Bundinha nas vascas, golfadas de sangue" [Oh, Nena, how could I leave the boy alone like that? I never abandoned anyone, not even my friend Lorde Bundinha, in the convulsions, the spurts of blood] (53).

The pathos of this scene is that Manguari does not abandon anyone, yet he remains apart. This is implied as the hero's dilemma: in a certain sense he is condemned by need for action to make a virtue of hope at the expense of clear vision. This becomes apparent in the long segment, totally in the present, that ends the scene in which Manguari carefully explains to Luca how to organize his protest. (Manguari himself will write the editorials.) Approximation and alienation merge in one image as Manguari confides to Luca (closeness) about watching the neighbor (alienation).

Scene 6 begins with one of the longest segments in the realist mode of the play. This is a dual segment. In the first part, Manguari's view of reality is contested by the students, a view that Vianinha distances by stage directions that call for slides behind Luca, Milena, and Camargo Moço portraying students meeting in an elegant apartment. Significantly, the only segments of the present staged outside of the spatial parameters of the apartment emphasize the ideological distance between father and son. It is also the first time we see Camargo Moço, who defends Manguari against the other students' ridiculing a cautious and reformist strategy. (Manguari wants to compile documents about the right to use long hair, write editorials, circulate petitions, etc.)

There are only two brief intersplices from the dramatized past, both of which show Manguari and Camargo Velho armed in scenic opposition to Cott and 666, also with guns, an image that refers to the Intentona Comunista of 1935.

The contrasting parts of this segment present the theme of the revolutionary traditions of Brazil. In the second part, Manguari and Luca argue. Luca heatedly questions the validity of this tradition: "Fora a Cabanagem, fora Canudos, que morreu ali o último, até o último, fora isso o que é [the revolutionary tradition]? Calça arriada! Não é mais ou menos essa a tua herança, Manguari Pistolão?" [Except for Cabanagem, except for Canudos, where the last one died, even to the last one, except for them, what is it (the revolutionary tradition)? Dropped drawers! Isn't that more or less your heritage, Manguari Pistolão?] (62).

Manguari sadly notes that he, too, was hotheaded when he was young. However, Luca, who doesn't see the whole staged story as we do, fiercely denies his father's experience, countering with a shout for "Ação direta!" [direct action!] (62). The lights go out abruptly in preparation for the next scene.

This scene (7) contains the most intensely violent images of the play, in which the rhythm and Bundinha's singing and dancing on a center-stage platform make a macabre reversal of the *revista* technique used earlier. Allocation of stage space is particularly important. In the first segment, which depicts parallel torture sequences, we see Manguari on one side suffering an interrogation marked by blows. A disciplined revolutionary, he answers only with his name and place of work, repeating "não tenho mais nada a dizer" [I don't have anything else to say] (63). Camargo is thrown into the same stage space, having undergone the same interrogation and provided the same answers. Their solidarity is contrasted by the intercut with Luca's interrogation on the other side of the stage.

Action is focused into the present through the intermediary of Nena in the apartment, learning through a phone call of Luca's arrest for invading Cott's office. Nena explains that her husband can't come to the phone right then because "está com dores" [he's in pain] (63). The explanation for Manguari's absence from the scenic space of the apartment is used to connect the different levels of his pain.

On Luca's side of the stage, we see Cott conducting an interrogation. The students buckle under Cott's authority (he needs no physical gestures), reneging on their participation. In the first interrogation, Milena denies that she destroyed anything. When Luca comes in, he pretends that he doesn't know whose idea it was to invade the school but rather quickly concurs that it might have been Milena's after Cott insinuates that the other students have already betrayed her.

The second and closing segment, the longest on the present plane without interruption from the past, is the sequence in which Camargo Moço and Manguari exchange ideas on generational differences, the importance of doubt, and continuity of struggle commented in the introductory discussion of *Rasga coração*. The shift from past to present to future focus is integrated by a sharing of values that starts the segment. Camargo Moço has come to see Luca because someone has betrayed him. Although he insists that it was not he, Luca breaks down in sobs: he cannot quite understand the base of his father's and Camargo Moço's rage at betrayal, nor their code of honor. In despair, Luca justifies himself by saying that all protest leads to violence and that "é a terra deles" [that land is theirs] (66).

Returning to Luca's argument, the first segment of scene 8 shows concurrent dropout sequences. After his torture, Manguari assuages his pain by "tripping" with Bundinha on morphine. Among the other specifics of his torture, we learn that Manguari's nails were ripped out. This is juxtaposed to Milena and Luca licking their psychological wounds by obliterating themselves with drugs.

This switches to a segment between Manguari and Nena, back in the central scenic space of the apartment. Manguari has come to comprehend his son, but through his own system of values. He tells Nena:

> E isso é derrota, sabe? Quando a gente é derrotado, fica com nojo da existência normal, precisa de outras portas pra se sentir separado, entende? Não derrotado. . . . Aconteceu exatamente isso comigo quando eu saí da cadeia, lembra? Não ia trabalhar, dias com a mesma roupa no corpo, lembra, tomei até morfina.

> [And that's defeat, you know? When you're defeated, you feel sick about normal existence, you need other doors to feel separate, understand? Not defeated. . . . That's exactly what happened to me when I got out of jail, remember? I wouldn't go to work, days wearing the same clothes, remember, I even took morphine.] (70)

Manguari tells her that what brought him back to reality was Bundinha's death. Stoned and incapable of judging his friend's state,

Manguari had interpreted Bundinha's death agonies as simply the need to sleep. The memory is so forceful that it occasions a convergence of scenic space. Bundinha enters the present to embrace his friend, as Manguari laments to Nena, who cannot see Bundinha, that "estava morto nos meus braços, Nena, e eu pedindo pra ele dormir" [he was dead in my arms, Nena, and me asking him to go to sleep] (70).

This memory structures a further encounter between Manguari and Luca. Searching for some common ideological ground beyond the negative desperation of a dropout mentality, Manguari begs Luca to explain his actions. Luca, also wishing to find some correspondence to his father's values, responds that he has not totally dropped out, but that his activism has taken other paths: "Eu não estou largando pai, ontem estive na porta de uma fábrica de inseticida, fui explicar pros operários que eles não podem produzir isso" [I'm not dropping out, Dad, yesterday I was at the gate of an insecticide plant, I went over there to explain to the workers that they can't make that stuff] (72).

For the first time, Manguari turns his back on his son: the pain and the ideological distance are too much for him. Going over to embrace his father, Luca sees that he is crying. Through his tears Manguari tells his son: "Na porta das fábricas pedir pros operários largarem seus empregos, são tão difíceis de conseguir, rapaz!" [At the factory gates asking workers to quit their jobs, they're so hard to get, son!] (72).

From the past, a staccato and pathetic image of Bundinha dying is counterposed to Camargo Velho, who closes the scene by proclaiming:

> É preciso fazer campanha de solidariedade às famílias dos presos políticos, companheiros . . . está havendo uma grande ascensão do movimento de massas com a campanha da entrada do Brasil na guerra contra a Alemanha . . . acho que este vai ser o nosso ano . . . as perspectivas são todas favoráveis a nós!

> [We must put together a solidarity campaign for the families of the political prisoners, comrades . . . there's a great ascension of movement of the masses with the campaign for Brazil's entry into the war against Germany . . . I think this is going to be our year . . . the perspectives are all in our favor!] (73)

Of course, history has proved Camargo's optimism wrong.

However, it is interesting that Bundinha's death coincides with Brazil's declaration of war, which was in effect a reentry into active participation in the international arena. As the figure through whom most of the references to exotic imagery of Brazil is filtered, Bundinha's apolitical cultural hedonism is symbolic of isolationism, and his brand of isolationism reflects on Vargas's populist and nationalist policies.

The penultimate scene of the play (9) elaborates the discussion of scene 6 regarding what constitutes revolutionary action. The stage is brilliantly lit. This is the scene in which Camargo Moço confirms Manguari as a true revolutionary against Luca's assertion of what he considers a revolutionary attitude toward life. Luca takes his own principled stand:

> Vocês lá, ensinam essa vida que está morta, essa vida de esmagar a natureza, de super-homens neuróticos, lá vocês querem dominar a vida, eu quero que a vida me domine . . . não é revolucão política, é revolução de tudo, é outro ser!

> [Over there, you teach this dead life, this life that crushes nature, of neurotic supermen, you want to dominate life, I want life to dominate me . . . it's not political revolution, it's the revolution of everything, it's another being! (another thing altogether).] (74)

Manguari, resigned to their differences, replies: "Está certo, Luis Carlos, está certo, eu não discuto mais! Você faz como quiser, faz como decidir, tem todo o meu respeito, mas agora é fora de minha casa, menino, entendeu?" [All right, Luis Carlos, all right, I won't discuss it any further! Do whatever you please, do whatever you decide, you have all my respect, but now get out of my house, understand?] (74).

Luca's expulsion, which really starts with scene 6, has reference to Bundinha's agony and death. In a certain sense, Manguari has lost a friend whom he loved despite their differences. Although Luca is more articulate (or sophistic) in his philosophy than the ever-joking Bundinha, the similarity is explicit as Manguari remarks to his son: "você não é revolucionário, menino, sou eu, você no meu tempo chamava-se Lorde Bundinha que nunca negou que era um fugitivo, você é um covardezinho que quer fazer do medo de viver, um espetáculo de coragem!" [you're no revolutionary, kid, I am, you, in my day, called yourself Lorde Bundinha, who never denied being a fugitive, you're a little coward who wants to make a spectacle of courage out of his fear of living!] (75).

A wrap-up scene of the play's message, scene 9, is very short. It only one segment in the realist mode, except for several incursions of 666 and Bundinha that comment on 666's expulsion of Manguari, thereby ironizing the relationship between the political and the personal (666, we recall, expelled his son for finding him in bed with a woman). Beginning with brilliant lighting, it ends as the lights descend slowly.

The last scene of the play really serves as an epilogue. The only action or stage movement on the reality plane reflects resolution and forgiveness as Nena begs Manguari to reconsider. He refuses but accepts Luca's farewell kiss without rancor. The sense of epilogue is augmented by the fact that words englobe action. This takes place on the plane of Manguari's dogged determination in the present, and in Camargo Velho's faulty prediction that closes the play's dialogue. (As discussed, the curtain comes down with the singing of the theme verse.)

In effect, this one-segment scene sums up Vianinha's concept of the primacy of the theatrical word. Manguari's last dialogue is not encoded narration, but rather action epitomized and directed through verbalization. The gestural act reveals intention and direction: Manguari picks up the phone. The verbal action gives meaning to the gestural act, as Manguari speaks:

Marco Antônio? Custódio . . . como vai? . . . os pensionistas do Departamento de Limpeza Urbana não estão recebendo pensão há dois meses . . . que há gente em situação desesperadora . . . vamos reunir agora à noite, você pode?

[Marco Antônio? Custódio . . . how are you? . . . the pensioners from the Department of Urban Sanitation haven't received their pensions for two months . . . there are people in desperate situations . . . we're getting together tonight, can you make it?] (77)

It is, I think, reflective of Vianinha's consistent tendency to put his own theory into a questioning perspective that the last dialogue of the play presents a kind of reversal of the above argument, although it by no means negates it. Again, we hear Camargo Velho pontificating with an erroneous assessment of the historical moment:

"Agora, com o fim da guerra contra a Alemanha, há grandes perspectivas de ascensão do movimento democrático . . . esse vai ser o nosso ano, companheiro! . . . as perspectivas são todas favoráveis a nós!" [Now, with the end of the war against Germany, there are great perspectives for the rise of the democratic movement . . . this is going to be our year, comrade! The perspectives are all in our favor!] (77). The action implied by Camargo's inflammatory words never came to pass.

The quiet determination that permeates Manguari's last dialogue carries over to comment Camargo's remark, however, transmitting the author's perspective on political and theatrical matters. For Manguari/Vianinha, revolution is not a pyrotechnic affair, but the result of nonvoluntaristic, day-to-day commitment. Vianinha is not negating Camargo's struggle, but comprehending and temporizing a view of revolution that he once shared.

Furthermore, the inflammatory element of Camargo's statement sets up a correspondence with a dialogue between Manguari and Luca of the previous scene that puts this argument in the framework of theatrical practice. As indicated, this is the scene that confirms Manguari's (and Vianinha's) ideas on what is revolutionary. Manguari tells Luca: "Revolução pra mim já foi uma coisa pirotécnica, agora é todo dia, lá no mundo, ardendo, usando as palavras, os gestos, os costumes, a esperança desse mundo" [Revolution for me used to be something pyrotechnic, now it's an everyday thing, burning there in the world, using the words, the gestures, the customs, the hope of this world] (75).

This declaration alludes to theatrical as well as to the political practice. It calls to mind Vianinha's objections to the methods of the theater of aggression, which in previous statements he had categorized as pyrotechnical.[18] If we translate Manguari's affirmation of how the truly "burning" *(ardendo)* revolutionary proceeds into theatrical terminology, we have a clear view of Vianinha's theory of dramatic action. As in Manguari's definition of a revolutionary that gives syntactical priority to "usando as palavras," Vianinha gives priority to the conventions of the spoken word.

For Vianinha, the word has to be relevant to, and revealing of, objective historical reality ("desse mundo"), as do the theatrical gestures ("os gestos") that accompany and explicate the dramatic word. As Manguari's definition continues to include "os costumes, a esperança desse mundo" in the tools a revolutionary must use, we can hear Vianinha speaking about the importance of recognizing social and cultural values in the formation of perceptions of reality.

This interpretation is born out by fragments of a prologue in verse with which Vianinha had at one time intended to introduce *Rasga coração* (*Vianinha* 188–92). Speaking against the abusive techniques of ritualized aggression, he declares the theater a sacred place of contemplation that should lead to comprehension, starting with the three knocks that announce the beginning of communication:

Essas batidas indicam que um momento sagrado
vai começar
quando os homens se reúnem para se contemplarem a si mesmos
a contemplação
portanto, nada de esgares, agressões
corridas pela platéia
nada que perturbe a contemplação
não viemos aqui para julgar, nem para condenar, nem participar
viemos para compreender
obstinados procuradores da compreensão
a compreensão parece que é uma forma de debilitamento da
    ação
um enfraquecedor da luta
ao contrário, achamos que é o seu deflagrador

[These knocks indicate that a sacred moment
Is about to begin
When men gather together to contemplate themselves
Contemplation
Therefore, no grimaces, no aggressions
Running around in the audience
Nothing that perturbs contemplation
We have not come here to judge, nor to condemn, nor
    participate
We have come here to understand
Obstinate seekers of comprehension
Comprehension seems to be a way of debilitating action
An enfeebler of struggle
On the contrary, we think it's what sets it off]

Thus, when Vianinha states in the preface to *Rasga coração* that he wanted to write a play that studied the difference between "o novo" and "o revolucionário," categorically adding that what is new is not always revolutionary, nor is what is revolutionary limited to what is new, we see that this applies to his concept of theater as well as to his definition of political responsibility.

Rasga coração presents, intentionally, an amalgamation of the new and the old. Its dramatic characterization is essentially one of psychological realism, while its presentational style strives to create a critical distancing effect through the collage technique of intersplicing conventions of illusionist theater common to Brazilian social realism with *revista* and Brechtian devices. In brief, *Rasga coração* is a dialogue with tradition, and when Vianinha says that it is necessary to include history as a category of representation, he refers not only to historical fact as perceived and lived by individuals and societies, but also to the history of theatrical conventions that interpolate historical experience.[19]

Production and Critical Appraisal

Rasga coração was written between 1972 and 1974, censored in 1974, and released for production only with the political opening of 1979. It first opened in Curitiba in 1979 and played in Rio de Janeiro and in São Paulo in 1979 and 1980 to full houses.[20] It was a very large and expensive production, with twenty-one actors (most of them often onstage in musical numbers or as background figures), four musicians, and an elaborate set, with tiers rising behind the low, revolving platform that represented Manguari's living room. It cost three million *cruzeiros* to produce, a portion of which was initially financed by the Serviço Nacional de Teatro (SNT) and the state government of Paraná. It was directed by José Renato, a companion of Vianinha's since the days of Arena, in a style that gave crisp attention to the dramatic scenes of Manguari's everyday life and that opened up to a festive interpretation of the irreverent scenes involving Lorde Bundinha.

Part of its popularity can be explained by its cast of television stars and by its author's reputation as a *telenovela* writer, as well as being a folkloric figure within resistance mythology. However, a more significant factor in the success of the play was that, after almost sixteen years of censorship, the public was again seeing plays that dealt directly with Brazilian social reality, and this public was immensely hungry to see its own history portrayed onstage.

The Brazilian stage of the first few year of redemocratization produced a number of plays with similar themes, such as Dias Gomes's *Campeões do mundo* (Champions of the World), that were also written by highly visible television authors and had all-star casts. None reached such broad audiences or provoke the same discussion about recent Brazilian history, social reality, and theater that *Rasga coração* did. As a group, these plays represent an important process of revindication and recuperation of historical themes and recommence a tradition of direct investigation and interpretation of national identity that has characterized contemporary Brazilian (and Spanish American) theater—a tradition either absent, or obscured by, metaphorical displacement during the 1960s and 1970s. Interviews with authors and actors of these plays make it clear that the predominant dramatic structure of the historical mosaic was designed to reincorporate a sense of history into Brazilian drama. However, when considered solely in terms of their individual merits, and not as a dramatic tendency, few of these plays besides *Rasga coração* present any significant dramatic interest beyond their instructive purposes. As a rule, dramatic action and didactic narrative are privileged at the expense of dramatic tension, and the plays present a closed reading of dramatic events.

Rasga coração, on the other hand, was generally hailed as a landmark contribution to Brazilian theater, critics signaling the importance of its historical treatment. In a eulogy to Vianinha's produced and unpublished work, Sábato Magaldi in 1974 categorically stated: "*Rasga coração* é, no teatro brasileiro, a mais completa sondagem do país, desde a conturbada década de trinta até os nossos dias [*Rasga coração* is, in Brazilian theater, the most complete sounding of the country, from the troubled 1930s to our days] ("Vianinha" n.p.). Yan Michalski seconded this opinion in an article from 1980 that discusses dramatic structure and historical reference in the play ("Como acompanhar o quebra-cabeça" n.p.).

Michalski starts by commenting on the almost overwhelming quantity of historical information: "Talvez a obra mais virtuosisticamente construida de toda a dramaturgia brasileira, *Rasga Coração* exigirá do espetador desejoso de captar toda a enorme riqueza do seu conteúdo um certo esforço de atenção" [Perhaps the most virtuosically constructed work in all of Brazilian playwriting. *Rasga Coração* will demand a particular effort of attention from the spectator who wishes to receive all the enormous wealth contained in it]. For Michalski, the expert use of the collage technique is the basis for the play's success in aesthetically organizing fact and personal experience:

O fundamental dessa estrutura é que ela permite encenar para-lela e simultaneamente acontecimentos que, na ordem cronológ-ica natural, seriam sucessivos. E esse é, na verdade, o grande achado formal de *Rasga Coração*. Claro que milhares de outros autores já o usaram antes. Mas não me lembro de nenhuma peça em que ele tenha sido orquestrado de modo tão sistemático e sugestivo.

[What is fundamental about this structure is that it allows for the parallel and simultaneous staging of events that, in natural chronological order, would be successive. And this, in truth, is the great formal discovery of *Rasga Coração*. Sure, a thousand other authors used it before. But I don't remember any play in which it was orchestrated as systematically or suggestively.]

Edélcio Mostaço, on the other hand, takes a harsh look at both the play's intentions and the production, finding both lacking coherence and innovation ("Rasga coração, fígado, cérebro" [Rip Your Heart, Liver, Brain]). He contends, first of all, that *Rasga cora-ção* presents nothing original in terms of its narrative process of flash-backs and that, furthermore, it fails to synthesize adequately the historical treatment to which it pretends. In his view, the fact that historical moments are all filtered through Manguari's memories lim-its the possible interpretations of history the audience might have.

Mostaço argues that this focus is inevitable, due to the essen-tially illusionist dramatic depiction of the central character: "Vianna, ao optar pelo realismo psicológico como forma teve de aceitar as re-gras cênicas e de carpintaria compatíveis com esta opção" [Vianna, in opting for psychological realism as a form, had to accept all the rules of staging and carpentry compatible with that option] (5). Referring to the Brechtian distinction between dramatic and epic genres, he sug-gests that the play should have opted for an epic analysis:

Se a via escolhida tivesse sido a épica a História ficaria num en-tremeio entre o palco e a platéia, num espaço aberto às interpret-ações da consciência, tanto da personagem principal (e das demais personagens do presente) como dos espectadores. Como está, permanece fechada em seu círculo de ficção, acreditando-se, porém, um painel realista e dialético do passado brasileiro.

[If the chosen path had been the epic, History would remain somewhere between the stage and the audience, in a space open to the interpretations of consciousness, as much that of the main character (and of the other characters in the present) as of the spectators. As it is, it remains closed within its circle of fiction, believing itself, however, to be a realistic and dialectic panel of the Brazilian past.] (5)

Following this line of reasoning, he credits José Renato's production with being "funestamente fiel ao autor" [fatally faithful to the author], adding that the only real, or true, scenic space is Manguari's living room. He thinks that the scenic emphasis on this space is appropriate to the treatment of the main character, who "plenamente inserido dentro de uma problemática pequeno-burguêsa que não vendo saídas de ação no presente refugia-se num passado mais honroso, dentro dos limites estilísticos daquilo que se convencionou chamar de drama-burguês" [totally situated within a petit bourgeois problematic, and who, seeing no chances for action in the present, seeks refuge in a more honorable past, within the stylistic limits of what has been traditionally called bourgeois drama] (5).

Mostaço's comments provide for a fitting end to this chapter. For, although he is implacable in his judgment, they raise important considerations. Moreover, it should be noted that they are made in good faith, from his point of view of what Brazilian theater should be. He feels that Manguari is anachronistically kin to figures of social realism such as Willy Loman and that the political positions that Vianinha espouses through his portrayal of this "anonymous revolutionary hero" have played a large role in holding back the growth of Brazilian theater. Specifying that theater should again take up the threads of invention of the tropicalist-aggressive works of the late 1960s, Mostaço ends his arguments by proclaiming: "Resta-nos, agora, procurar a lucidez para levar adiante o combate contra a herança ideológica com que a Velha Guarda embaralhou os caminhos" [It remains to us, now, to seek for lucidity to carry on the battle against the ideological heritage with which the old guard mixed up the paths] (5).

I think, however, that *Rasga coração* is more appropriately seen in the context of its author's intentions of 1974 and in that of the reality of the theatergoing public of 1980, when it was first performed. In this regard, it is precisely the problematic mixture of illusionist dramatic traditions with conventions associated with the epic theater proposed by Brecht that gives the play a theatrically coherent nexus, providing it with a high degree of dramatic tension and structurally opening the play to permit multiple readings. Vianinha's intentions were to reach an audience whose patterns of perception were formed by illusionist theater. Wishing to avoid both didacticism and facile dramatic identification, he aimed at the perceptual field of his audience by positioning his anonymous revolutionary hero, Manguari Pistolão, at the core of the most common quotidian contradictions of his real audience. Hoping to expand perception to a *contemplação* of the larger political issues that configure Brazilian reality, as well as Manguari's, Vianinha placed Manguari's dramatic conflict in a hybrid structure of Brechtian distancing techniques and *revista* elements. This is not a theater that proposed any abrupt or radical departures from traditional values and conventions, but rather one of conscious transition that struggled to avoid voluntaristic stances, be they political or aesthetic.

Conclusion

Speaking about form and subject matter, Bertolt Brecht commented in 1929 that

> Difficulties are not mastered by keeping silent about them. Practice demands that one step should follow another; theory has to embrace the entire sequence. The new subject matter constitutes the first stage, the sequence however goes further. The difficulty is that it is hard to work on the first stage (new subjects) when one is already thinking about the second (humanity's new mutual relationships). (29)

This study, taking its inspiration from Brecht's ideas on form and subject matter, has been designed to be as comprehensive as possible, both in the sense of its understanding of Vianinha's work, and in the sense of encompassing its broader cultural and social context. To that end, I have structured it as two intertwining studies designed to explicate each other: one study being of the cultural space and theatrical conventions of the time in which he lived, a study that necessarily entails an analysis of the historical circumstances that delineate that space; and the other being a discussion of Vianinha's theory and practice within that framework, which has been textually separated in my analysis to help distinguish his admittedly partisan view from those of other cultural analysts, including myself.

Agreeing with Brecht that "theory has to embrace the whole sequence," my hypothetical position regarding the importance of cultural space and theatrical conventions in Brazilian and Spanish American theater, an issue by no means exclusive to Vianinha's work, represents a beginning attempt to articulate a theory adequate to this theater's practice.

This hypothesis develops, first of all, from theories that space is the primary structuring element of theater, that the theatrical act is spatially represented (place and stage) and spatially transacted (the literal and figurative communicative distance/approximation between play and audience). Furthermore, the playwright deals with these concepts as he or she organizes the images that focus his or her own understanding of their importance. Second, I have held that theatrical conventions arise mainly from spatial exigencies and from cultural values as these values are spatially demonstrated.

I have found the juxtaposition of cultural space and theatrical conventions particularly applicable to the study of Brazilian theater because, as I have sought to demonstrate, a major factor in the growth of its traditions has been the continuous struggle for a space of practice.

Vianinha cited Brecht frequently, acknowledging him as one of his major teachers, and what Brecht said in 1929 goes far to illuminate Vianinha's theatrical trajectory. From the moment he started in theater (1954) until the day he died (July 16, 1974), Vianinha certainly never kept silent about the difficulties and inconsistencies he perceived in his own and others' attempts to find an adequate dialectic between theatrical and political practice. At every point in his theoretical development he turned back to embrace the sequential steps of his practice, rethinking and revising his positions in the context of a more subtle evaluation of the perceptual patterns of his real audience.

Theoretical communalities with Brecht take significantly different form in the case of Vianinha. This is largely a question of contextual emphasis. Whereas Brecht's subject matter was the study of social behavior in a capitalist society, Vianinha took a somewhat different route. He set as his specific task the analysis of Brazilian social behavior in the context of underdevelopment. The difference is important on many levels.

First of all, the development of Brecht's theatrical practice observes an organicity of theory and practice that indicates a context of continuity in the transformations of cultural patterns. For, despite the upheavals of the era in Germany, and despite the conflagration that brought with it real cultural ruptures, Brecht created within a social environment in which theater has had continuous and autochthonous traditions.

As with most Europeans, he can claim or disclaim this heritage from a perspective of continuity that affords a certain generalization, or universalization, of cultural specificity. In other words, there is an operant solidity of cultural identity regardless of one's readings of the values that inform that identity. Thus, in his oppositional ideas regarding the manner in which theater mediates objective reality, the artist has a *sense* of continuity in practice obtained from his or her cultural context even if the artist's own path be interrupted by historical catastrophes, economic difficulties, or personal hardships of a different nature.

This is not the case in Brazil and Spanish America, where the context for theater is discontinuous, often in obsessive dialogue with questions of cultural identity and dependency. Constantly interrupted by the economic and spatial constraints of underdevelopment and repression, theater's evolution has been sporadic. Given these circumstances, the forging of new theatrical conventions involves a comprehensive dialogue with the *discontinuities* of traditions.

There is a baroque complication in much of Vianinha's better work, particularly in *Rasga coração*, that reflects this dialogue. This is seen first of all in the variety of his work. As Juca de Oliveira, an actor who worked with Vianinha, observed: "Tudo que ele fez . . . tudo de propósito era para encontrar um caminho pela dramaturgia brasileira, pelo ator brasileiro" [Everything that he did . . . everything was meant to find a path for Brazilian dramaturgy, for the Brazilian actor] (interview by author).

As did Brecht, Vianinha believed in a theater of comprehension in which attention to new subject matter would generate new theatrical forms. Whereas Brecht stressed economic infrastructure as a category of representation in his investigation of social behavior (as did Vianinha did in his early plays), Vianinha came to emphasize historicity, both as subject matter and as a category of representation.

This emphasis makes sense for him in two interrelated aspects. It speaks to the discrepancy between official (and authoritarian) interpretations of historical fact and the unofficial history of underdevelopment in Brazil. It allows him to validate the experiential component of the unofficial history, to analyze "os valores . . . toda a vida . . . todas as conexões de valores, de éticas, de comportamentos a que são submetidas o homem subdesenvolvido brasileiro" [the values . . . all life . . . all the connections of values, of ethics, of behavior to which the Brazilian of underdevelopment is submitted] (*Vianinha* 166). Secondly, interpolating an explicitly historical perspective into the dramatic text allows him to posit a view of continuity in theatrical traditions by showing that the ruptures and inconsistencies (in sum, the discontinuities) are not gratuitous, but rather accompany the continuity or discontinuity of the historical process.

Vianinha's understanding of historicity is equally as specific in his allusions to local structurings of cultural space as it is comprehensive in terms of national, and more global, analysis. Thematically, he often posited the discontinuities of underdevelopment in a scenario of interpersonal spaces in shock with cultural and economic exigencies of mass communication, as is exemplified in his last interview, where he comments on the reduction of Brazilian society to its market and of the effects of mass communication as mediating perceptions of social reality:

> Para reduzir uma sociedade de mais de cem milhões de pessoas a um mercado de vinte e cinco milhões de pessoas é preciso um processo cultural muito intenso, muito elaborado e muito sofisticado, muito rico, para manter, para fazer com que as pessoas aceitem ser parte de um país fantasma, de um país inexistente, de um país sem problemas, a não ser os problemas de trânsito, da poluição, do próprio crescimento, da falta da matéria-prima mundo. . . . A sociedade brasileira está sendo um pouco reduzida a isso: à ambição individual da ascensão social como um valor supremo reduzido num setor muito pequeno.

> [In order to reduce a society of more than a hundred million people to a market of twenty-five million people it is necessary [to have] a very intense cultural process, very elaborate and very sophisticated, very rich, to maintain, to get people to accept being a part of a phantom country, of an inexistent country, a country without problems, unless [they are] problems of traffic, of pollution, of its own growth, of a lack of first world materials.

. . . Brazilian society is becoming somewhat reduced to this: the individual ambition of social ascension as the supreme value reduced to a very small sector [of the population.] (*Vianinha* 180-81)

Although Vianinha wrote several successful plays that targeted rural society and problems, his major works dissect urban space and culture, centering on a very localized conflict within the nuclear family. Indeed, we see that his career begins and ends with stage focus on the almost minuscule confines of a middle class Copacabana apartment. His first play, *Bilboa via Copacabana,* uses the farcical misadventures of the inhabitants of an ordinary apartment building as a rather simplified microcosm exploring aspirations and contradictions of social ascension. However, his last drama, *Rasga coração,* presents a panorama of social and theatrical history whose interpolation into the constrictions of the social, political and economic circumstances of contemporary urban reality is in part achieved by observations framed by, and directed from, Manguari and his family's view from their modest thirteenth floor windows, as short, but visceral, reports are given on the violence and alienation of the street scene below. This somewhat alienated perspective theatrically creates a tension between empathic and distancing elements that also affords, and frames, his broader interweaving analyses of private and public spaces and actuation.

Concomitant with Vianinha's dramatic goal to provide both synthesis and detail (imbedded theory and explicit practice), his conventions of characterization are often complex and agglomerative. He considered theater a transitional enterprise and sought provisional solutions. However, for reasons already noted, Vianinha looked to incorporate the lessons and conventions of the past, for in his reading of Brazilian social reality it was essential to discuss "present-day action" by the motives and features of the previous generation. This was Vianinha's way of trying to make a serious contribution to Brazilian dramatic literature, and in this he was successful.

Notes

Chapter 1

1. I refer the reader to the following writings on culture that have been consulted for my discussion. In his short entry in the *Encyclopedia of Philosophy* ("Culture and Civilization"), Raymond Williams deals with concepts of culture and methodological problems synchronically. See also Williams, *Culture and Society*, and Geertz.

2. This is the relationship that Bernard Dort considers to be essential to the Brechtian actor. He uses this as part of his definition of epic representation, which is in part "An attempt to offer to a socially aware audience a representation which is mediated by actors who, while being specialists, nonetheless remain delegates of this audience" ("Site of Epic"). This role of social mediation is, of course, applicable to much, if not most, theater.

3. When considering how economic conditions delimit theater's activities, we must consider to what degree these conditions are determining, or shaping, influences. The relationship is rarely directly causal, but usually mediated by other factors, including ideological values. Raymond Williams makes the point in the following manner: "The shaping influence of economic change can of course be distinguished. . . . But the difficulty lies in estimating the final importance of a factor which never, in practice, appears in isolation" (*Culture and Society* 280).

4. Fergusson's concept of analogy and anagogue ("the ultimate meaning of the play" [140]) is dense. For a synthesis of his thought on this matter,

see pages 224–36 of the appendix he devotes to the technical concepts used in *The Idea of a Theater.*

5. Fergusson, of course, deals with how "histrionic sensibility" is solicited by a performance. However, for my purposes here, I prefer Williams's categories since they deal more closely with concepts of cultural insertion in the sociological and political terms important to the Brazilian theater.

6. Williams also uses the term *structure of feeling* outside the context of theater. However, in discussing the structure of feeling represented in novels, for example, my interest here is in how he applies this concept to theater.

7. See Berger's *Ways of Seeing* for an exceptionally well explicated discussion, through selected illustrations, on how this works in the visual arts and advertisement.

8. Keir Elam, in *The Semiotics of Theatre and Drama*, stresses this intertextuality, which he considers a problematic relationship that structures the theatrical experience:

> Each text [written text/performance text] bears the other's traces, the performance assimilating those aspects of the written play which the performers choose to transcodify, and the dramatic text being "spoken" at every point by the model performance—or the *n* possible performances—that motivate it. This intertextual relationship is problematic rather than automatic and symmetrical. Any given performance is only to a limited degree constrained by the indications of the written text, just as the latter does not usually bear the traces of any *actual* performance. It is a relationship that cannot be accounted for in terms of facile determinism. (209)

   See also Pavis and particularly Ubersfeld, in her two volumes of *Lire le théâtre,* for further discussion of this intertextuality from a semiotic approach.

9. The introduction and conclusion of Williams's *Culture and Society* are particularly useful expositions of his viewpoint.

10. For more detail, see Brecht, the sections "The Modern Theatre Is the Epic Theatre" (33–43) and "A Short Organum for the Theatre" (179–209).

11. How theatrical conventions can embody and promote a system of values of a culture can be clearly seen in the case of the Broadway musical. This, the quintessential American theatrical form, hones in on the "American way of life" and the "American dream" in every possible level, and its cultural insertion is indeed broad. Musicals may get their stamp of approval on Broadway, where audiences are limited by geographical accessibility and ticket prices, but they filter through the whole culture, appearing as movies, television specials and—in limited form—as recordings that include some text as well as songs. Traveling casts make theatrical productions geographically more accessible and are usually cheaper. Community theaters produce musicals more than anything else.

   Besides catchy songs, what is the mass appeal of the musical? A show such as *Oklahoma!* can give us an idea. The exuberance and hope of the frontier dream of a new life and all that is associated with it—success, love, friendship, and community—achieved by individual merit and democratic cooperation is amply transmitted by movement, dance, and song. Conflicts occasioned by opposing individual and group interests are resolved, in the end, by cooperation and belief in the democratic system. The cowboys and the farmers can be friends because there is (at least in the musical) space enough for everybody to expand, attend to their personal needs, and still live by the golden rule. *Oklahoma!* provides the optimum mixture of democratic participation and responsibility with individual opportunity and even unbridled and eccentric individualism (Poor Jud).

Even *Hair*, the antiwar musical that portrays the darker side of the Vietnam War years, trades on these values. The hero of the show is typical of the musical comedy hero, remarkable for his spunk, ingenuity, in short for his heightened and theatrically communicated sense of individuality. The fact that he comes home in a casket is not a commentary aimed at the organizing values of the American way of life, but rather serves as an indictment of how these values have gone awry. There is no deep analysis of the economic and social formation of American culture. In this musical, as in others, to say that power and money corrupt is, in combination with the portrayal of the hero, an inverted way of emphasizing the primary formula: individual character is what truly counts.

12. See Luzuriaga for one of the first overall views, in English, of this focus. See also Pianca, Albuquerque, and Arrabal and Alves de Lima for discussion of theater and social commitment from the 1960s through the mid-1980s.

13. These categories are indeed applicable to most countries' theaters but are particularly useful in analyzing Brazilian theater given the importance that smaller spaces, such as university and amateur houses, have had in the growth of its traditions.

14. Perhaps the most famous recent example of this is found in Antunes Filho's theatrical adaptation of *Macunaíma* (first staged in 1978). Antunes used a variety of innovative scenic solutions to portray a sense of cultural movement. For example, he organized stage movement to suggest the *blocos* of Carnival, having the actors, in groups, move in diagonals across the stage as action and dialogue occurred. This and many other scenic solutions developed by Antunes have now come to constitute a recognizable school of staging in Brazil. For more on the work of Macunaíma, see D. George, *The Modern Brazilian Stage*.

15. By way of parenthetical rhetoric here, I'd like to state that the shift in verb tenses regarding the existence of these institutional spaces is only partly due to the difficulties of updating information. Perhaps more important for our discussion here are the institutional changes that have occurred in cultural allocation since the euphoria and cultural expansion of the early 1980s. Since its reformulation in 1981, responding to institutional modifications brought by the political opening, the INACEN has been transformed twice. Due mostly to internal ministerial changes that accompanied the Sarney presidency, INACEN was reorganized as FUNDACEN in 1985–86 and met its official death along with many other cultural programs during the brief Collor de Mello presidency (1990–

92). Federal institutional care of the scenic arts has regrouped, as FUNARTE.

16. One of the consistent projects of the various incarnations of the SNT, against almost all the odds of financial feasibility, has been the documentation of the schools and groups most important to Brazilian theater. From the bibliography, see the special issues of *Dionysos* that document theater schools. Theater schools in Brazil, as in the United States, will often have an emphasis on either the academic or professional aspects of theatrical activity. For example, there are two schools connected to the University of São Paulo: ECA (Escola de Comunicação e Artes), that awards graduate degrees in academic studies on theater, and EAD (Escola de Arte Dramática), which grants a non-academic, professional degree in threatrical practice.

17. For more information on the *revista,* see Maria Helena Kühner, *O teatro de revista,* and Roberto Ruiz, *O teatro de revista no Brasil.* The *revista* could be described as a historicized vaudeville, since many of the reviews were satires, or parodies, of current political events. These formulas of historical satire, which also provided a pre-Brechtian sense of Brechtian theatrical values, flowed naturally into the later political theater of the 1960s.

18. Hermilo Borba Filho, in *Apresentação do Bumba-meu-Boi* and *Fisionomia e espírito do mamulengo,* gives a rich description of these forms, linking their theatrical effects to more contemporary or urbanized phrasings of these conventions, such as Brechtian alienation techniques. For a more continental vision of the admixture process of popular and elite forms in the traditions of Latin American theater, see J. Weiss et.al.

19. Maria Helena Kühner documents this movement in Brazil very well in *Teatro amador,* describing, among other things, how organization of the amateur-independent groups proposed a theater circuit alternative to the commercial, sometimes using amateur status as a springboard to the professional. For a history of this movement in Spanish America, see Pianca, *El teatro de nuestra América.*

20. In respect to funding policies, a full comparison of the political ramifications of the large discrepancies between municipal, state, and national funding would be illustrative of the nonhegemonic nature of the cultural links between state policies and local funding as implemented during the dictatorship. For instance, in 1974 the municipality of São Paulo, under Cultural Secretary Sábato Magaldi, helped fund the International Festival Ruth Escobar of that year.

21. Kier Elam cites Edward T. Hall's categories of the proxemic relationships possible on stage as being intimate distance, personal distance ($1\frac{1}{2}$ feet), social distance (4–12 feet), and public distance (12–25 feet) (Elam 64–65).

22. See Elam 138–48 for a discussion of deixis. Elam comments: "It is important now to note that the drama consists first and foremost precisely in this, an *I* addressing a *you here* and *now*" (139), which echoes Bentley's formulation in linguistic terms.

23. This is clearly true in Robert Wilson's productions, where the significance of his minimalist text is largely spun through emphatic changes in the key

deictic words of repetitious phrases in conjunction with small gestures or movements in stage space.

Chapter 2

1. The diminutive, Vianinha, is used to distinguish him from his father, Oduvaldo Vianna, who was also a playwright. The name can be found spelled both Viana and Vianna. In this book, however, the spelling had been standardized to *Vianna*.

2. Vianinha's writings on theater, television, and politics have been laboriously collected and excellently edited and commented upon by Fernando Peixoto in *Vianinha: Sobre teatro televisão e política*. Except when otherwise noted, quotes from Vianinha's theoretical writings are taken from this edition rather than from primary sources. The decision to cite from Peixoto's volume was made both because of the coherence of vision found in this book and because of the relative inaccessibility of individual articles, notes, letters, and interviews—some unpublished except in Peixoto's volume, others published in scattered journals and newspapers or as program notes to plays. Articles used from *Vianinha* for discussion in this study have been checked with the originals made available to me from Peixoto, from the archives of *O Estado de São Paulo* and *Jornal do Brasil* and INACEN (Instituto Nacional de Artes Cênicas).

    In respect to the manner in which texts are cited in this study, it should be noted that accentuation is according the original text, not current usage.

3. This title was given by Fernando Peixoto to twenty-two pages of uncorrected typewritten manuscript (edited by Peixoto). As Peixoto observes, these notes seem to have been destined for internal discussion by participants of Arena, although it is uncertain that they were used for this purpose. Several of the articles used in this overview of Vianinha's theoretical thought have turned up in unpublished form. In a certain sense the indeterminate nature of the use and destination of these articles would seem to make them specious resources for an evaluation of his critical thought. However, I have found the contrary: these unpublished pages of theoretical analysis are among those that give us the clearest picture of Vianinha's insistence and honesty in grappling with the more difficult aesthetic problems that a committed political writer confronts. This will be the case of the several articles—or manuscript pages—used in this presentation of his theoretical preoccupations.

4. It is likely that, at least here, Vianinha's understanding of the movement of consciousness, as well as of aesthetics as a category of knowledge, owes much to Sartre, whom Vianinha, like most Brazilian intellectual activists of the 1960s, read. This supposition of dialogue with Sartrian theory is enforced by the inclusion of a discussion of *Huis clos* in the article (67), which Vianinha ends by stating: "Não sei até que ponto podem nos interessar—como artistas que pretendem extrair do nosso contato sensível com a realidade seus movimentos necessários mais profundos para entregar ao homem uma liberdade cada vez mais ampla—a filosofia e a arte

de Sartre" [I do not know to what point the philosophy and art of Sartre can interest us—as artists who intend to extract from our sensitive contact with reality its most profound necessary movements to give to man an ever greater freedom] (67).

5. This debate will be analyzed and documented in the following chapters.

6. The imprecision of dates is due to the fact that these pages—pages typewritten with handwritten corrections—have no specific references that would indicate their date. Peixoto does not give a date to this article, which he entitles "A ação dramática como categoria estética" (Dramatic action as an aesthetic category), nor to its following companion pages, to which he gives the title "A cultura proprietária e a cultura desapropriada" (Proprietary culture and disappropriated culture). Relying on the evidence of their fit in the evolution of Vianinha's theory as well as on Peixoto's chronological placement, I date these pages roughly as written in 1971 or late 1970.

7. It is quite possible that Vianinha uses "systems of representation" in the Althusserian sense. It is probable that he was familiar with *For Marx*, first published in France as *Pour Marx* (Paris: François Maspero S.A., 1965) and published in translation in Brazil in 1967 under the title *Análise crítica da teoria marxista* (Rio de Janeiro: Zahar Ed.). The following definition, given by Althusser in "Marxism and Humanism," speaks to Vianinha's arguments in this article:

> There can be no question of attempting a profound definition of ideology here. It will suffice to know very schematically that an ideology is a system (with its own logic and rigor) of representations (images, myths, ideas or concepts, depending on the case) endowed with a historical existence and role within a given society. Without embarking on the problem of the relations between a science and its (ideological) past, we can say that ideology, as a system of representations, is distinguished from science in that in it the practico-social function is more important than the theoretical function (function as knowledge). (*For Marx* 231)

And Althusser goes on to say that ideology "is a structure essential to the historical life of societies" (232). Within this view, a system is *not* reducible to its elements; it is more the dynamic of these elements' interrelation, how they are functionally perceived.

The dichotomy "unconscious/conscious" as pertaining to theatrical conventions is discussed by Althusser in the article "The 'Piccolo Teatro': Bertolazzi and Brecht" (129–51).

8. This article, in large part, revolves around a critique of political theater of the 1964–68 period. He criticizes the lack of analysis of the relationship of underdevelopment to value systems and gives what he sees as two major reasons for this oversight of analysis: *(a)* sectarianism; *(b)* lack of possible continuity of artistic output necessary to clarify such complex issues in theater. He speaks of the manner in which dominant ideology justifies itself in cultures of underdeveloped nations, needing even more than in other cultures to assume the characteristic of absolute truth. Indeed, he affirms that Brazilian culture is doubly a culture of adaptation

to the status quo, a culture twice removed, an imitation ("a cultura prati-
cada no Brasil é não-brasileira" [the culture practiced in Brazil is non-
Brazilian] [146]), of a culture already bankrupt (or very problematic) on
its home ground.

A useful work that treats questions of adaptation versus transformation
in European theater is George H. Szanto's *Theater and Propaganda.*
Szanto approaches the analysis of social theater by making distinctions
between agitation (transformative) propaganda and integration (adap-
tive) propaganda.

9. He makes this clearer in "A cultura proprietária." Speaking of the problems that workers face in creating a viable culture that speaks to their
   concerns, Vianinha says that the workers' energies are consumed in a
   manner that promotes their alienation: "Sua necessidade de adaptação
   ao meio o [the worker] nega como transformador, como conhecedor do
   meio. Seu meio natural não é humano." Therefore, "a cultura que cria
   tem um baixo teor racionalizado. Só a sua vanguarda ideológica conse-
   gue formulá-lo com lucidez" [His need for adaptation to the environment denies the worker as transformer, as knowledgeable of the
   environment. His natural environment is not human. . . . The culture
   he creates has a low reasoned content. Only his ideological avant-garde
   successfully formulates it with lucidity] (144).

   He goes on to elaborate on the relationship of the vanguard to the
   worker: "Para que ele [the worker] consiga transformar-se em produtor
   do meio em que vive, em transformador dele, ele precisa uma programa-
   ção, uma racionalização dos fenônemos da realidade. Essa é a tarefa dos
   seus ideólogos e dos seus artistas" [So that the worker may transform
   himself into a producer of his environment, into a transformer of it, he
   needs a programming, a rationalization of the phenomena of reality. This
   is the task of his ideologues and of his artists] (145).

   Clearly, this is a problematic stance, to be discussed in the body of this
   analysis as it pertains to Vianinha's assessment of the cultural space available (and potential) for practice of such vanguard positions.

10. Techniques of aggression designed to provoke audience reaction and
    thought were common to alternative and politically motivated occidental
    theater of this period. This will be discussed in the Brazilian context in
    chapter 5.

11. He refers often to Brecht, acknowledging him to be his major influence
    in theater, and specifically mentions Lukács and Marx at points in his
    writings. Perhaps Hauser was his favorite, a supposition supported by his
    widow, Maria Lúcia Marins, in a personal interview by the author. Peix-
    oto corroborates this by quoting Gianfrancesco Guarnieri as saying that
    during the 1960s, *A história social da literatura e da arte* (The Social
    History of Art) was a kind of Bible for Vianinha (*Vianinha* 54).

12. Although Vianinha's work lends itself extraordinarily well to a biographi-
    cal-autobiographical approach, I have included relatively little biographi-
    cal material here, wishing to devote more space to his theoretical
    concerns, as shown earlier in this chapter. For further biographical back-
    ground see the autobiography of his mother, Deocília Vianna, *Compan-*

heiros de viagem; Dênis de Moraes, *Vianinha;* and Carmelinda
Guimarães, *Um ato de resistência.*

13. In an interview with the author, his mother gives fourteen as the age. In
an interview with Carmelinda Guimarães (18), the age is given as twelve.

Chapter 3

1. *Teatro de Arena* 7. All general information regarding Arena is taken from
this volume. For other critical studies that specifically focus on Arena's
importance in Brazilian theatrical history, see Boal, *Teatro do oprimido;*
Magaldi, *Um palco brasileiro;* Mostaço, *Teatro e política.*
2. This was the intent of the Arena staging. Photographs included in this text
indicate these stagings for *Chapetuba Futebol Club* and *Eles não usam
black-tie.*
3. Martins Pena (1815–48) is considered the founder of the Brazilian *comédia de costumes* (comedy of manners) by most critics (Magaldi, *Panorama* 40–58). Magaldi also considers him the true founder of "o teatro
nacional" (40), the author who first created Brazilian characters within a
satirical framework of Brazilian social institutions.
4. For example, Joracy Camargo's *Deus lhe pague* (God Will Reward You),
first produced in 1932 by Procópio Ferreira. This social comedy revolves
around the resolution of a love triangle in which the primary character
(played by Procópio) is a millionaire social "philosopher" who proffers
simplistic communist analyses of Brazilian society while amassing a fortune "working" as a beggar.
      For a history of *teatro de revista,* the Brazilian vaudeville form that
incorporated social commentary, see Kühner, *O teatro de revista.*
5. *Os Comediantes.* For a good historical overview of contemporary Brazilian
theater, with attention to the groups that constitute theatrical moments
or movements from 1927 (Teatro de Brinquedo) until 1968, see Doria.
Very appropriately, Doria stresses the importance of interchange between
amateur, student, and professional groups in the growth of theatrical
traditions in Brazil. For further documentation on student theater, see
Teatro do Estudante do Brasil.
6. For detailed analyses of developmental nationalism of the Kubitschek
years, see Cardoso; Flynn; all Skidmore references; Burns; dos Santos;
and Mota.
7. A discussion of the Vargas legacy and of the operant differences between
Vargas's brand of nationalism and that of Kubitschek would be essential
to full development of this question, but beyond the scope of the present
work. Discussion of the Vargas years will be found in chapter 5, in context of Vianinha's reading of history in *Rasga coração.*
8. Toledo, particularly "Anexo" 184–92. For further reading on the ISEB,
see Sodré, *A Verdade sobre o ISEB;* and Mota 154–81.
9. For a history and posterior analysis of the theory and practice of the CPC,
see Hollanda; Hollanda and Gonçalves; Pereira and Hollanda; *Teatro/
Ensaio* no. 3; *Arte em Revista* 1, nos. 1 and 2; Berlinck; Martins, *A
questão da cultura popular;* and Morel.

10. For what is probably the most accessible printing of the "Anteprojeto" for study, see Hollanda 121–44.
11. This is an elementary definition of what would be considered the petite bourgeoisie in Brazil at the time. However, it is the one then most generally held by Brazilian intellectuals and artists, most of whom include themselves in that group (Costa, interview by author). For a larger treatment, see Sodré, *História da burguesia brasileira.*
12. How Boal takes his own counsel—a discussion outside of the realm of this analysis—is indeed important to Brazilian theater and can be found, theoretically elaborated, in *Teatro do oprimido* and other texts of his. We see the problems that both Boal and Vianinha pose in their assessment of *Chapetuba* discussed by Vianinha in the theory he puts forth in 1960, treated in chapter 2 of this study.
13. Chico de Assis also points out that the theatrical techniques of the play vacillated between Brecht and those of the Dramatic Seminars of Arena (215). This mixture requires attention that, although pertinent to Vianinha's aesthetic, would expand discussion of the play beyond appropriate measure here.
14. Speaking very eloquently (and I believe correctly) to this point, Carlos Estevam Martins expresses his resentment at limited hindsight analyses of CPC activity in 1981:

> Quando hoje alguém me diz que se estivesse lá no CPC não teria agido da mesma forma como nós agimos, acho isso um absurdo, ou melhor dizendo, uma arbitrariedade, uma violência. Porque simplesmente não havia ninguém propondo fazer outra coisa maior ou melhor, e se houvesse, não há nenhuma dúvida de que nós faríamos essa coisa maior ou melhor, pois era disto que estávamos a fim. O que é preciso entender é isso: nós estávamos atuando no limite do nosso tempo histórico.

> [When someone says to me today that if he had been right there at the CPC he wouldn't have acted in the way we did, I think that's absurd, or better yet, arbitrary, a sort of violence. Because there just wasn't anyone proposing something bigger or better, and if there were, there isn't any doubt that we would do that bigger, better thing, because that's what we wanted to do. What must be understood is this: we were acting at the limit of our historic moment.] (Qtd. in Morel 5)

15. Although it is what is of interest here, theater was not the only cultural activity that the CPC engaged in. Film was extremely important, and CPC work became the basis for the movement known in the mid-1960 as Cinema Novo (see Johnson and Stam). Poets were also heavily involved, most significantly those of the group Violão da Rua. Musicians and musical groups contributed their time, talent, and energy not only to theater, but with local shows that also went on tour. Workshops, courses, and schools were set up in all the arts in the CPC centers as well as in union halls and in *favela* and suburban community cultural spaces.

As indicated by this brief description, the CPC constituted a movement of considerable cultural mediation and mobilization.

16. *O filho da besta torta do Pajéu* was written around late 1962 or early 1963, first produced in 1963, and later published under the name *Quatro quadras de terra,* the title under which it won the Cuban Casa de las Américas prize. The plot tells a tragic story of generational conflict within the context of social injustice and revolt: rural workers are in the process of organizing resistance to expulsion from the land they have worked for generations. The father of the family around which the play centers, Jerônimo, continues to believe in the *patrão* and the benefits of the archaic paternalistic structure of the *latifúndio,* even though it is apparent that this system is no longer economically viable. His son Demétrio speaks of the injustice of this system and of the hope of collective revolutionary action. Jerônimo shoots Demétrio, preferring to see him dead than a rebel. Jerônimo is left alone on the farm. The others have been expelled to look for work in some other equally desperate region. The play ends with the hope that rural unionization can provide the collective strength to change the situation of the rural worker.

Os Azeredos mais os Benevides, written somewhat later and published in 1966, tells a similar story from a slightly different perspective. Questions and schematic analysis regarding the economic and social interrelationship between the city and rural regions are posited in the story as it tells of the fluctuations in the economic fortunes of an absentee landlord. Since their economic star now is in decline, the Azeredo family sends its son, Espiridião, to a cacao plantation in the interior in order recuperate their losses. While there, Espiridião makes friends with a worker, Alvimar, making Alvimar the foreman of the plantation after Espiridião's economic success allows him to resume his life in the city (Salvador, Bahia). Regional political alliances are also treated: part of Espiridião's success is due to his marriage into the Benevides family, whose head is the political chief *(coronel)* of the area. Alvimar has a son, for whom Espiridião acts as godfather, a serious quasi-familial relationship in Brazil, particularly in the interior. The son spends time with the Azeredo family in the city.

Time passes. The son, now grown, is back on the plantation. No longer needing the income from the plantation, which has become a financial burden, Espiridião no longer provides for its maintenance, and the workers are starving. Alvimar's son leads a group of peasant workers in the pillage of the plantation warehouse. Espiridião returns and orders the police to shoot the son, alleging to Alvimar that he would have done the same had it been his own flesh and blood. Espiridião closes the plantation, and the workers are forced to leave. The play ends as Espiridião gives Alvimar and his wife money to start life anew elsewhere.

17. The radical government of Miguel Arraes in Pernambuco had already instigated a series of agrarian reforms. The Ligas Camponesas, mainly led by Francisco Julião, had made giant inroads in grassroots organization among the peasants and rural poor throughout the Northeast. Pernambuco was also the center of operations of the sociologist and educator Paulo Freire, who directed the Movimento de Cultura Popular, a movement much akin to the CPC in its activities and programs. So, in this

regard, the plays did capture and transmit "reality in movement" despite their aesthetic limitations. For more on the MCP, see *Movimento de Cultura Popular.*

Chapter 4

1. The full text of Linz's article, in English, can be found in Stepan 233–54.
2. For an analysis of "sobornism," its beginnings in 1946, and the impossible task of conciliation of liberal legal process with governmental control, see Limoeiro Cardoso as well as Velasco e Cruz and Martins.
3. As indicated before, Boal's theories on theater, particularly as expounded in *Teatro do oprimido, e outras poéticas políticas,* were of profound importance to Spanish American theater as well as to Brazilian theater and also influenced thought and practice in Europe (mainly in France, where Boal spent his years of exile). It should also be signaled that his "sistema do coringa" and his subsequent experiences with forms such as "teatro-foro," "teatro jornal," "teatro invisível," and later use of techniques of psychological sensitivity training influenced the work of Brazilian theater activists after 1964 on a much larger scale than can be discussed here. His theories continue to generate much discussion—pro and con—that have added to the body of practical theory in Brazilian theater. Of Boal's writings, see also: *Técnicas latino-americanas de teatro popular; 200 exercícios e jogos para o ator e o não-ator com vontade de dizer algo através do teatro;* and *Stop: c'est magique.* For several retrospective evaluations of his work, see *Boal/Brook* and Mostaço, *Teatro e política.*
4. This distinction between what might be called "theater of action" as opposed to that of the word will be taken up more extensively in chapter 5. As in the case of Boal, it is important to note, here, that the limitations of this analysis preclude giving the work of Oficina the space that it would deserve in a specifically comparative study of the conventions of the contemporary Brazilian stage. For more information on Oficina, see *Teatro Oficina* and da Silva. For a treatment of the impact of the production of *O rei da vela,* see George, "Reinterpretation." For a comparative, if somewhat harsh, posterior analysis of the work of Arena, Oficina, and Opinião, see Mostaço, *Teatro e política,* as well as José Arrabal's article "Anos 70," in *Teatro. Anos 70.* Arrabal rightly considers that the three most important theatrical tendencies of the late 1960s that carried over into the early 1970s are represented by the work of Boal, Zé Celso, and Vianinha. (The name of Plínio Marcos should be listed here, if extending "theatrical" back into the dramatic text, even though Marcos did not work, in group, as a "theatrical tendency.")
5. *Moço em estado de sítio* was produced in 1981, *Papa Highirte* in 1979; therefore they will not be analyzed in the body of this study.
6. The published version of the play list the authors in the following order: Armando Costa, Oduvaldo Vianna Filho, and Paulo Pontes.
7. Directed by Augusto Boal and produced under the banner of Arena, *Opinião* was credited by some critics to Boal. This error was undoubtedly due to the legal aspects of the joint venture: the writers, all well-known activ-

ists of the CPC, knew that the censors would never allow them to produce a show at that moment. Opinião was able to surface as a group after
the enormous public success of the show.

8. The literal translation of *morro* is "hill" or "hillside," where many slums
are located, even though by U.S. standards this is often prime vista property, such as seen in the French-Brazilian film *Black Orpheus.*

9. Life = sadness = scar. Sung by itself, "Cicatriz" admits an interpretation
of a lament of poverty, where the social message is to move the hearer
about the extensiveness of poverty. By this interpretation, the "coragem"
mentioned later refers mainly to the will to survive. As woven into the
show, however, this lament distinctly becomes an optimistic call to the
possibilities of collective protest.

10. Dias Gomes, a party compatriot of Vianinha's, accentuates the conflict
between moral vision—exemplified by the need for continual self-exami-
nation—and political pragmatism as being operant in Vianinha's aesthetic (interview by author). He also emphasizes the part Vianinha's
parents played in the formation of this moral conviction toward political
commitment, where the normal pressures experienced between parents
and children were played out or contributed to the tension in the political realm.

11. The most famous and successful play of this genre is Ariano Suassuna's
Auto da Compadecida (1955). Suassuna's trickster, João Grilo, always
manages to stay one step ahead of the earthly power structure but finds
in the scene of the final judgment (Heaven) that morality can't be negoti-
ated, although transgressions can be forgiven.

12. Fernando Peixoto gives this explanation, stressing that many people saw
this article as the beginning of a political *involução,* while others saw it as
a mature *evolução* in Vianinha's thought (*Vianinha* 129)

13. Dias Gomes, who was also an active member of the PCB at the time and
a close friend of Vianinha's, remarks that he (Dias) and other young
cultural activists in the party considered Vianinha's position considerably
changed from a radical analysis to a conciliatory, and even overly moderate, view of social and cultural reality in 1967–68. Dias also admits that
in retrospect, he sees that Vianinha was more perceptive about the real
problems of Brazilian theater than the more radical leftists (interview by
author).

Chapter 5

1. Correspondences between the Vargas era and the period after 1964 will
be discussed in chapter 6 in context of *Rasga coração.*

2. This argument complements, rather than contradicts, Skidmore's assertions regarding the authoritarian structure inherited by Vargas. As
Skidmore points out in "Politics," the authoritarian institutions of Vargas were largely created by acts or decrees, although many of them were
"legitimized" by incorporation into rewrites of the constitution. In this
respect, it is important to note that although these constitutions (as well
as constitutional modifications after 1964) left much leeway for imple-

mentation of authoritarian strategies, their basic political structure adheres to the tenets of democratic process.

3. My analysis here is a continuation of discussion of Velasco e Cruz and Martins's ideas in the beginning of the last chapter of this study, as set forth in their article "De Castello a Figueiredo."

4. This also coincides with Linz's theory that authoritarian rule is sustained, in significant part, by its efficacy in finding the slogans and symbols that will give it popular legitimization (237–38).

5. The authors point out that many of these programs, particularly the Transamazônica, ended as economic and planning disasters, but served the ideological ends of the "Brasil Grande" myth (42).

6. For details on the extent and kind and flux of torture that went on throughout the dictatorship, see Dassin, *Torture in Brazil.*

7. Institutional Act 5 was revoked October 13, 1978, several months after General João Baptista Figueiredo was named next president. Political persecution and *cassações* of mandates continued almost up until the moment of its revocation.

8. Besides which, the plan's definition of fundable popular culture carefully defangs the element of social commentary in it, focusing on artisans and excluding or limiting forms more propitious to social criticism. For a discussion of this plan, see Sumner and Camargo Costa.

   The theater class, responding to "normalization" and to cultural planning, proposed measures to strengthen its own position. In October 1973 the ACET (Associação Carioca de Empresários Teatrais [impresarios association]), under the presidency of Orlando Miranda, sent a document of protest to the minister of education, Jarbas Passarinho. This statement, elaborated by Paulo Pontes but taking many of its issues from Vianinha's ideas, analyzed the situation of Brazilian theater, relating the economic crisis caused by censorship. It called for nonpaternalistic forms of financing by the government, subsidies that would allow theater to create a viable autonomous infrastructure not prey to the arbitrary decisions of the Ministry of Justice. This document became the base program of the SNT when Orlando Miranda took over administration of that organ beginning in 1974.

9. For discussion of television and T.V. Globo, see Pereira, and Kehl.

10. This best example of this was Teatro Ipanema's 1974 production, *Hoje é dia de rock* (Today Is a Day for Rock) an invigorating hit whose slim text centered on its protagonist's dreams of being a rock star. The primary and ritualistic use of music in these shows, although having some precedence in Opinião's work, is quite different from that exemplified by *Opinião,* where music and dialogue were used contrapuntally to explicate each other's significance.

11. See Luciano Martins's article "A geração AI-5 (um ensaio sobre autoritarismo e alienação)" (The AI-5 Generation [An Essay on Authoritarianism and Alienation]) for further discussion of language and the counterculture in Brazil after 1968.

12. He also authored a play first called *Nossa vida em família* (Our Family at Home) (staged with that name in 1970), and restaged in 1972 under the title *Em família.* It is a moving drama that treats problems of old age

and separation (the devoted old couple have to separate, one going to a son's house, the other to an geriatric home). However, it will not be discussed here since, despite its thematic interest, it is not as pertinent to Vianinha's development of conventions and characterization as the other plays of this period.

13. The conventions of *Alegro Desbum* are more sophisticated versions of those discussed in chapter 3 in connection with *Bilbao. Alegro Desbum* is mentioned here as further evidence of Vianinha's wish to stretch out to find a broader audience and as further notation of the importance of figures of mass communication in his dramatic characters after 1968.

14. It is improbable that Vianinha knew Berger's work, or at least this book, since it was published in Britain in 1972. However, besides being avowed Marxists (and Marxists do not necessarily agree on these matters), their application of Marxists concepts to art, perception, and societal values would seem to concur all the way down the line.

15. He shows ads of panty hose and girdles that promise revolutionary freedom. One also thinks of the commodification of the revolutionary heros of the 1960s: Che Guevarra appearing in expensively framed posters, as a figure in the play *Evita,* and so forth. In the art of choosing images for co-optation, it is significant that Che—although far more politically radical than Fidel—is dead, and Fidel still very much presenting an image difficult to reinterpret for sale.

16. These ideas culled and synthesized from the "Polemical Introduction" to *Theater and Propaganda,* where they are given preliminary definition in pages 6–9.

17. As seen in his preface to the play, Vianinha himself considered *Corpo a corpo* a modest experiment in theatrical clarity and an attempt to reformulate the traditions of the Brazilian social drama in dialogue with the theatrical advances of the vanguard.

Chapter 6

1. The title is emblematic of the visceral force of the tensions of the play: *Rasga coração,* which I have loosely translated as "Rend Your Heart." Although the Portuguese title, *Rasga coração,* does not include the article "o" that would make it a true imperative, I have chosen the imperative sense of the play's theme song: interpreted as an imperative, you must rip apart your heart to reach connection with life. Even interpreting the title as the "Heart Rips" (or as Severino Albuquerque suggests, "Heart Rending"), we are still advised that the heart will rip, if or when confronted with the significance of our lives.

2. The autobiographical aspects of the play will not be specifically developed here. However, it should be noted that the generational conflicts in *Rasga coração* have two significant parallels with Vianinha's life: his own relationship with his father (and to a lesser degree his mother), who was a PCB activist and writer (see chap. 2); and his son, Vinicius, born in 1958, to whom the play is dedicated. In a sense, Manguari is a composite of Vianinha and his father. The conflict between Luca and Manguari has

its autobiographical base in Vianinha's concern to understand his own son, who in the early 1970s defended the counterculture against his father's concept of activism (interviews by the author with Deocélia Vianna and with Ferreira Gullar and Teresa Aragão).

The tone of the play also expresses Vianinha's "inner" biography: Manguari's autocriticism and doubts, always in confrontation with the necessity of practice, are also the psychological mechanism of Vianinha's political and artistic evolution. In this sense, the structured fragmentation of the collage effect is emblematic of Vianinha's process of constant revaluation and assessment of subjectivity/objectivity in his own perceptions of reality.

3. As seen in the previous chapter, Vianinha questions the political efficacy of this movement in its co-optability and its gestural abstraction. However, it is important to restate that he did recognize it as a forceful, if problematic, voice. His treatment of Luca furthers his metaphorical presentation in *Corpo a corpo*.

4. See Pavis, *Dictionnaire* 82–83, for a brief discussion of the concept of the implicit receptor. According to Pavis, the "récepteur implicite" is the character in a play who represents the author's ideal spectator. He is the one whose presence transmits the message of the play to the audience, without necessarily being the author's spokesperson. Pavis comments: "on sent que c'est à ce type de personne que s'adresse le message de la pièce: ainsi Trofimov et Anna dans La ceriseraie de Tchekhov qui symbolisent la nouvelle génération révolutionnaire" [one senses that this is the type of person to whom the message of the play is addressed: thus Trofimov and Anna in the cherry orchard of Chekhov symbolize the new revolutionary generation].

5. Historical data used in this section is compiled from Burns, Flynn, and Skidmore, *Politics in Brazil* and *The Politics of Military Rule*.

6. Although there is no direct reference to it in the play, undoubtedly the sobriquet 666 refers to the apocalyptic sign of the "beast." Often in his plays, Vianinha used symbolic references that alluded to historical moments of great repression without further explanation. In this manner, the title of his play *A long noite de Cristal* serves as a possible analogical warning to "Krystal Nacht," the name given to the November 1938 mass destruction of Jewish property that marked the beginning of the holocaust in Germany.

7. Manguari is played by a child actor here (Vianinha's second son in the original cast), but the teenage and the adult Manguari are portrayed by the same actor. This casting gives continuity to his political personage.

8. See Chilcote, *The Brazilian Communist Party;* Konder; and A. Pereira for further studies on the formation of the PCB. In addition, for the perspective of a former militant, see Peralva. Chilcote observes that the PCB rose partly as a consequence of the failure of the socialist and anarchist movement of the first decade of the century, that it pushed participation in the electoral system as early as 1927, and that it is essential to remember that the PCB has had connections with military men since the 1930s (a result of Prestes's popularity) (4–7).

Chilcote also makes a statement that is most pertinent to understanding Manguari's persistence. In answer to his own question as to why people continued in the Party despite political conditions and revelations of the Party's internal distress (Stalin, etc.), Chilcote remarks: "In a society in which alternatives to existing conditions are rarely feasible, a conscious commitment to social change might well be retained only within the refuge of the party itself" (7).

In regards to the "Semana de Arte Moderna," the polemical cultural event that marked a turn toward forming a "national aesthetic," as opposed to a European one, there are many published studies. For a study on theater during this period of Brazilian modernism, see Lara.

9. The Ação Integralista was founded in 1932 by Plínio Salgado, a politician, essayist, and poet whose work exalted the Integralist program and glorified Brazil. Their symbol was the Σ (obviously akin to the swastika); they wore green shirts (a link with Mussolini); their salute was an Indian word, *anauê* (nationalist reference); and their motto, Deus, Pátria, e Família (God, Country, and Family). They stressed order, hierarchy, and obedience. The political program aimed at an "integral" state under a single authoritarian head of government, and their declared enemies were democrats, Communists, Jews, and Masons (Burns 295). For a full-length study of the Integralists, see Trindade.

10. The histrionic quality of this note bears witness to the charismatic force that Vargas exercised over the nation much more than many pages of textual analysis could. It is therefore worth quoting here:

> Once more the forces and interests against the people are newly coordinated and raised against me . . . I follow the destiny that is imposed on me. After years of domination and looting by international economic and financial groups, I made myself chief of an unconquerable revolution. I began the work of liberation, and I instituted a regime of social liberty. I had to resign. I returned to govern on the arms of the people. A subterranean campaign of international groups joined with national groups revolting against the regime of workers' guarantees. . . . I have fought month to month, day to day, hour to hour, resisting a constant aggression, unceasingly bearing it all in silence, forgetting all and renouncing myself to defend the people that now fall abandoned. I cannot give you more than my blood. . . . I offer my life in the holocaust, I choose this means to be with you always. When they humiliate you, you will feel my soul suffering at your side. When hunger beats at your door, you will feel in your chests the energy for the fight for yourselves and your children. When they humiliate you, you will feel in my grief the force for reaction. My sacrifice will maintain you united, and my name will be your battle flag. . . . I fought against the looting of Brazil. I fought against the looting of the people. I have fought bare breasted. The hatred, infamy, and calumny did not beat down my spirit. I gave you my life. Now I offer my death. Nothing remains. Serenely I take the first step on the

road to eternity, and I leave life to enter history. (Cited in Burns 327, from the *New York Times,* August 25, 1954).

11. See Flynn 145 for a brief but good discussion on Vargas populism. For further discussion see Skidmore, *Politics in Brazil;* Weffort; and Ianni, *O colapso do populismo no Brasil.*

12. I have been unable to determine to what extent censorship influenced the structure and focus of the play. There is a considerable difference of opinion about whether Vianinha really expected this play to be performed. José Renato asserts that Vianinha was hoping to hang on to life long enough to see it in production and that in order to feed this hope he, Renato, lied to him on his deathbed, telling him that it had been liberated by the censors (interview by author).

13. It is interesting that Cott comes out as a more rounded character in the play than both Camargos. This is partly because of his continuity from plane to plane, but also possibly because in the original version he had a much larger role. José Renato mentions that Vianinha had long scenes, which he later cut for structural unity, in which Manguari and Cott disputed Nena's love (the ideological choice verified by the romantic choice) as well as several encounters in which Manguari bested Cott—one in which Manguari literally left Cott without his pants in the middle of Avenida Rio Branco (Renato, interview by author).

14. These are the only two women in the play. A study of the female presence in Vianinha's work would reveal that, as a rule, the women are seen in the traditional roles of housewife, lover, sounding board—in short, in their roles of illuminating the predominant male figures.

15. Vargas also loved to see himself presented in the *revista* sketches, laughing at the caricatures made of him. In José Renato's production, an extra clearly dressed as Vargas enters this scene, directing stage movement with a whip.

16. The choppiness of the second act also reflects Vianinha's haste. His illness, I believe, also influenced the rhythm changes and difference of degree of emphasis put on pain, as a theme, in the two acts. Vianinha was in extreme pain as he completed the last act, a pain that fragmented his periods of productivity.

17. Since this is one of the few major scenes that calls for slides, Vianinha obviously meant this as a distancing and differentiating technique from the same contrasts in illusion and reality that the leftist activists present. Feeling this to be a cooling effect on the play, José Renato replaced all indications of slides in the text with background movement involving extras (interview by author).

18. See the discussion on the preface to *Corpo a corpo* in chapter 5.

19. The breadth and depth of historical and cultural research that went into *Rasga coração* was tremendous, as can be seen in the appendices of historical fact, slang, newspaper notices, song verses, and other cultural references that comprise more than two-thirds of the SNT published edition of the play.

20. According to statistics taken form records collected by the Sociedade Brasileira de Autores Teatrais (SBAT) and the Instituto Nacional de Artes

Cênicas (INACEN), cited in Maria Helena Kühner's study, *A communi-cação teatral*, *Rasga coração* gave 100 performances at 102.2 percent house capacity in 1979 at the Villa-Lobos theater, one of Rio's largest and most prestigious professional theaters. In 1980 it was presented 302 times, in the same theater, at 97.9 percent house capacity. This was a phenomenal record, and the play had only one close "competitor": a boulevard comedy, *Pato com Laranja*, more within the conventions of the usual *carioca* (Rio de Janeiro) theatergoing public.

Bibliography

General Cultural and Theatrical Theory

Althusser, Louis. *For Marx.* Trans. Ben Brewster. 1969. New York: Vintage Books, 1970.

Aronoff, Myron J., ed. *Culture and Political Change.* Vol. 2 of *Political Anthropology.* New Brunswick, N.J.: Transaction Books, 1983.

Benjamin, Walter. *Understanding Brecht.* Trans. Anna Bostock. New York: New Left Books, 1973.

Bentley, Eric. *The Life of the Drama.* London: Methuen, 1965.

———. *The Theatre of Commitment, and Other Essays on Drama in Our Society.* New York: Atheneum, 1954.

Berger, John. *Ways of Seeing.* New York: Viking Press, 1973.

Boal, Augusto. *Stop: c'est magique.* Rio de Janeiro: Editor Civilização Brasileira, 1980.

———. *Técnicas latino-americanas de teatro popular.* São Paulo: Editor Hucitec, 1979.

———. *Teatro do oprimido, e outras poéticas políticas.* 2d ed. Coleção Teatro Hoje, vol. 27. Rio de Janeiro: Editôra Civilização Brasileira, 1980.

———. *200 exercícios e jogos para o ator e o não-ator com vontade de dizer algo através do teatro.* Rio de Janeiro: Editor Civilização Brasileira, 1980.

Bibliography

Brecht, Bertolt. *Brecht on Theatre: The Development of an Aesthetic.* Ed. and trans. John Willet. New York: Hill and Wang, 1964.

Carlson, Marvin. *Theories of the Theatre: A Historical and Critical Survey from the Greeks to the Present.* Ithaca, N.Y.: Cornell University Press, 1984.

Dort, Bernard. "The Site of Epic Representation." Trans. Loren Kruger. *Communications* 1, no. 2 (1985): 3–18.

———. *O teatro e sua realidade.* Trans. Fernando Peixoto. Coleção Debates. São Paulo: Editóra Perspectiva, 1977.

Durand, Régis, ed. *La Rélation théâtrale.* Lille: Presses Universitaires de Lille, 1980.

Duvignaud, Jean. *Sociologie du théâtre: Essai sur les ombres collectives.* Bibliotèque de Sociologie Contemporaine. Paris: Presses Universitaires de France, 1965.

Elam, Keir. *The Semiotics of Theatre and Drama.* New York: Methuen, 1980.

Fergusson, Francis. *The Idea of a Theater: A Study of Ten Plays.* Princeton: Princeton University Press, 1949.

Geertz, Clifford. *The Interpretation of Cultures: Selected Essays.* New York: Basic Books, 1973.

Gramsci, Antonio. *Selections from the Prison Notebooks of Antonio Gramsci.* Ed. and trans. Quintin Hoare and Geoffrey Nowell Smith. London: Lawrence and Wishart; New York: International Publishers, 1971.

Jameson, Fredric. *The Political Unconscious: Narrative as a Socially Symbolic Act.* Ithaca, N.Y.: Cornell University Press, 1981.

Luzuriaga, Gerardo, ed. *Popular Theater for Social Change in Latin America: Essays in Spanish and English.* University of California at Los Angeles Latin American Studies, vol. 41. Los Angeles: University of California at Los Angeles Latin American Center Publications, 1978.

Pavis, Patrice. *Dictionnaire du Théâtre: Termes et concepts de l'analyse théâtre.* Paris: Editions Sociales, 1980.

———. *Languages of the Stage: Essays in the Semiology of the Theater.* New York: Performing Arts Journal Publications, 1982.

Pianca, Marina. *El teatro de nuestra América: Un proyecto continental: 1959–1989.* Minneapolis, Minn.: Institute for the Study of Ideologies and Literature, 1990.

Piscator, Erwin. *The Political Theatre: A History, 1914–1929.* Trans. Hugh Rorrison. New York: Avon Books, 1978.

Sartre, Jean-Paul. *Sartre on Theater.* Ed. Michel Contat and Michel Rybalka, trans. Frank Jellineck. New York: Pantheon Books, 1976.

Szanto, George W. *Theater and Propaganda.* Austin: University of Texas Press, 1978.

Ubersfeld, Anne. *Classiques du peuple: Critique.* Vol. 1 of *Lire le théâtre.* Paris: Éditions Sociales, 1978.

Bibliography

————. *L'école du spectateur.* Vol. 2 of *Lire le théâtre.* Paris: Éditions Sociales, 1981.

Weiss, Judith, Leslie Damasceno, Donald Frischmann, Claudia Kaiser-Lenoir, Marina Pianca and Beatriz J. Rizk. *Latin American Popular Theatre: The First Five Centuries.* Albuquerque: University of New Mexico Press, 1993.

Williams, Raymond. "Culture and Civilization." In *The Encyclopedia of Philosophy,* ed. Paul Edwards, 2:273–76. New York: Macmillan and Free Press, 1967.

————. *Culture and Society, 1780–1950.* 1958. New York: Columbia University Press, 1960.

————. *Drama in Performance.* Middlesex: Penguin Books, 1972.

Brazilian Theater and Culture

Albuquerque, Severino João. *Violent Acts: A Study of Contemporary Latin American Theatre.* Detroit: Wayne State University Press, 1991.

Arrabal, José and Mariângela Alves de Lima. *Teatro: O nacional e o popular na cultura brasileira.* São Paulo: Editora Brasiliense, 1983.

Bader, Wolfgang, ed. *Brecht no Brasil: Experiências e influências.* Rio de Janeiro: Paz e Terra, 1987.

Benevides, María Victoria de Mesquita. *A UDN e o udenismo: Ambigüedades do liberalismo brasileiro (1945–1965).* Coleçao Estudos Brasileiros, vol. 51. Rio de Janeiro: Paz e Terra, 1981.

Berlinck, Manoel Tosta. "Um projecto para a cultura nos anos 60: análise sociológica do Centro Popular de Cultura." Unpublished manuscript, n.d. Later revised and published as *CPC: Centro Popular de Cultura.* Campinas: Papirus, 1984.

Boal/Brook. Special issue of *Ensaio/Teatro* 4 (1981).

Borba Filho, Hermilo. *Apresentação do Bumba-meu-Boi.* Recife: Imprensa Universitária, 1966.

————. *Fisionomia e espírito do mamulengo.* São Paulo: Editôra da Universidade de São Paulo, 1966.

Brandão, Tânia. "A estática da palavra." *Ensaio/Teatro* 5 (1983): 13–20.

Burns, E. Bradford. *A History of Brazil.* New York: Columbia University Press, 1970.

Butler, Ross Erin, Jr. "Artistic Exploration of Unifying Themes in the Contemporary Brazilian Protest Theater." Ph.D. diss., University of Arizona, 1972.

Cacciaglia, Mário. *Pequena história do teatro no Brazil (quatro séculos de teatro no Brasil).* Trans. Carla de Queiroz. São Paulo: Editora da Universidade de São Paulo, 1986.

Campos, Augusto de. *Patrícia Galvão: Pagu, vida, obra.* 2d ed. São Paulo: Editôra Brasiliense, 1982.

Campos, Cláudia de Arruda. *Zumbi, Tiradentes.* São Paulo: Perspectiva/Editora da Universidade de São Paulo, 1988.

Cardoso, Miriam Limoeiro. *Ideologia do desenvolvimiento—Brasil: JK-JQ.* 2d ed. Coleção Estudos Brasileiros, vol. 14. Rio de Janeiro: Paz e Terra, 1978.

Chilcote, Ronald H., ed. *Brazil and Its Radical Left: An Annotated Bibliography on the Communist Movement and the Rise of Marxism, 1922–1972.* Millwood, N.Y.: Kraus International Publications, 1980.

———. *The Brazilian Communist Party: Conflict and Integration 1922–1972.* New York: Oxford University Press, 1974.

Ciclo de debates do Teatro Casa Grande. Coleção Opinião. Rio de Janeiro: Editôra Inúbia, 1975.

Os Comediantes. Special issue of *Dionysos* 22 (December 1975).

Corbisier, Ronald. *Os intelectuals e a revolução.* Coleção Depoimentos, vol. 17. Rio de Janeiro: Avenir Editora, 1980.

Costa, Iná Camargo. "A crise do drama em *Eles não usam black-tie:* Uma questão de classe." *Discurso* 20 (1993): 147–55.

Cruz, Sebastião C. Velasco e, and Carlos Estevam Martins. "De Castello a Figueiredo: Uma incursão na pré-história da 'Abertura.'" In *Sociedade e política no Brasil pós 1964,* eds. Bernardo Sorj and Maria Herminia Tavares de Almeida. São Paulo: Editôra Brasiliense, 1983.

Dassin, Joan, ed. *Torture in Brazil.* Trans. Jaime Wright. New York: Vintage Books, 1986.

Dionysos 17 (July 1969).

Doria, Gustavo A. *Moderno teatro brasileiro: Crônica de suas raízes.* Coleção Ensaios. Rio de Janeiro: Serviço Nacional de Teatro, 1975.

Dramaturgia brasileira hoje. Special issue of *Ensaio/Teatro* 5 (1983).

Escola de arte dramática. Special issue of *Dionysos* 29 (1989).

Favaretto, Celso F. *Tropicália: Alegoria, alegria.* Coleção Traços. São Paulo: Kairos Livraria e Editora, 1979.

Fernandes, Florestan. *Mudanças sociais no Brazil: Aspectos do desenvolvimiento da sociedade brasileira.* São Paulo: Difusão Europeia do Livro, 1960.

Fernandes, Rofran. *Teatro Ruth Escobar: 20 anos de resistência.* São Paulo: Global Editora, 1985.

Ferreira Gullar. *Cultura posta em questão.* Coleção Vera Cruz (Literatura Brasileira), vol. 81. Rio de Janeiro: Editôra Civilização Brasileira, 1965.

———. *Vanguarda e subdesenvolvimento: Ensaios sobre arte.* Coleção Perspectivas do Homem, vol. 57. Série ensaio. 2d ed. Rio de Janeiro: Editôra Civilização Brasileira, 1978.

Bibliography

Flynn, Peter. *Brazil: A Political Analysis.* Nations of the Modern World. London: Ernest Benn; Boulder, Colo.: Westview Press, 1978.

Freire, Paulo. *Pedagogy of the Oppressed.* Trans. Myra Bergman Ramos. New York: Seabury Press, 1970.

Furtado, Celso. *Formação econômica do Brasil.* Biblioteca Fundo Universal de Cultura, Estante de Economia. Rio de Janeiro: Editôra Fundo de Cultura, 1959.

Galante de Souza, J. *O teatro no Brasil.* Vol. 1: *Evolução do teatro no Brasil.* Vol. 2: *Subsídios para uma bibliografia do teatro no Brasil.* Rio de Janeiro: Instituto Nacional do Livro, 1960.

Garcia, Silvana. *Teatro da militância.* São Paulo: Perspectiva/Editoria da Universidade de São Paulo, 1990.

George, David. *The Modern Brazilian Stage.* Austin: University of Texas Press, 1992.

————. "The Reinterpretation of a Brazilian Play: *O Rei da Vela.*" *Ideologies and Literatures* 2, no. 8 (September–October 1978): 55–64.

Góes, Walder de. *O Brasil do General Geisel: Estudo do processo de tomada de decisão no regime militar-burocrático.* Coleção Brasil Século 20. Rio de Janeiro: Editôra Nova Fronteira, 1978.

Guzik, Alberto. *Teatro Brasileiro de Comédia: Crônica de um sonho.* São Paulo: Editôra Perspectiva, 1986.

Hollanda, Heloísa Buarque de. *Impressões de viagem: CPC, vanguarda e desbunde: 1960–1970.* São Paulo: Editôra Brasiliense, 1980.

Hollanda, Heloísa Buarque de, and Marcos Augusto Gonçalves. *Cultura e participação nos anos 60.* Tudo é História, 41. São Paulo: Editôra Brasiliense, 1982.

Ianni, Octavio. *O colapso do populismo no Brasil.* 4th ed. Coleção Retratos do Brasil, vol. 70. Rio de Janeiro: Editôra Civilização Brasileira, 1978.

————. "O estado e a organização da cultura." *Encontros com a Civilização Brasileira* 1 (July 1978): 216–41.

Johnson, Randal, and Robert Stam, eds. *Brazilian Cinema.* East Brunswick, N.J.: Associated University Presses, 1982.

Kehl, Maria Rita. "As novelas, novelinhas e novelões: mil e uma noites para as multidões." In Kehl et al. *Anos 70—televisão,* 49–73. Rio de Janeiro: Europa, 1979–80.

Khéde, Sônia Salomão. *Censores de pincené e gravata: Dois momentos da censura teatral no Brasil.* Coleção Edições do Pasquim, vol. 113. Rio de Janeiro: Codecri, 1981.

Konder, Leandro. *A democracia e os comunistas no Brasil.* Biblioteca de Ciências Sociais, Série Política, vol. 15. Rio de Janeiro: Edições Graal, 1980.

Kühner, Maria Helena. *A comunicação teatral: De 1980 a 1983.* Rio de Janeiro: Associação Carioca dos Empresários Teatrais, 1983.

————. *O teatro de revista e a questão da cultura nacional e popular.* Rio de Janeiro: Fundação Nacional de Arte, 1979.

————. *Teatro amador: Radiografia de uma realidade (1974–1986).* Rio de Janeiro: Instituo Nacional das Artes Cênicas, 1987.

Lacerda, Carlos. *Depoimento.* Coleção Brasil Século 20. Rio de Janeiro: Editôra Nova Fronteira, 1977.

Lara, Cecília de. *De Pirandello a Piolim: Alcántara Machado e o teatro no modernismo.* Rio de Janeiro: Instituto Nacional de Artes Cênicas, 1987.

Linz, Juan J. "The Future of an Authoritarian Situation or the Institutionalization of an Authoritarian Regime: The Case of Brazil." In Stepan 233–54.

Magaldi, Sábato. *Panorama do teatro brasileiro.* Coleção Ensaios, vol. 4. Rio de Janeiro: Serviço Nacional de Teatro, 1962.

————. *Um palco brasileiro: O Arena de São Paulo.* São Paulo: Editôra Brasiliense, 1984.

Martins, Carlos Estevam. "Historia do Centro Popular de Cultura." *CPC.* Depoimento ao Centro de Estudos de Arte Cont. 78.

————. *A questão da cultura popular.* Rio de Janeiro: Edições Tempo Moderno, 1963.

Martins, Luciano. "A geração AI-5: Um ensaio sobre autoritarismo e alienação." *Ensaios de opinião* 11, nos. 2–9 (1979): 72–102.

Mendes, Antonio, Jr., and Ricardo Maranhão, eds. *Era de Vargas.* Vol. 4 of *Brasil História: Texto e consulta.* 2d ed. São Paulo: Editôra Brasiliense, 1982.

Michalski, Yan. *O palco amordaçado: 15 anos de censura teatral no Brasil.* Coleção Depoimentos, vol. 13. Rio de Janeiro: Avenir Editora, 1979.

————. *O teatro sob pressão: Uma frente de resistência.* Rio de Janeiro: Jorge Zahar Editor, 1985.

Michalski, Yan, and Rosyane Trotta. *Teatro e Estado: As companhia oficiais de teatro no Brasil.* São Paulo: Hucitec/Instituto Brasileiro de Arte e Cultura, 1992.

Morel, Marco, ed. "Está no hora de repensar o CPC." Unpublished report of the Comissão Organizadora do seminário "Repensando o CPC." N.d.

Mostaço, Edélcio. *O espetáculo autoritário: Pontos, riscos, fragmentos críticos.* São Paulo: Proposta Editorial, 1983.

————. *Teatro e política: Arena, oficina e opinião (uma interpretação da cultura de esquerda).* São Paulo: Proposta Editorial, 1982.

Mota, Carlos Guilherme. *Ideologia da cultura brasileira, 1933–74: Pontos de partida para uma revisão histórica.* 4th ed. Ensaios 30. São Paulo: Editôra Atica, 1980.

Bibliography

Movimento de Cultura Popular: Memorial. Recife: Fundação de Cultura Cidade do Recife, 1986.

Partido Communista Brasileiro: Vinte anos de política 1958–1979 (documentos). Coleção A Questão Social no Brasil, no. 7. São Paulo: Livraria Editôra Ciências Humanas, 1980.

Peixoto, Fernando. *Teatro em movimento: 1959–1984.* São Paulo: Editoria Hucitec, 1986.

―――. *Teatro em pedaços (1959–1977).* Coleção Teatro. São Paulo: Editôra Hucitec, 1980.

―――. *Teatro em questão.* São Paulo: Editora Hucitec, 1989.

―――, ed. *O Melhor teatro do CPC da UNE.* São Paulo: Editora Hucitec, 1986.

Peralva, Osvaldo. *O retrato.* Belo Horizonte: Editôra Itatiaia, 1960.

Pereira, Astrojildo. "A formação do PCB." In *Ensaios históricos e políticos.* Biblioteca Alfa-Omega de Ciências Sociais: Política, Série 1, vol. 9. São Paulo: Editôra Alfa-Omega, 1979.

Pereira, Carlos Alberto M., and Heloísa Buarque de Hollanda. *Patrulhas ideológicas, marca reg.: Arte e engajamento em debate.* São Paulo: Livraria Brasiliense Editora, 1980.

Pereira, Carlos Alberto M., and Ricardo Miranda. *Televisão: O nacional e o popular na cultura brasileira.* São Paulo: Editora Brasiliense, 1983.

Prado, Décio de Almeida. "A personagem no Teatro." In *A Personagem de ficção.* São Paulo: Editôra Perspectiva, 1992.

―――. *O teatro brasileiro moderno.* São Paulo: Editôra Perspectiva, 1988.

―――. *Teatro em progresso: Crítica teatral (1955–1964).* São Paulo: Livraria Martins Editôra, 1964.

Prado Junior, Caio. *A revolução brasileira: Perspectivas em 1977.* 6th ed. São Paulo: Editôra Brasiliense, 1978.

Praia do Flamengo, 132: Ensaio/Teatro, no. 3. Rio de Janeiro: Edições Muro, 1980.

Questão popular. Special issue of *Arte em revista* 2, no. 3 (March 1980).

Reilly, Charles A. "Cultural Movement in Latin America: Sources of Political Change and Surrogates for Participation." In *Culture and Political Change,* vol. 2 of *Political Anthropology,* ed. Myron J. Aronoff, 127–53. New Brunswick, N.J.: Transaction Books, 1983.

Rosenfeld, Anatol. "Héroes y coringas." *Conjunto* 9 (1970): 29–45.

―――. "O herói humilde." *Revista Civilização Brasileria* 2 (1968): 79–91.

―――. *Texto/contexto.* Coleção Debates. 3d ed. São Paulo: Editôra Perspectiva, 1976.

Roux, Richard. *Le Théâtre Arena (São Paulo 1953–1977).* Aix-en-Provence: Université de Provence, Service des Publications, 1991.

Ruiz, Roberto. *Hoje tem espetáculo? As origens do circo no Brasil.* Rio de Janeiro: Instituo Nacional das Artes Cênicas, 1987.

———. *Teatro de revista no Brasil: Do início à la Guerra Mundial.* Rio de Janeiro: Instituto Nacional de Artes Cênicas, 1988.

Salgado, Plínio. *O ritmo da história.* 3d ed. São Paulo: Editôra Voz do Oeste, 1978.

Santos, Fernando Augusto Gonçalves. *Mamulengo: Um povo em forma de bonecos.* Rio de Janeiro: Fundação Nacional de Arte, 1979.

Santos, Theotônio dos. "Brazil: The Origins of a Crisis." In *Latin America: The Struggle with Dependency and Beyond,* ed. Ronald H. Chilcote and Joel C. Edelstein, 409–90. New York: John Wiley and Sons, 1974.

Schoenbach, Peter Julian. "Modern Brazilian Social Theatre: Art and Social Document." Ph.D. diss., Rutgers University, 1973.

Schwarz, Roberto. *Ao vencedor, as batatas: Forma literária e processo social nos inícios do romance brasileiro.* São Paulo: Livraria Duas Cidades, 1977.

———. *Misplaced Ideas: Essays on Brazilian Culture.* Ed. with intro. by John Gledson. London: Verso, 1992.

———. "Cultura e política, 1964–69." In *O Pai de família,* 61–93.

———. *O pai de família, e outros estudos.* Coleção Literatura e Teoria Literária, vol. 27. Rio de Janeiro: Paz e Terra, 1978.

Segatto, José Antonio. *Breve história do Partido Communista Brasileiro.* Coleção A Questão Social no Brasil, no. 8. São Paulo: Livraria Editôra Ciências Humanas, 1981.

Silva, Armando Sérgio da. *Oficina: Do teatro ao te-ato.* São Paulo: Editôra Perspectiva, 1981.

———. *Uma oficiana de atores: A Escola de Arte Dramática de Alfredo Mesquita.* São Paulo: Editora da Universidade de São Paulo, 1989.

Silva, Hélio. *Vargas.* Coleção Pensamento Político Brasileiro, vol. 1. Porto Alegre: L&PM Editores, 1980.

Silveira, Miroel. *A contribuição italiana ao teatro brasileiro (1895–1964).* Coleção Logos (Teoria Crítica e Histórica). São Paulo: Edições Quiron; Brasília: Instituto Nacional do Livro, Ministério da Educação e Cultura, 1976.

———. *A outra crítica.* São Paulo: Edições Símbolo, 1976.

Singer, Paul. *A crise do "Milagre": Interpretação crítica da economia brasileira.* 5th ed. Rio de Janeiro: Editôra Paz e Terra, 1977.

Skidmore, Thomas E. "Politics and Economic Policy Making in Authoritarian Brazil, 1937–71." In Stepan 3–46.

———. *Politics in Brazil, 1930–1964: An Experiment in Democracy.* New York: Oxford University Press, 1967.

———. *The Politics of Military Rule in Brazil, 1964–85.* New York: Oxford University Press, 1988.

Bibliography

Soares, Álvaro Texeira. *O Brasil no conflito ideológico global: 1937–1979.* Coleção Retratos do Brasil, vol. 140. Rio de Janeiro: Editôra Civilização Brasileira, 1980.

Sodré, Nelson Werneck. *A verdade sobre o ISEB.* Coleção Depoimentos, vol 4. Rio de Janeiro: Avenir Editora, 1978.

———. *História da burguesia brasileira.* 2d ed. Retratos do Brasil, vol. 22. Rio de Janeiro: Editôra Civilização Brasileira, 1967.

———. *Quem é o povo no Brasil?* Cadernos do Povo Brasileiro, vol. 2. Rio de Janeiro: Editôra Civilização Brasileira, 1962.

Sorj, Bernardo, and Maria Herminia Tavares de Almeida, eds. *Sociedade e política no Brasil pos-64.* São Paulo: Editôra Brasiliense, 1983.

Stepan, Alfred, ed. *Authoritarian Brazil: Origins, Policies, and Future.* New Haven: Yale University Press, 1973.

Sumner, Anne-Marie and Iná Camargo Costa. "Da hegemonia cultural a uma política para a arte." In *Teatro.* Special issue of *Arte em revista,* 62–69.

O Tablado. Special issue of *Dionysos* 27 (1986).

Teatro. Anos 70 3. Rio de Janeiro: Europa Empresa Gráfica e Editora, 1979–80.

Teatro. Special issue of *Arte em revista* 6 (October 1981).

Teatro Brasileiro de Comédia. Special issue of *Dionysos* 25 (September 1980).

Teatro de Arena. Special issue of *Dionysos* 24 (October 1978).

Teatro e Realidade Brasileira. Special issue of *Revista Civilização Brasileira* 2 (July 1968).

Teatro do Estudante do Brasil; Teatro Universitário; Teatro Duse. Special issue of *Dionysos* 23 (September 1978).

Teatro Oficina. Special issue of *Dionysos* 26 (January 1982).

Tinhorão, José Ramos. *Música popular: Um tema em debate.* 2d ed. Rio de Janeiro: JCM Editores, n.d.

Toledo, Caio Navarro de. *Instituto Superior de Estudos Brasileiros: Fábrica de ideologias.* Ensaios 28. 2d ed. São Paulo: Editôra Atica, 1978.

Trindade, Hélgio. *Integralismo: O fascismo brasileiro na década de 30.* 2d ed. São Paulo: DIFEL/Difusão Editorial, 1979.

Vasconcellos, Gilberto. *Música popular: De olhos na fresta.* Rio de Janeiro: Edições do Graal, 1977.

Weffort, Francisco Correia. *O populismo na política brasileira.* 2d ed. Coleção Estudos Brasileiros, vol. 215. Rio de Janeiro: Editôra Paz e Terra, 1980.

Oduvaldo Vianna Filho: Plays and Theory

Allegro desbundaccio (Se Martins Pena fôsse vivo). Manuscript copy, Serviço Nacional de Teatro.

Os Azeredo mais os Benevides. Rio de Janeiro: Ministério da Educação e Cultura, Serviço Nacional de Teatro, 1968.

Bilbao via Copacabana. In *Teatro.*

Brasil-versão brasileira. In Peixoto, *CPC da UNE* 249–317.

Chapetuba Futebol Clube. In *Teatro.*

Corpo a corpo. Revista de Teatro 387 (May–June 1972): 31–43.

Em família. Manuscript copy, Edições Muro.

A longa noite de Cristal. Manuscript copy, Serviço Nacional de Teatro.

A mais-valia vai acabar, seu Edgar. In *Teatro.*

"O meu Corpo a corpo." *Revista de Teatro* 387 (May–June 1972): 29–30.

Moço em estado de sítio. Manuscript copy, Edições Muro.

Papa Highirte. Rio de Janeiro: Ministério da Educção e Cultura, Serviço Nacional de Teatro, 1968.

O melhor teatro. Ed. Yan Michalsky. São Paulo: Global, 1984.

Quatro quadras de terra. In *Teatro.*

Rasga coração. Rio de Janeiro: Serviço Nacional de Teatro, 1980.

Teatro. Vol. 1 of *Oduvaldo Viana Filho.* Ed. Sônia Faerstein, org. Yan Michalski. Rio de Janeiro: Ilha, 1981.

Vianinha: Sobre teatro televisão e política. Ed. Fernando Peixoto. São Paulo: Editôra Brasiliense, 1983.

Vianna Filho, Oduvaldo, Armando Costa, and Paulo Pontes. *Opinião: Texto completo do "Show."* Rio de Janeiro: Edições do Val, 1965.

Vianna Filho, Oduvaldo, and Ferreira Gullar. *Se correr o bicho pega se ficar o bicho come.* Coleção Teatro Hoje, vol. 1. Rio de Janeiro: Editôra Civilizaçao Brasileira, 1966.

Vianna Filho, Oduvaldo, Paulo Pontes, and Armando Costa. *Dura lex sed lex no cabele so Gumex: Revista musical.* Manuscript copy, Edições Muro.

Oduvaldo Vianna Filho: Biography and Critical Evaluation

"Armando Costa: Contestar é preciso." *Jornal do Brasil, caderno* B, 14 December 1979, n.p.

Assis, Chico de. Preface to *A mais-valia vai acabar, seu Edgar.* In Oduvaldo Vianna Filho, *Teatro,* 213–16.

Bárbara, Danúsia. "Rasga coração liberado: Um marco do teatro brasileiro sai das gavetas para a boca de cena." *Jornal do Brasil,* 21 April 1979, n.p.

Bastos, Mauro Martins, and Antônia Eliana Chagas. "Mea máxima culpa." *Isto é,* 13 October 1979, 40–41.

Brandão, Ignácio de Loyola. "Uma das peças mais lindas dos últimos tempos." *Folha de São Paulo,* 10 May 1979, n.p.

"Comédia satiriza o consumo." *Estado de São Paulo,* 13 March 1976, n.p.

"*Corpo a corpo:* A bola no chão." *Globo,* 16 February 1975, n.p.

Del Rios, Jefferson. "Beleza e emoção na obra-prima de Viana." *Globo,* 9 October 1980, n.p.

———. "A derrota política de uma geração." *Isto é,* 13 October 1979, 44.

———. "Este é seu último aceno de esperança." *Folha de São Paulo,* 16 October 1980, n.p.

———. "Vianinha, no coração da história." *Folha de São Paulo,* 4 May 1979, n.p.

"Depoimento de Vianninha a Marcílio Eiras Morães." *Jornal do Comércio,* 29 July 1973, n.p.

Dines, Alberto. "Rasgando corações: A política como arte." *Folha de São Paulo,* 14 October 1979, n.p.

Ferreira Gullar. "O alvo da repressão." *Jornal do Brasil,* caderno B, 14 December 1979, n.p.

Gagno, Carmem. "Um painel de quarento anos de Brazil, uma cascata de emoções." *Jornal da Tarde,* 17 October 1980, n.p.

Guimarães, Carmelinda. *Um ato de resistencia: O teatro de Oduvaldo Vianna Filho.* São Paulo: MG Editores Asociados, 1984.

Gropillo, Ciléa. "Moços em estado de sitio: Texto inédito de Vianinha estréia no SESC da Tijuca." *Jornal do Brasil,* 26 November 1981, n.p.

Ishmael-Bissett, Judith. "Brecht e Cordel: Distanciamento e protesto em *Se correr o bicho pega.*" *Latin American Theatre Review* (fall 1977): 59–64.

Jafa, Van. "*Chapetuba F.C.:* Teatro de verdade." *Correio da Manhã* 6 March 1960, n.p.

Leite, Luiza Barreto. "Ainda o Teatro de Arena." *Jornal do Comércio,* Folhetim, 6 November 1959, n.p.

———. "Teatro do Arena." *Jornal do Comércio,* Folhetim, 15 September 1959, n.p.

Magaldi, Sábato. "Problemas de *Chapetuba F.C.*" *Estado de São Paulo,* 4 April 1959, n.p.

———. "*Rasga coração,* um momento de perfeição do nosso teatro." *Jornal da Tarde,* 23 October 1980, n.p.

———. "Vianinha: O tempo trará mais sucesso." *Jornal da Tarde,* 18 July 1974, n.p.

———. "Vianinha volta ao palco." *Jornal da Tarde,* 14 July 1979, n.p.

Macksen, Luiz. "*Papa Highirte* em cena, cinco anos depois da morte de Vianinha." *Jornal do Brasil,* 13 July 1979, n.p.

Maciel, Luiz Carlos. "O bicho que o bicho deu." *Revista Civilização Brasileira* 7 (May 1966): 289–98.

Mendes, José Guilherme. "*Papa Highirte,* viva Vianninha!" *Revista Ela Ela* 11, no. 125 (September 1979): 27–28.

Mendes, Oswaldo. "O novo nem sempre é revolucionário." *Folha de São Paulo,* 6 May 1979, n.p.

Michalski, Yan. "Brasil, 1930–1972: Como acompanhar o quebra-cabeça." *Jornal do Brasil,* 31 July 1980, n.p.

———. "De volta, *Opinião.*" *Jornal do Brasil,* 27 May 1975, n.p.

———. "Longa jornada estado de sítio adentro." *Jornal do Brasil,* 30 November 1981, n.p.

———. "O passado carioca numa pesquisa de Vianinha." *Jornal do Brasil,* 14 August 1977, n.p.

———. "Símbolo de uma boa causa." *Jornal do Brasil,* 21 April 1979, n.p.

Moraes, Dênis de. *Vianinha: Cúmplice da paixão.* Rio de Janeiro: Nórdica, 1991.

Morães, Luiz Carlos. [Ensaio sobre *Papa Highirte* de Oduvaldo Vianna Filho]. *Ensaio/Teatro* 2 (n.d.): 56–62.

Mostaço, Edélcio. "Rasga coração, fígado, cerebro." *Revista Teatro* 4 (May–June 1981): 5.

Neto, Licínio. "Aspectos do processo dramático no teatro de Oduvaldo Viana Filho." *Revista de Teatro* 423 (May–June 1978): 6–11.

"Os olhos de tragédia." *Visão,* 5 August 1974, 70.

Renato, José. "Tempos de desencanto: *Rasga coração.*" Interview. *Globo,* 9 October 1979, n.p.

Ventura, Mary. "Oduvaldo Vianna Filho: A paixão do encontro do intelectual com o povo." *Jornal do Brasil,* 6 November 1979, n.p.

Vianna, Deocélia. *Companheiros de viagem.* São Paulo: Editôra Brasiliense, 1984.

Xexéo, Artur, and Jairo Arco e Flexa. "A batalha de Vianninha." *Veja,* 10 October 1979, 86–91.

Interviews by Author

Aragão, Teresa (with Ferreira Gullar). 14 November 1981.

Boal, Augusto. 10 August 1981.

Cortez, Raul. 14 December 1981.

Costa, Armando. 16 November 1981; 12 December 1981.

Dias Gomes, Alfredo. 17 December 1981.

Ferreira Gullar (with Teresa Aragão). 14 November 1981.

Guimarães, Carmelinda. 2 December 1981.

Marins, Maria Lúcia. Numerous interviews, spring and fall 1981.

Michalski, Yan. 15 December 1981.

Neves, João das. 18 February 1981.

Oliveira, Juca de. 5 December 1981.

Peixoto, Fernando. 5 December 1981.

Prado, Décio de Almeida. 3 December 1981.

Renato, José. 20 November 1981.

Teixeira, Maria Célia. 8 December 1981.

Vianna, Deocélia. 8 December 1981.

Index

Latin American Literature and Culture Series

Books in this series